D0004876

CONTENTS

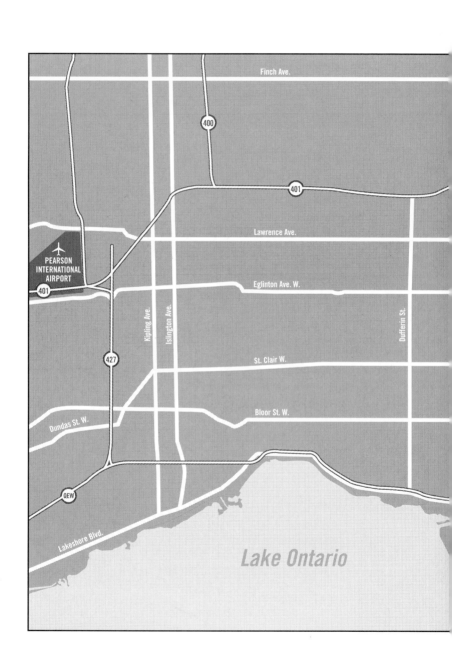

Lake Ontario

TORONTO

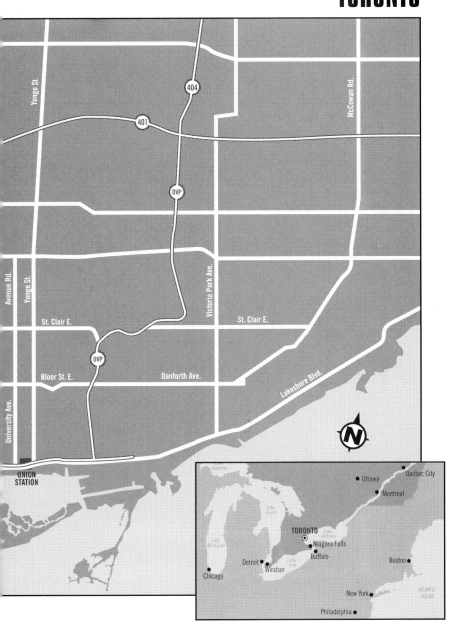

Yonge St.

404

401

McCowan Rd.

DVP

Avenue Rd.

Yonge St.

Victoria Park Ave.

St. Clair E.

St. Clair E.

DVP

Bloor St. E.

Danforth Ave.

University Ave.

Lakeshore Blvd.

UNION
STATION

Lake Superior

Ottawa

Quebec City

Montreal

Lake Huron

TORONTO

Niagara Falls

Buffalo

Lake Michigan

Detroit

Windsor

Lake Erie

Lake Ontario

Boston

Chicago

New York

ATLANTIC
OCEAN

Philadelphia

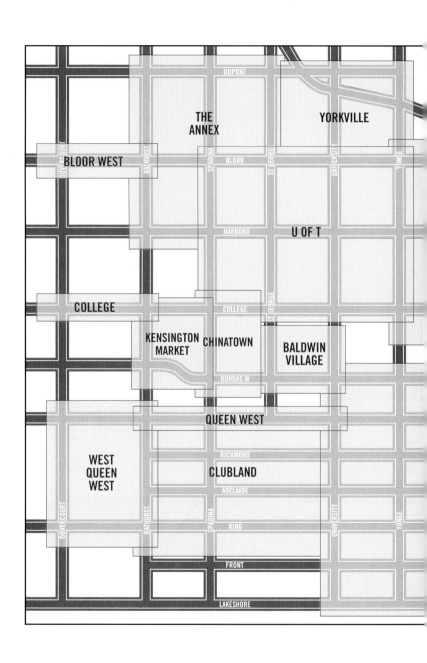

TORONTO'S NEIGHBOURHOODS

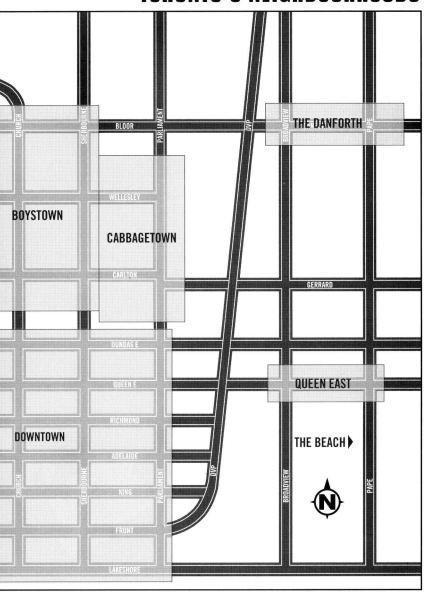

BOYSTOWN

CABBAGETOWN

THE DANFORTH

WELLESLEY

CARLTON

GERRARD

DUNDAS E

QUEEN E

QUEEN EAST

RICHMOND

DOWNTOWN

THE BEACH ▶

ADELAIDE

KING

FRONT

LAKESHORE

BLOOR

SHERBOURNE

PARLIAMENT

CHURCH

BROADVIEW

PAPE

DVP

TORONTO INSIDERS FOR 18 YEARS

Welcome to the inaugural edition of the **NOW CityGuide** to Toronto, a book that gives you an insider's view of one of North America's most vibrant cities — seen through the eyes of the people at NOW magazine, who know the city best.

Every week for more than 18 years, NOW magazine has published the real lowdown on what's happening in the city. Our comprehensive arts and entertainment coverage makes NOW the first place people turn for essential information on what's going on in and around Toronto. But NOW isn't just an entertainment guide — it's also Toronto's most trustworthy source of news about the people and events that mainstream newspapers ignore. We're proud of NOW's long-standing reputation for printing stories that take on the powerful, challenge public opinion, and open debate on local and international issues.

The **NOW CityGuide** continues this tradition of exploring and explaining the city from a fresh viewpoint. Both first-time visitors to Toronto and long-time residents will find the **CityGuide** an invaluable handbook on the best places to eat, party, dance, shop, and generally have fun in the city. Whether you're here for a weekend, a month, or the foreseeable future, you can rely on the **NOW CityGuide** to show you a side of Toronto that goes beyond tourist traps and picture-postcard places. Journey through the best Toronto has to offer, neighbourhood by neighbourhood.

And for the latest up-to-date info on what's happening in Toronto, don't forget to pick up your free copy of NOW magazine, available every Thursday at over 2,000 locations — including restaurants, clubs, and retail outlets, as well as from our distinctive green street boxes.

Michael Hollett
Editor/Publisher

Alice Klein
Editor/CEO

INTRODUCTION

Back in the 1960s, British actor Peter Ustinov rather disdainfully described Toronto as "New York operated by the Swiss." This may have been true 40 years ago, but Toronto today is more like Zurich run by New Yorkers: sure, some traditional British reserve remains from Toronto's early days, but beneath its stiff facade lies North America's most cosmopolitan city — and, thanks to the likes of Ustinov, a city often unfairly dissed and dismissed.

Since the Second World War, immigrants from all over have made Toronto their home — so many that the United Nations declared Toronto the most culturally diverse city in the world. Nowhere is this variety more evident than in the broad range of food available in Toronto restaurants. While much of North America still thinks that fine dining means surf 'n' turf, Torontonians routinely chow down on such varied cuisines as pad thai, jerk chicken with rice 'n' peas, tandoori cauliflower, Vietnamese submarines, and incendiary Ethiopian wat.

But more than its disparate population, it's the lay of the city itself that makes Toronto unique. Unlike other major North American metropolises, Toronto's downtown neighbourhoods have not been bulldozed to make way for corporate skyscrapers. Instead, old office and industrial spaces — parking lots, too! — have been converted into loft-style condominiums. In reverse of the trend in other burgs, Torontonians have escaped the suburbs to live downtown where they can party into the early hours at the innumerable late-night spots that flourish in Clubland, along Queen Street West, and on College Street.

It's not just the downtown core that's happening. The city is made up of a network of neighbourhoods, each surprisingly different from the next, many proudly ethnic, and all vibrant. There are great places to live (Cabbagetown and Riverdale off the Danforth), to shop (Yorkville and Kensington Market), or just kick back (the Toronto islands and the Beach) — all linked by bicycle lanes and public transit. American sociologist and author Jane Jacobs discovered this side of Toronto while writing her acclaimed study *The Death and Life of Great American Cities*, and — recognizing a good thing when she saw one — moved her family to a house in the Annex, two blocks away from Honest Ed's and the Brunswick House.

Toronto, a city once completely dead on Sundays, now rocks 24-7. In the summer, sidewalk cafés line tree-shaded streets, and every few weeks some major event or other keeps the city hopping. Toronto hosts Caribana, the largest carnival north of Trinidad, the North by Northeast music festival, attended by thousands of musicians both local and international, the Gay Pride weekend-long extravaganza, and the International Film Festival, North America's premier cinematic celebration. And that's not all.

The **NOW CityGuide** is completely unlike the usual stuffy city guide that tells you all about tedious tourist traps. Instead, it's an irreverent impression of the Toronto that the conventional guides don't know. The **CityGuide** doesn't take itself seriously but it's serious about having a good time. And whether you've lived here all of your life or you're planning your first visit, you'll find the **CityGuide** is your best partner in discovering the city. Up till now — and NOW — Toronto itself has been Torontonians' best-kept secret. Promise you won't tell anyone else about us, okay? Otherwise, everybody will want to live in what *Utne Reader* calls "North America's most liveable city."

HOW TO USE THIS GUIDE

The Maps

The best place to start is with the neighbourhood maps. You'll notice that along most of the streets on the map there are numbers set within three different shapes. The three shapes correspond to the three sections that all the listings in each chapter fall under:

Food & Drink **7**   **Entertainment** **31**   **Shopping** **75**

The numbers within the symbols correspond to the various listings and are arranged in the order you'll come across them on the street. The maps are not to scale and, for reasons of space, the location of some listings isn't exact. Only the relevant intersections are indicated. If a listing has more than one location, the main listing appears in the neighbourhood where its most prominent outlet is found — its other locations are cross-referenced, and the map reference indicates its location.

Ͳ indicates a subway station

Access

After talking with the people at the Centre for Independent Living Toronto (CILT), an advocacy group for people with disabilities, we ditched the terms "wheelchair accessible" and "inaccessible." Instead, at the end of each listing we describe the actual access you'll encounter. By doing so, we let those for whom mobility is a concern know in advance what kind of obstacles — or lack thereof — to expect. **Barrier-free** means that there are no steps or obstructions at a listing's entrance and that its washrooms are located on the same floor, but it doesn't necessarily mean that these washrooms are equipped for wheelchair users. This first edition provides access information only for the Food & Drink and Entertainment sections of the CityGuide. (In future editions we'll add the access to shops, too.) We've done our best to verify this information, but it might be worth a phone call to the listing before you go just to check — please inform us of any discrepancies so that we can update the next edition of the CityGuide.

Other Info

At the end of each listing, you'll find other information in short form:

Fully licensed means that the business is licensed to sell all types of alcohol. Because it goes without saying that all bars are fully licensed, we've dropped that information from bar listings. **Beer and wine** indicates that, although the place is licensed, it may only sell beer and wine. And **unlicensed** means just that — no booze whatsoever.

Cigarette smoking is prohibited in all public buildings and stores throughout the city, but most restaurants and bars have a designated smoking area. Those that don't are listed in the CityGuide as **smoke-free**.

Most businesses accept some kind of credit or direct-payment card, but those that don't are listed as **cash only**.

If a restaurant or bar has an outdoor serving area, we say **patio**.

The dollar signs at the end of the Food & Drink listings indicate the cost of eating there — $ means cheap, $$ is reasonable, and $$$ warns you it's expensive.

Black Bull

QUEEN WEST

Think of Queen West as Toronto's version of Hollywood's Melrose, minus the palm trees. And Heather Locklear. Whether for shopping or people-gawking, Queen West is Toronto's hippest strip.

FOOD & DINING

RESTAURANTS

65 **THE BAMBOO**
312 Queen W, 593-5771

Built on the site of a former wicker-furniture store, the 'Boo resembles a tacky, tiki rec room from the '50s crossed with a Jamaican jerk shack. The menu is a culture clash, too. Pad thai bumps up against barbecued burgers and Island-spicy jerk chicken. Upstairs, there's a breezy rooftop patio — scene of many summertime showbiz parties — and downstairs, the evening's entertainment is irie, mon. Local and international reggae stars appear regularly, and there's a weekly big-band Swing Night. Roots and zoot suits! Closed Sunday.

Two steps at door, washrooms on same floor. Fully licensed. Patio. $$

59 **THE BISHOP AND THE BELCHER**
361 Queen West, 591-2352

Although it might look like one of those pre-fab English pubs that come out of a crate — the Duke of Wotsit, perhaps? — the Bishop is the local for many non-Brits. Satellite TV pulls in sports action, and plush couches are arranged around a fireplace at the restaurant's rear. In summer, enjoy the fenced-in patio out back. Year round there's $5.95 Pasta Night on Tuesday and $9.95 Steak Fest on Wednesday, and the kitchen stays open every night till last call at 2 a.m.

One step at door, washrooms in basement. Fully licensed. Patio. $$

98 **THE CAMERON HOUSE**
408 Queen West, 703-0811

When this rococo hangout announced it would start serving Sunday brunch, the ultra-jaded yawned in unison, "Whatever." To everyone's amazement the Cameron has become Toronto's hottest brunch ticket. Floral arrangements and linen tablecloths skilfully disguise the room's shortcomings, and now the $11.95 all-inclusive brekkie gets the late-night crowd up early in the morning. Noon's early, right?

One step at door, washrooms on same floor. Fully licensed. Patio. $

6 **EMATEI**
30 St. Patrick, 340-0472

Stylish Japanese bistro.
Barrier-free. Fully licensed. $$$

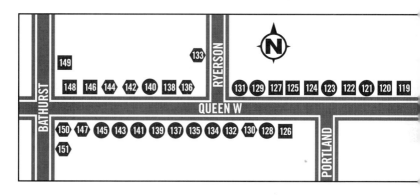

SIREN: Where the children of the night shop for crushed velvet merkins and pixie boots.

127 EPICURE
512 Queen West, 504-8942

Popular with the theatre crowd — Theatre Passe Muraille and the Factory Theatre are nearby — Epicure is a low-key bistro serving such classic French fare as grilled calf's liver and pâté à la campagne. Even with its two patios — one curbside, the other on the rear roof — you can expect crowds during their $3.99/lb. mussel festivals. Saturday and Sunday brunch.

Barrier-free, washrooms in basement. Fully licensed. Patio. $$

122 GOULASH PARTY HAUS
498 Queen West, 703-8056

Despite its grungy appearance, this eatery serves some of the heartiest food on Queen. Rib-sticking goulash (what else?), massive burgers, and legendary former owner Leslie's special — goulash soup, garlic bread, wiener schnitzel, paprika'd home fries, garden salad, and strudel — turn strangers into regulars, despite the decor. Opens early and closes daily at 4 a.m.

One step at door, washrooms in basement. Fully licensed. $

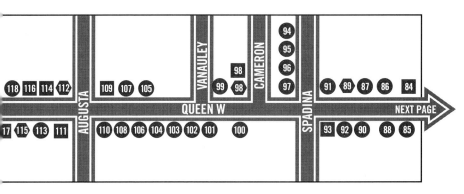

HOT SPOT

116
RED CAT TRADING COMPANY
478 Queen West, 504-5127

Outfitted in chic chinoiserie — paper lanterns stencilled with calligraphy cast romantic shadows on Chinese-red walls — the Cat serves pan-Asian tapas to some of Queen West's hippest customers. Operated by the people responsible for Taro, Red Cat keeps costs down but expectations high. Signature dish: lime-marinated broiled baby calamari served with ripe-mango salsa and Asian noodle salad. Reservations recommended for the prime front-window booth.

One step at door, washrooms in basement. Fully licensed. $$

74
LE SELECT
328 Queen West, 596-6405

One of Queen West's oldest establishments, this Parisian bistro features cookbook-classic cassoulet and steak bavette avec frites. With its *fin de siècle* atmosphere — the nineteenth, that is — Le Select's most charmingly eccentric touch is a hanging breadbasket at each table that you pull down from the ceiling with a hand-operated winch.

Barrier-free. Fully licensed. Patio. $$

124
MASSIMO PIZZA & PASTA
504 Queen West, 703-1803

See listing page 153.

Barrier-free, washrooms in basement. Fully licensed. $$

61
PETER PAN
373 Queen W, 593-0917

In a revitalized diner that first opened in 1880 you'll find Peter Pan, the restaurant that kick-started trendy Toronto 20 years ago, and continues to define hip today. You can't go wrong with the Peter Pan burger, but the merit of dinner mains can be uneven. Rule of tongue: the simpler, the better. Saturday and Sundays brunches are extremely popular, and the weekday $6.95 pasta-and-salad lunch specials can cause long lineups.

Barrier-free, washrooms in basement. Fully licensed. Patio. $$

11
QUEEN MOTHER CAFE
208 Queen West, 598-4719

Taste what Canada considered cutting-edge 20 years ago. The Queen Mum's Cosmic Burger — a patty made of lotsa ground nuts, flakes, and sprouts, slathered in Thousand Island dressing and served on a sesame-seed bun — is still offered in this funky bistro that, fortunately, has mostly moved beyond health food. Although you can get the real Asian thing just a couple of blocks north in Chinatown, the Mum offers a serviceable take on Thai and Laotian specialties that won't frighten your wallet or your date. Brunch Sunday.

Barrier-free, washrooms in basement. Fully licensed. Patio. $$

116
RED CAT TRADING COMPANY
478 Queen West, 504-5127

See Hot Spot listing this page.

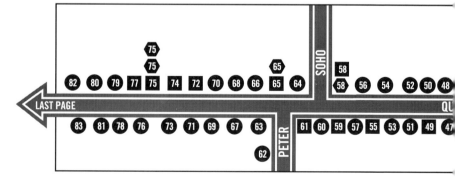

75 THE RIVOLI
332 Queen West, 597-0794

The Riv offers mainstream Pacific Rim fare —
pad thai, Laotian spring rolls — as well as a terrific namesake burger with baked Yukon Gold
frites. The reason for the crowd has little to do
with the action on the plates, however. Out front,
on what might be the coolest patio on the city's
hippest street, you can ogle the passing parade
— from behind shades, of course. Or, upstairs,
shoot a game of snooker on one of 17 antique
pool tables. In the back room, catch a rising out-
there comic — Kids in the Hall got their start
here — or nod to cutting-edge combos that play
everything from heaving hardcore to sophisticated nouveau lounge.

Barrier-free. Fully licensed. Patio. $$

9 SUSHI BISTRO
204 Queen West, 971-5315

Sleek and modern, the Bistro is one of the busiest
fish 'n' rice palaces on Queen West. Expect long
lineups at lunch or dinner but, once seated at a
black lacquered table or the sushi bar, expect
first-rate fare. A pair of cone-shaped temakisushi
stuffed with rice and shrimp tempura, fish roe, or
avocado makes a super light supper.
Closed Sunday.

Barrier-free. Beer and wine, smoke-free. $$

49 SUSHI TIME
339 Queen West, 977-2222

This minimally decorated grey eatery may be
unknowingly fashionable. Did the restaurant

BAMBOO: An Island oasis of irie grooves.

designers guess that grey is the new brown now
that brown is no longer the new black? Style notes
aside, this straight-ahead sushi-and-sashimi
emporium offers combination dinners that,
despite their odd names — Hockey Sushi? Golf
Combo? — provide good bang for the buck.
Closed Sunday.

One step at door, washrooms in basement. Fully
licensed. $$

120 TARO
492 Queen West, 504-1320

Sister restaurant to the nearby Red Cat, Taro has a
more cosmopolitan roster than its sibling's Asian
menu. Against a backdrop of exposed brick, sten-

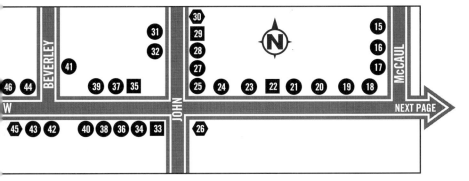

cilled hardwood floors, and tapestries, Taro serves up such contemporary grub as tempura-veggie salad, seared New Zealand lamb tenderloin with an apple-tamarind glaze, and apple-stuffed pork cutlets. Popular on weekends for brunch.

Barrier-free, washrooms in basement. Fully licensed. Patio. $$

10 TIGER LILY'S
257 Queen West, 977-5499

Owner and chef Dinah Koo takes lowly Asian-noodle fast food and makes it sparkle at this small eatery. The decor's not much — bamboo curtains and a poster for Woody Allen's *What's Up, Tiger Lily?* — but Koo's take on Vietnamese pho soups updates these meal-in-one dishes with good ingredients and results. Try spring rolls packed with shrimp, daikon, and sprouts before tucking into a better-than-average pad thai. Weekend brunches now feature Koo's inventive dim sum — hoisin-duck quesadillas, Hawaiian-inspired pineapple congee.

One step at door, washrooms on same floor. Fully licensed, smoke-free. $$

28 YOUNG THAILAND
165 John, 593-9291

See listing page 109.

13 steps at door, washrooms on same floor. Fully licensed. $$

CAFES AND COFFEE HOUSES

149 AZUL
181 Bathurst, 703-9360

You can't fault Azul for its decor — there isn't any, just burlap-covered walls, shaky stacking chairs, and wobbly tables that wouldn't find their

way into *Architectural Digest*. Solid smoothies and shakes like the Hangover Helper go well with the mostly organic mains and starters. Racks of magazines and a motorcycle add atmosphere. Weekend brunch on the patio — an alleyway, really — packs in regulars. *Frasier*'s Kelsey Grammer hangs here when he's in town.

One step at door, washrooms on same floor. Unlicensed, smoke-free. Patio. $

55 COFFEE CONNOISSEUR
357 Queen West, 595-7323

Two steps at door, washrooms in basement. Unlicensed. $

111 JAVA HOUSE
537 Queen West, 504-3025

With its large street-side patio, Java is a popular student spot perfect for making a cuppa coffee last all afternoon while watching the passing Queen Street parade. Straightforward wraps, veggie salads, and simple noodle combos round out the mostly Asian menu.

Barrier-free, washrooms in basement. Unlicensed. Patio. $

93 LETTIERI
441 Queen West, 592-1360

The corner of Queen and Spadina is ground zero for squeegee kids. Since Lettieri's patio fronts on the action, you can get a curbside view of their panhandling and window-washing year round. Indoors, steaming cappuccinos and lattes complement a pizza and panini menu.

Barrier-free. Fully licensed. Patio. $

Other locations:
94 Cumberland (see page 176)
544 Danforth (see page 191)

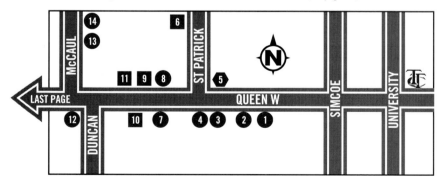

117 LOST CAMEL
559 Queen West, 703-5275

One of Queen's best beaneries, Lost Camel brews up a terrific cup of joe. There are the customary caps, lattes, and espressos, as well as sandwiches — try the Godfather, with salami, mozzarella, and bitter greens — and spicy chickpea wraps. Noodle salads, quiche Florentine, and flatbread pizza, too.

Barrier-free, washrooms in basement. Unlicensed, smoke-free. $

35 L'EXPRESS
254 Queen W, 596-0205

Glaringly painted in Gucci citrus colours — lime, orange, and lemon — this popular pasta, pizza, and panini spot caters to an informal crowd. Quite often the tables in the striped back room are full of rich high-school girls gossiping on cell phones. Out front, more mature patrons opt for Energy veggie burgers, twisted chicken on braided bagels, and six-cheese Tuscan pizzas built to share or hog.

Barrier-free. Fully licensed. Patio. $$

33 SECOND CUP
307 Queen West, 598-5641

Canada's premier chain of coffee houses seems to have an outlet on every corner in town. And the Queen and John location is one of the best. Not only does it have a covered and fenced-in patio that's open almost every day of the year, but customers get a front-row seat for the shenanigans outside music-video superstation MuchMusic across the street. If you're ever trying to track down Second Cup's Yankee competitors — Starbucks — they're nearly always located next door.

Barrier-free. Unlicensed. Patio. $

119 TEQUILA BOOKWORM
490 Queen West, 504-7335

You won't run out of reading material at this coffee 'n' panini house — there's a magazine stand brimming with the latest issues of fashion and music mags, a basket stuffed with dailies, used hardcovers in the library at the rear of the room, and a stack of NOW magazines, of course. Brunch and lunch are as laid-back as the café's design — high tin ceilings, kitchen tables, couches, and a lunch counter with revolving stools.

Barrier-free, washrooms in basement. Unlicensed. Patio. $

DELIS AND DINERS

114 THE BLUE JAY
472 Queen West, 703-0517

Barrier-free, washrooms in basement. Unlicensed. $

84 THE STEM OPEN KITCHEN
354 Queen West, 593-0530

Long before Queen West was a street anyone would want to visit — let alone live on — the Stem was serving all-day breakfasts to regulars. They fight over the two-seater booths to this day. Even if you don't score the primo window seat, you can still perch on a red-vinyl stool at the lunch counter, read the morning papers, and savour a grilled cheese sandwich — true comfort food.

One step at door, washrooms in basement. Unlicensed. $

JUICE BARS

77 JUICE FOR LIFE
336 Queen West, 599-4442

See listing page 166.

Barrier-free. Unlicensed, smoke-free. $

TAKEOUT

138 AMATO PIZZA
534 Queen West, 703-8989

Amato serves some of the biggest pizza slices in town — and these amply proportioned quarter-pies will set you back all of three bucks. Toppings range from the traditional pepperoni and mozzarella to the more exotic grilled eggplant, artichokes, and "salty sardo" cheese. Once past the busy takeout counter, you'll find a casual dine-in area where the menu expands to include pastas and salads along with their super thin-crust pizzas.

One step at door, washrooms on same floor. Fully licensed. $$

Other locations:
429 Yonge (see page 118)
380 College (see page 83)

126 CARIBBEAN ROTI CORNER
607 Queen West, 504-9558

If the Corner were any more laid-back, it would be horizontal. Service here is very slow — regulars know to phone their takeout orders far in advance, giving the cook at least half an hour to assemble the sizable rotis that make the wait worthwhile. The gigantic shells can hold carefully curried callaloo, turnip, or excellent eggplant. On weekends, the Corner serves Jamaican dishes like jerk chicken or fried salt fish with dumplings, but the menu also includes Lebanese falafels. Just don't be in a hurry!

One step at door, no washrooms. Unlicensed, smoke-free, cash only. $

148 FALAFEL QUEEN
576 Queen West, 504-9736

Shawarma, shish kebab, and souvlaki are served up every night until 4 a.m. at this mostly Middle Eastern eatery. Get your food to go or eat in — the resto's interior (textured mocha walls, large gilt-framed mirrors) is surprisingly swank for such a grungy intersection.

Barrier-free. Unlicensed, cash only. $

146 GANDHI
554 Queen West, 504-8155

A plain storefront with a few bare tables in the window, Gandhi is brought to you by the folks from the far pricier Babur down the street. Rotis are the thing here: huge wrappers holding mostly vegetarian goodies such as chickpea channa, spinach with mild paneer cheese, or curried eggplant. Meat eaters can tear into versions full of lamb, shrimp, and deboned chicken.

Barrier-free. Unlicensed, cash only. $

BARS

22 THE BEVERLEY TAVERN
240 Queen W, 598-2434

Twenty years ago, the Queen West scene started here. When it was a divey beer hall, students from the nearby Ontario College of Art staged music shows here. Soon-to-be household names the Dishes, the Viletones, and Martha and the Muffins trod the boards for the first time on the second floor's wobbly stage. That's all gone now, and to-day the Bev is gentrified and generic. The rooftop patio gets heavy summer action and every Friday night the first-floor window offers a ringside view of the desperate hijinks being taped across the street for Citytv's dance show *Electric Circus*. If the bartender's in a good mood, he just might spin the Demics' circa-'78 "I Wanna Go to New York City." Closed Sunday.

One step at door, washrooms on same floor. Patio.

58 THE BLACK BULL
298 Queen West, 593-2766

Established in 1883, the Bull goes in cycles from being extraordinarily hip to being the last place on earth you'd want to be seen. Indoors, it's ye olde taverne, complete with neon beer signs and an '80s-rock soundtrack. Thursday's Karaoke Night and bluesy roots rockers play on the weekend. But the real action happens on the 200-seat patio when summer hits. Try getting a table there once a gang of wannabe Hell's Angels — most likely dentists in real life — descend after parking their $30,000 Harley hogs on the sidewalk!

One step at door, washrooms on same floor. Patio.

142 BOVINE SEX CLUB
542 Queen West, 504-4239

From the outside, the Bovine looks like the aftermath of an accident in an ironworks. Bits of scrap steel, bicycle wheels, and wrought-iron railings have been welded to form a heavy metal facade that protects the equally heavy-drinking clientele from the real world outside. Inside, where it's dark, dank, and down-and-dirty, DJs spin vintage AC/DC, Alice Cooper, or whatever's loud and happening. Sunday nights there's a free brunch — toast with Cheez Whiz. And no, cattle have never been seen shagging here.

Barrier-free.

98 THE CAMERON HOUSE
408 Queen West, 703-0811

The definitive Queen West bar, the Cameron's wild decor — check out the ceiling mural — and art installations have long made it the lounge to be scene in. Prince once took over the entire place for a private party of five — his Purpleness and four models. Where did he sit? Nowhere — he danced. What did he drink? Water.

One step at door, washrooms on same floor. Patio.

109 **THE DUKE OF CONNAUGHT**
460 Queen West, 504-6462

One of the few remaining vestiges of Queen West before it was hip. Don't miss its punk-rock jukebox.

One step at door, washrooms on same floor. Patio.

144 **SAVAGE GARDEN**
550 Queen West, 504-2178

Undead! Undead! Undead! Are the Sisters of Mercy the soundtrack to your sad life? Are you a fan of Anne Rice novels? Do you fancy yourself in a cinched corset, pixie boots, and a Robert Smith–style psycho-wig? Goth lives on in an eternal-death sorta way at this groovatorium à gogo, where persons of indeterminate sex writhe in cages. The horror! The hubris! The hilarity!

Nine steps at door, washrooms on same floor.

72 **THE 360**
326 Queen West, 593-0840

Once home to the Canadian Legion — well, it still is, but the war vets have moved upstairs — this punky watering hole showcases up-and-coming hardcore bands and fringe-theatre performances. Big, comfortable booths out front and pool tables and a stage in the back mean the 360 is always jumping. The street-side summer patio is the perfect spot for sneering at the bourgeoisie promenading past.

Barrier-free, washrooms in basement. Patio.

125 **VELVET UNDERGROUND**
508 Queen West, 504-6688

Behind its rusted steel facade, V.U. is decorated with spiky angel statuary by Floria Sigismundi, the multidisciplinary Toronto artist famous for the gothic videos she directed for David Bowie and Marilyn Manson. The club's a raucous frat-boy beer hall where off-work strippers come to dance to loud top-40 alternative rock. If the music's volume suddenly drops, it's just the sound system's over-ride kicking in — wouldn't want to annoy the neighbours!

Barrier-free, washrooms in basement.

89 **THE HORSESHOE**
368 Queen West, 598-4753

For more than 50 years, the 'Shoe has been presenting rockin' performances. Everyone from Loretta Lynn to the Rolling Stones has played here. Once Stompin' Tom's stomping ground, this neon-lit honky-tonk has lost some of its historic cachet, but still offers gigs by the likes of Grant Lee Buffalo, the High Llamas, and secret shows by the Tragically Hip. Sightlines are limited, but no matter who's playing, the vibe is always true 'Shoe.

Barrier-free, washrooms in basement. Fully licensed. Patio.

ENTERTAINMENT

LIVE MUSIC

58 **THE BLACK BULL**
298 Queen West, 593-2766
See listing page 18.

98 **THE CAMERON HOUSE**
408 Queen West, 703-0811

The back room of the Cameron has launched many music careers. Handsome Ned, Molly Johnson, and Big Sugar's Gordie Johnson all started out in this intimate room. After Sunday brunch, Cameron co-owner — and former disco diva — Cindy Mathews shakes the room up with the old-time Cameron Family Singers.

One step at door, washrooms upstairs. Fully licensed. Patio.

45 **CHICAGO'S**
335 Queen West, 598-3301

A *Cheers*-style bar with an upstairs performing space, Chicago's features blues jams and r 'n' b shootouts nightly. The downstairs menu doesn't stray from pub grub — beefy burgers, nachos and chili-cheese poppers, a coupla pizza combos — but the atmosphere is always upbeat, especially for a place that's home to the blues.

Barrier-free, washrooms upstairs. Fully licensed.

THE CAMERON: Barbra Streisand and date.

⒀ EXIT 609
609 Queen West, 504-8356

A murky joint hidden behind blacked-out windows, 609 focuses on rhythm and blues and the funk, y'all. Mondays, they host a blues jam, Tuesdays are open mic and Thursday showcases funk guitarist Alix Anthony — "Prince meets Hendrix" (his modest description). Saturdays, Snooky Tynes takes over for a night of soul testifying. Closed Sunday.

Barrier-free, washrooms in basement. Fully licensed.

⒂ HOLY JOE'S
651 Queen West, 504-0744

A third-floor walk-up, Holy Joe's is an intimate room that's often used as the dressing room for headliners at the Reverb club downstairs. The decor amounts to some twinkly Christmas lights, and the entertainment runs to up-and-coming acoustic acts.

35 steps at door, washrooms on same floor. Fully licensed.

⒆ THE HORSESHOE
368 Queen West, 598-4753

See Hot Spot listing page 19.

⒄ REVERB
651 Queen West, 504-0744

Up a claustrophobic flight of stairs, you'll find one of Queen West's best music venues. Great sightlines, two bars, and excellent sound make Reverb a great spot to catch local bands or concerts by such international headliners as Crowded House's Neil Finn, American rockers Wilco, or hometown hero Ron Sexsmith. Although upwards of 500 club-goers can be squeezed into the space, most nights the room is comfortably uncrowded.

16 steps at door, washrooms on same floor. Fully licensed.

❺ THE REX HOTEL
194 Queen West, 598-2475

One of Queen West's oldest watering holes, the former dingy tavern has reinvented itself as the street's premier jazz venue. Jazz and blues performers — including big-band swingers, jump-joint jivers, and merengue maniacs — rock the house seven nights a week. And when the weather allows, office workers from nearby towers fill the sunny patio while chowing down on the Rex's cosmopolitan lunch menu.

Barrier-free. Fully licensed. Patio.

⒂ THE RIVOLI
334 Queen West, 596-1908

The Riv's rear performance space is an intimate venue spotlighting local and international musicians and comedians — the Kids in the Hall got their start in this 125-seat room. Monday night's ALT.COMedy Lounge showcases the best of Toronto's comedy scene as well as star turns from visiting out-of-town talent like *Saturday Night Live*'s Janeane Garofalo and Will Ferrell. Past musical performers include Patti Smith and Iggy Pop.

Barrier-free. Fully licensed.

DANCE CLUBS

⒂ THE BIG BOP
651 Queen West, 504-6699

A black hole of a room popular with the suburbanite S & M — Scarborough and Mississauga — crowd, the Bop is as cutting-edge as the latest Céline Dion remix (i.e. not very). Early shows are more street — hip hop, old-school rappers, and breakers — while weekend jams are positively mainstream. Lots of alternative rock and '80s hits, although no Swing Nights. Yet.

Barrier-free. Fully licensed.

136 ZOO BAR
526 Queen West, 703-9453

Closed Sunday to Wednesday.

16 steps at door, washrooms on same floor. Fully licensed.

POOL HALLS

112 CENTRAL BILLIARDS
468 Queen West, 504-9494

A sign by the locked front door pointedly states "Members only." As you peer through the cigarette-stained windows at the bleary pool sharks who roam from table to table, cue in hand, you may find yourself thinking maybe it's just as well that they don't admit the general public.

Barrier-free. Fully licensed.

115 CLUB 24-7
553 Queen West, 361-6354

Unlike its grungy neighbour — Central Billiards across the street — 24-7 is a stylishly appointed four-table pool hall complete with video screens, overstuffed black leather couches, and a small snack menu. And, as its name suggests, the place is open around the clock.

Barrier-free. Fully licensed.

75 THE RIVOLI
332 Queen West, 596-1501

A very cool space with great tunes, this major hang attracts a stylish crowd with more than the white ball on their minds.

20 steps at door, washrooms on same floor. Fully licensed.

GALLERIES AND MUSEUMS

30 JANE CORKIN GALLERY
179 John, 979-1980

Featuring some of the great names of photography — Edward Steichen, Irving Penn, Man Ray — in their permanent collection, this internationally renowned gallery also exhibits work that ranges from 19th-century Japanese prints to glamour snaps of Madonna by Herb Ritts. Closed Saturday and Sunday.

THEATRE

133 THEATRE PASSE MURAILLE
16 Ryerson, 504-7529

Literally "theatre without borders," T.P.M. has been presenting contemporary Canadian drama since the late '60s. Originally a collaborative devoted to works by emerging playwrights, the company is now part of Canada's dramaturgical establishment. Two stages — the Main Space and the more intimate Back Space — present pay-what-you-can Sunday matinees.

Some areas barrier-free.

ATTRACTIONS

26 MUCHMUSIC
299 Queen West, 597-5757

A news truck bursting through a brick wall marks the home of MuchMusic, Bravo!, and Citytv television stations. Friday nights, you can dance outside with club kids not groovy enough to be invited inside to dance on *Electric Circus*. Or stand behind crowd barriers to await the arrival of the Backstreet Boys or the Spice Girls. For a loonie, you can sit down in the *Speaker's Corner* video booth and tell media mogul Moses Znaimer what you think of his empire. Or say hi to your mom.

SHOPPING

AROMATHERAPY

123 OSMOSIS
336 Queen West, 408-3500

North America's first full-concept aromatherapy store, Osmosis's motto is "Smell locally, shop globally." As well as products that nourish and please the body — nose elixirs, aromatic eye pillows, and botanical body lotions — the staff offer seminars on the Art of Perfume and on aphrodisiacs.

ART SUPPLIES

82 CURRY'S
344 Queen West, 260-2633

See listing page 155.

BICYCLES

(141) DUKE'S CYCLE
625 Queen West, 504-6138

One of the city's finest bike shops, Duke's also has a fast repair service. Although they also sell hockey equipment and sharpen skates — and exchange them, too — the main attractions are the top-of-the-line mountain, hybrid, and road bikes. Frames by Cannondale, Gary Fisher, Specialized, and Rocky Mountain; cool shades from Oakley, Arnette, and Spy; and Louis Garneau cycling duds, as well.

(31) URBANE CYCLIST
180 John, 979-973

BOOKS AND MAGAZINES — NEW

(13) ANOTHER MAN'S POISON
29 McCaul, 593-6451

Specializing in books on historical and contemporary design, graphics, and architecture, this cluttered bookshop also houses a collection of everyday objects that are considered works of art: merry-go-round ponies, modernist Olivetti typewriters from the '60s, '50s Philco Predicta TVs, coffee makers, and a postwar Wurlitzer jukebox. Closed Sunday.

(37) PAGES
256 Queen West, 598-1447

A one-stop local bookstore with a focus on contemporary art and popular culture, Pages also stocks a comprehensive selection of local and international magazines and newspapers. In addition to NOW magazine — and the lesser freebie weeklies — it also gives shelf space to other gratis journals that cover the Toronto literary, sexual politic, and alternative-music scenes. Don't miss its intriguingly offbeat window displays.

BOOKS AND MAGAZINES — USED

(106) ABELARD
519 Queen West, 504-2665

Scholarly tomes and antiquarian titles.

(80) DAVID MASON BOOKS
342 Queen West, 598-1015

Antiquarian and first-edition literary titles.

(102) STEVEN TEMPLE BOOKS
489 Queen West, 703-9908

Rare and antiquarian tomes. By appointment only.

(4) VILLAGE BOOK STORE
239 Queen West, 598-4097

New and used Canadian titles with a focus on art.

COMIC BOOKS AND 'ZINES

(18) 3RD QUADRANT
226 Queen West, 974-9211

Heavily secured — almost everything here is under lock and key — this new- and used-comic-book emporium retails superhero posters and bubble gum cards, plus *Star Trek* commemorative plates and coffee mugs. Warning: "Shoplifters will be vaporized."

(60) SILVER SNAIL
367 Queen West, 593-0889

A two-storey store, the Snail deals in more than just new and used comic books. Displayed throughout the building are exclusive imported action figures and limited-edition titles long sold out at other outlets. Not that the shop is dedicated to traditional comic-book icons — you'll find doll replicas of *All My Children*'s soap-opera diva Susan Lucci next to Barbie Loves Elvis and Talking G.I. Joe.

Other location:
2374 Yonge (see page 227)

DRUGS

(20) THE FRIENDLY STRANGER
226 Queen West, 595-1749

Bongs, chillums, and stoner gear are the raison d'être of this drug store. Ostensibly a purveyor of fine hemp goods — hippie dashikis, itchy towels, and macraméd belts — it's the rolling papers and marijuana paraphernalia that draw the stoners. We used to call these places head shops, but at least they got rid of those appalling psychedelic posters. Closed Sunday.

FASHION — ACCESSORIES

(108) ARTON
523 Queen West, 504-1168

Beads, baubles, and buttons — Arton sells everything a do-it-yourself jeweller needs to get started. As well as selling bead looms, they have a wide selection of bracelet charms — guns, skulls, happy faces — and goth crosses and pentagrams. Ooo, scary! Closed Sunday.

⑮ MALABAR
14 McCaul, 598-2581

Torontonians think of Malabar as the place to rent a Halloween costume, but it sells stuff, too. The retail half of the store concentrates on theatrical makeup and apparel — many members of the National Ballet buy their pointe shoes here. If you want to fashion your own tutu, they've got shiny fabrics, sew-on sequins, and marabou feathers for you. Danskin fishnet tights, punky Manic Panic hair dye, Darth Vader headgear, and red plastic clown noses, too. Closed Sunday.

⑪⓿ NIK NAK
525 Queen West, 703-1092

As its name suggests, this boutique features fashionable whatnots — groovy shades, Guess bags, and butterfly hair-clips.

Other locations:
412 Danforth (see page 195)
450 Eglinton West (see page 223)

㊸ SILVER CROSS
331 Queen West, 599-3311

Need a new pair of handcuffs? A studded dog collar or a skull-and-crossbones ring? Silver Cross is your gothic one-stop shop. Straddling the blurred line between heavy-metal fashion and that just-crawled-out-from-under-a-rock look, this baroque boutique will appeal to Metallica headbangers and Bauhaus gravediggers alike. Remember, vampires aren't real, but black is forever.

⑬⓹ SIX DEGREES
613 Queen West, 504-8479

A retail space, an art gallery, and a millinery, Six Degrees wears many hats — and sells them, too. Owner and designer Suzanne Paquette's chic *chapeaux* are both whimsical and wearable. The boutique also features womenswear by Bravery, hair jewellery by Metal Maiden, and knitted caps by Jaqui.

㊺ STORM
292 Queen West, 340-8579

Already a chain in swinging London, Storm has fi-

⑨⓿ GET OUT SIDE
437 Queen West, 593-5598

From the street this shoe store appears to be stocked with the same platform trainers that all its competitors sell, but don't be deceived — G.O.S. is one of the most cutting-edge fashion boutiques on a street known for its trendiness. Past the Spice Girls gear, you'll find Tokyo street fashion by Kirita and Prego — handmade asymmetrical boots, T-shirts plastered with holograms, and white vinyl nurses' bags complete with IV tubing and plastic syringes. More conservative shoes by Airwalk, Dr. Martens, Simple, and Le Freak, too.

nally opened shop in North America. The store specializes in pen sets, multi-faced high-tech watches, industrial-strength belts, and shiny quilted-vinyl wallets and handbags similar to the incredibly cool — and much bootlegged — Boy London–brand accessories. They also sell Licence carryalls, camera bags, and knapsacks.

㊴ SUNGLASS HUT
290 Queen West, 977-6921

Top-of-the-line shades from Oakley, Emporio Armani, Ray-Ban, Stussy, Vuarnet, Tommy Hilfiger, and Ralph Lauren are just some of the big-name eyewear carried at this boutique that also has a branch in Miami's South Beach.

FASHION — NEW CLOTHING

⑨⓻ APPLE'S HOUSE OF HIP HOP
162A Spadina, 203-2171

Powerful speakers blasting the latest jeepbeats inside this hip-hop shop make Apple's one very loud boutique. One-of-a-kind outfits from such hip-hop heavy hitters as Fubu, Phat Farm, and MeccaDNM line the walls of this tiny, minimalist space, and DJ-mix cassettes are piled high behind the sales counter. Especially dope: crocheted (!) b-boy hats with floppy rabbit ears.

㊾ BLUENOTES
349 Queen West, 593-2681

Although it appears to be an upscale international jeanery, this is really just a good ol' Thrifty's store under a different guise. Affordable and mainstream, their duds are best described by this over-

HOAX COUTURE: The designers who "do" Paul Schaeffer.

heard comment: "I'm buying these jeans to wear to an audition for a McDonald's commercial."

34 BOOMER
309 Queen West, 598-0013

Dealing exclusively in menswear, Boomer specializes in almost-conservative suits by Hugo Boss and Cinque and slightly flashier duds by Dubuc Mode De Vie and Denommé Vincent. The sparse shop's five-way mirror makes sure you get to see how you look coming, and, more importantly, going.

85 CHARMIS COUTURE
425 Queen West, 977-9990

Fashion queens with rich sugar daddies are about the only people who can afford to shop at this Big Name fashion boutique. Yes, everything is fabulous — sky-high rubber platforms by No Name, Helmut Lang belts, Paul Smith quilted jackets. But look at the prices! $170 for a gauze Dolce & Gabbana T-shirt silk-screened with the Virgin Mary? $200-plus Versace jeans? At Charmis, if you have to ask the price, you can't afford it.

79 CHÂTEAU WORKS
336 Queen West, 971-9314

Le Château has made its reputation in the fashion world with bargain-priced knock-offs of whatever's hip and happening. Taking a page from Urban Outfitters' style book, the Montreal firm recently branched out beyond just fashionable threads. While browsing to anonymous techno muzak, you'll find a juice bar, unisex hairdresser, inflatable furniture — oh, and clothes, too.

Other Le Château locations:
772 Yonge (see page 181)
328 Yonge (see page 121)

92 CITY OF ANGELS
439 Queen West, 408-0111

Angels specializes in fly threads for superfly gals — skimpy PVC tops and jeans that r 'n' b crooner Barry White might suggestively describe as being "for the ladeez." Both sexy and sexist — one T-shirt declares "Slut!" — this is club gear with a hip-hop flava.

76 CLUB MONACO
403 Queen West, 979-5633

It's easy to dismiss the Club as a Canadian copy of the Gap, but it actually achieves what its American counterpart tries to do, with a lot more flash for a lot less cash. There's nothing preppy here; instead, you'll find upscale casual wear that you can easily wear from the office to a nightclub. Basic black, crisp whites, and classically formal grey flannel — no plaid or beige — make up Monaco's fashion palette.

Other locations:
157 Bloor West (see page 180)
Eaton Centre (see page 121)

8 ### DECIBEL
200 Queen West, 506-9648

Overheard comment from a shopper taking in the window display at Decibel: "Look, Kramer clothes!" Jerry Seinfeld's klutzy sidekick would feel right at home in this upmarket men's haberdashery with its retro-looking but completely contemporary fedoras, shirt jackets, and windbreakers. Its designer wear includes Fresh Baked Goods sweaters, Kangol caps and knapsacks, and Da Vinci of California bowling shirts. Cosmo would approve.

104 ### F/X
515 Queen West, 703-5595

The farther you travel past the tangle of soda-fountain stools that almost blocks your way into the store, the more interesting F/X gets. At the front, gaggles of preteens pig out on jawbreakers and homemade fudge. Mid-store you'll find rubber snakes, teddy bears, F/X's own kaleidoscopic line of nail polish, and a shoe department stocked with Underground and Swear. The rear of this hypermarket features the works of over 500 designers — Canadian and international — including Jean-Paul Gaultier, Vivienne Westwood, Anna Sui, Betsey Johnson, and, er, Hello Kitty.

71 ### FASHION CRIMES
395 Queen West, 592-9001

Fashion Crimes, Toronto designer Pam Chorley's fanciful boutique, features her imaginative line of womenswear. Taking her inspiration from turn-of-the-century — the last one, not this one — Titanic styles, Chorley has created a distinctive look that is all crushed velvet, feather headdresses, and beaded bodices. For extra effect, strap on a pair of angel's wings. Misdemeanours — her equally inventive children's-wear outlet — is right across the street (see listing page 26).

63 ### THE GAP
375 Queen West, 591-3517

From the Wal-Mart-like automaton who greets you

as you enter this Temple of Prep, to the cashier who wishes you a nice day, one thing's for sure — you'll never be lonely at the Gap. Some swear by the Gap's goods' longevity and timeless design. Others say the true spirit of Queen West died the day the Gap opened.

Other locations:
60 Bloor West (see page 180)
260 Yonge (see page 121)
302 Yonge (see page 121)

90 ### GET OUT SIDE
437 Queen West, 593-5598

See Hot Spot page 23.

40 ### GROOVY
323 Queen West, 595-1059

One of Queen West's oldest purveyors, Groovy stocks a wide array of men's and women's shoes, from casual Converse runners and retro Hush Puppies to the latest from Airwalk and Vans. They also peddle brothel creepers imported from the UK. But it's not all fashions for the feet at this esteemed shop — in addition to shoes, they also retail such upscale women's club wear as FreePeople, Doll House, and Cousto of Barcelona.

78 ### GUESS
409 Queen West, 979-1594

The jean company that brought Claudia Schiffer to the fashion world also gives Queen West one of its oddest stores. This Italian-owned boutique, resembling a pre-shootout OK Corral, attempts to recreate the Old West as a backdrop for its pricey denim togs. Overhead on video monitors, commercials for their cowboy-inspired duds play endlessly. Yeehaw, dude!

32 ### HOAX COUTURE
176 John, 597-8924

After a rickety ride on a one-person elevator to the fourth floor, fashion hounds can scope out the latest creations of Toronto design duo Jim Searle and Chris Tyrell. Known internationally as Hoax Couture, the two specialize in men's and women's clothes that are both upwardly mobile and down-to-earth funky. This informal workspace is where the designers come up with their runway apparel — there's even a rack of last year's castoffs marked down to ridiculously low prices. Among Hoax's celebrity clientele: David Letterman's band leader Paul Schaeffer and basketball bad boy Dennis Rodman. So this is where they get those crazy getups! Closed Sunday.

Other location:
114 Cumberland (see page 180)

27 LOUNGE
155 John, 351-7945

This top-of-the-line neon-lit b-boy boutique markets über-hip Toronto designers Too Black Guys' line of basketball-inspired sweats and tops. Although widely available in the States, since T.B.G. closed their Toronto store, their in-demand duds have been hard to find elsewhere locally. Also on hand at Lounge are club clothes by Dub Weather, Helly Hansen and Ralph Lauren (?!?).

70 MISDEMEANOURS
322-1/2 Queen West, 351-8758

Looking for the perfect outfit for your precious little angel? How about dressing the kid up in a pair of feathery angel wings? The kiddie offshoot of Pam Chorley's Fashion Crimes — which is right across the street — has just the thing for a budding Spice Girl or junior Courtney Love — feather boas, dalmatian-print coats, and over-the-top ballerina tutus.

42 MODROBES
329 Queen West, 340-1222

Pronounced "mode robes," this local designer's line of comfortable casual wear is retailed in over 160 stores across Canada, but the Queen West location is the only one dubbed a "design concept" outlet. Here, you can try out the likes of baggy-legged canvas cargo pants, body-snug tees silk-screened with the words "comfy crotch pleaser," or DJ carry-alls long before they hit the rest of the country. Queen Street's like that.

62 MS. EMMA'S DESIGNS
134 Peter, 598-2466

Housed in a space that resembles a warehouse loft, Ms. Emma carries its own handcrafted and custom-fitted women's apparel in natural fabrics. This Ms. — named for *The Avengers*' Emma Peel, although she wouldn't find any '60s garb here — offers sumptuous clothes made from richly textured velvets and brocades, and hand-printed silks.

Other locations:
480 Parliament (see page 130)
496 Danforth (see page 195)

12 NOISE
275 Queen West, 971-6479

Attention skate punks: wicked *Thrasher*-style threads and decks inside. Noise — the rambunctious kid brother to suave Decibel (or is it the other way round?) — carries the baggiest pants, the tightest tees, and the most trailblazin' trainers in town. Such essential names as Freshine, Quicksilver, Snug, Balzac, DCShoes, and Spiewak of New York City are all carried here. Celebrity shoppers: just about every musician or rapper who's ever visited MuchMusic next door. Plus Robin Williams and Farrah Fawcett — but not together!

25 NUMB
250 Queen West, 599-5424

Ever wonder where rave kids get the oversized getups they sport? Likely at Numb, which sells its own line of baggy club wear — lime-green fun-fur culottes, slinky marabou-trimmed tops, purple quilted ski pants, and butterfly hair-clips. Jungle, hardcore, and house compilation cassettes, too.

19 PABLO'S
226 Queen West, 260-6039

This second-storey cubbyhole's range of custom-made T-shirts may be limited, but their fashion-ability knows no bounds. Once the purveyor of tees bearing the face of then-unknown Spanish actor Antonio Banderas, Pablo's line now embraces martial-arts icon Bruce Lee and original riot grrrl Tank Girl.

103 PEACH BERSERK
507 Queen West, 504-1711

Madcap print designer Kingi Carpenter is one of Queen West's wackiest characters — and a successful businessperson to boot. She silkscreens campy patterns — among them "Eiffel for You" and "Naked Ladies" — onto cotton, cotton-Lycra, or silk, and then sews them into nifty designs you can buy off the rack. Or, if you prefer, she'll make something to order. She sells oven mitts, aprons, duvet covers, and sheets, too. Do-it-yourselfers can purchase the material separately and whip up their own creations.

⑤⑦ RAG TAG
359 Queen West, 979-3939

Visitors from the States are appalled at the price of clothing that hasn't been manufactured in Canada. First the cost is skyrocketed by a weak Canadian dollar, and then again by a surtax imposed on goods made beyond our borders. That's how a $30 U.S. pair of Levi's ends up costing $85 Canadian. But for those who insist on wearing a foreign label on their backside, Rag Tag has the names in demand — Todd Oldham, Big Star, Diesel, and Edwin. The very cool dressing rooms in the rear of the store have doors fashioned from fridges.

④⑦ REPLAY
337 Queen West, 979-9400

This beautifully appointed store caters to an older crowd with loadsa dough to spend. An outlet of the Italian sportswear company, Replay is much pricier than most jean retailers. $87 T-shirts? $200 satin hip-huggers? The firm's craftsmanship is top-notch — but then at these prices it should be.

Other location:
511 Danforth (see page 195)

④⑥ ROBIN KAY
276 Queen West, 585-7731

Since starting her business in 1976, Toronto knitwear designer Robin Kay has taken her distinctive cotton womenswear onto international fashion runways. Both consumer-friendly and ecologically sound, Kay's products reflect her personal philosophy: "Simplify life." Recently, her line has expanded to include home furnishings and botanical skin-care potions.

Other locations:
394 Spadina Rd. (see page 227)
2599 Yonge (see page 227)
348 Danforth (see page 195)

⑧⑥ ROOTS
356 Queen West, 977-0409

See listing page 121.

⑩⓪ SIREN
463 Queen West, 504-9288

Coffin-shaped black vinyl backpacks, vampire fangs, and Vlad the Impaler T-shirts — Siren is a goth superstore featuring silver jewellery by London's Alchemy, and Underground platform boots.

THEATRE PASSE MURAILLE: The play's the thing at this cutting-edge collective.

Siren's funereal owners Morpheus and Groovella Blak — real names, honest! — also stock hosiery by Fashion Heratix, Urban Decay makeup, and pentagram-engraved hip flasks. Beatle boots, to boot!

38 **SO HIP IT HURTS**
323 Queen West, 971-6901

Its owners may have been bragging when they came up with the name for their shop, but So Hip deserves its handle. The autographed Polaroids pinned to the wall attest to the shop's popularity with visiting rock stars. Korn, Blur, Offspring, and Rage Against the Machine have all shopped here for skate-inspired jackets, jeans, and trainers by PornStar, Serial Killer, and Lithium. Maybe it's the non-stop videos and leather couches that attract the famous clientele. Or the low prices for skateboard decks. Or more likely, the free bottle of beer with every $80 purchase — as long as you're at least 19!

88 **SPEED**
425 Queen West, 596-7609

This subterranean grotto not only houses a DJ-aimed record store but also a minimally appointed boutique stocked with raver threads. Among the club-kid labels they carry are Fiction, Yak Pak, and Ridiculous. Particularly groovy: camouflage bags by Safe and "Bodybag" form-fitting jumpsuits from Jade.

67 **UNCLE OTIS**
383 Queen West, 597-6847

This is hip-hop headquarters on Queen West. Happening threads by Stussy and Freshjive share space with graffiti-inspired artwork and a pair of turntables that get worked over by top international DJs promoting their in-town throw-downs at the mega-club Industry.

Other location:
26 Bellair (see page 181).

94 **X-LARGE**
170 Spadina, 203-2123

Under a twirling mirrored disco ball, X-Large is the Beastie Boys' Grand Royal clothing company's sole retail outlet in the world. As well as funky skateboard-inspired threads, it also stocks cool duds by Mini and custom-designed trainers by

Vans. In keeping with the street-music vibe, DJs occasionally drop by to throw down vinyl on the stores' twin turntables. Check out the Beasties' autographed photo hanging on the wall and the Vespa scooter in the window display.

FASHION — VINTAGE CLOTHING

39 **BLACK MARKET**
256 Queen West, 599-5858
319 Queen West, 591-7945

This is Toronto's largest vintage-clothing outlet, where you'll find racks of Levi's jeans — divided between those with zippers and them with buttons — as well as a better-than-average array of team jackets, western shirts, and overalls at cheaper-than-usual prices. Don't ignore the stacks of antique blankets, drapes, and still-in-their-original-wrapper '60s shirts (unfortunately, only available in boys' sizes). Odd — very odd — pieces of furniture occasionally appear. A thrift-store freak's paradise!

101 **BRAVA**
483 Queen West, 504-8742

You won't find many '70s or '80s polyester duds at Brava — though we did once spy a Diane von Furstenberg wrap dress — because most of this truly vintage shop's stock comes straight from the '30s, '40s, and '50s. Mint-condition men's gabardine shirts, police uniforms, clip-on bow ties, beaded cocktail frocks, clutch bags, and antique footwear are all lovingly displayed for easy fashion assembly.

107 **CIRCA 40**
456 Queen West, 504-0880

Circa 40 is mad for plaid — from the racks of so-ugly-they're-cool polyester pants out front to the rows of lumberjack shirts inside, it's obvious the owners have a thing for tartan. Especially popular with Queen West waiters, Circa stocks the servers' standard uniform of an oversized white cotton shirt and almost-new black Levi's. Funky '40s wide ties, too.

134 **PRELOVED**
611 Queen West, 504-8704

A lot of current big-name designers take their inspiration from the styles kids wear in the street.

And today, vintage — no matter what the decade — is where it's at. Former fashion models Julia Ricciardelli and Rena Cooke use this knowledge at their streetwise boutique to turn vintage clothing into the latest look. The duo also design a line of new clothes — called Loved — that reflects their fashion philosophy. Rena's hip mom, Peggy, crochets the teeniest of bikinis for the store. Cool sunglasses, too.

24 TRIBAL RHYTHM
248 Queen West, 595-5817

Anyone wanting to recreate the worst of '60s style should shop here. In one subterranean space you'll find the tackiest of hippie-era ephemera — stinky incense, patchouli oil, ugly wooden carvings, fringed suede jackets. Punk wars were fought to put an end to these far-out fashions!

Other locations:
27 Kensington (see page 87)
171B College (see page 157)

36 WORLD
321 Queen West, 599-5858

Affiliated with nearby Black Market, World features the cream of the crop of B.M.'s retro treasures. Western wear, embroidered Vietnam-vet jackets and crushed-velvet evening gowns may be pricier here than elsewhere, but World's gear is worth the extra expense for its quality.

FASHION — LEATHER

48 LACREEN LEATHER
278 Queen West, 348-8618

Don't let the hallway and rickety staircase leading to this second-storey atelier put you off — it might not look it, but this really is a store. Once you've found it, check out the racks of heavy-duty leather jackets, pants, and shoulder bags. And if you can't find what you had in mind, custom orders are accepted.

FASHION — SHOES

73 B2
399 Queen West, 595-9281

Don't expect a bargain basement when you hear B2 described as the discount outlet of high-end

shoe store Brown's — these are still some of the priciest platforms in town. True fashion fetishists will know the names — DKNY, Calvin Klein, and Charles Jourdan are some of the more famous labels — and yes, most are last season's runway models. But, style-wise, these shoes are still miles ahead of those on sale in neighbouring boutiques.

23 JOHN FLUEVOG
242 Queen West, 581-1420

An internationally cherished shoemaker, Vancouver's Fluevog opened his Toronto store on the premises of a former luncheonette. Since he didn't bother to rip out any of the old furnishings, custom-fit platforms, wacky wedgies, and sleek pointy-toed boots get displayed on the diner's former counter and refrigerated cases. Some fault the shoes' quality, but they look fan-tas-tic. Closed Sunday.

50 THE SHOW ROOM
278 Queen West, 340-8880

Colossal clodhoppers from the likes of Yellow Cab, Sketchers, Steve Madden, and Destroy are this platform-shoe boutique's stock in trade. The store also retails retro Hush Puppies and DKNY footwear and sweats.

68 TWINKLE TOES
320 Queen West, 977-6435

Dr. Martens, CAT Caterpillar, Mad Boy Stompers, and Steve Madden are just some of the brands of footwear you'll find at this smallish outlet — and often at discounted prices.

Other locations:
760 Yonge (see page 157)
2582 Yonge (see page 228)

HAIR — BARBERS

66 ARISTOTELIS
314 Queen West, 593-0856

Famous for its flat-tops, crew cuts and brush cuts, Aristotelis has been in business since 1935. With three chairs on the go, the wait is short — amuse yourself by scrutinizing the photos of local musicians and actors who make up the clientele. The plywood painting of Princess Diana is particularly eerie. Visiting MuchMusic celebs — notably the Backstreet Boys — have been clipped here, so sometimes you get a haircut accompanied by teenage screams. Closed Sunday.

RED INDIAN: Lava lamps, transistor radios, and Fiestaware.

HEALTH AND BEAUTY

52 THE BODY SHOP
286 Queen West, 599-4385

When you shop here, you're getting more than just shampoo, makeup, body scrubs, and essential oils. You're buying into a philosophy, as well. This English chain of boutiques has built long-term trading relationships with suppliers around the world who share its concern for the environment (you'll find refillable bottles, recycled catalogues, and no excess packaging) and its stand against animal testing. The chain also supports an in-house charity that funds STOP Women Against Violence.

Other locations:
86 Bloor West (see page 182)
1952 Queen East (see page 207)
71 Wellesley East (see page 144)
220 Yonge (see page 122)

95 LONGEVITY RESEARCH
162 Spadina, 504-6018

An oasis amidst the turmoil of Queen and Spadina, Longevity addresses the aging process with homeopathic therapies. While relaxing New Age

muzak tinkles in the background, clients sip complementary spring water, stock up on vitamins and anti-stress potions, and receive all-natural facials. Consultations by a registered aesthetician, too. Closed Sunday.

64 LUSH
312 Queen West, 599-5874

A favourite of Madonna, Kate Moss, and Sarah McLachlan, Lush is a UK manufacturer of preservative-free bath and beauty lotions and potions. All of their products' ingredients — mainly fruit and vegetable extracts and essential oils — are labelled, and everything's sold by weight. Much is suitable for vegans. Their motto: "Anything but ordinary."

Other locations:
116 Cumberland (see page 182)
2014 Queen East (see page 207)
663 Yonge (see page 157)

HIKING AND BACKPACKING

145 KING SOL
639 Queen West, 504-3333

Before businesses such as the Mountain Equipment Co-Op came to Toronto, King Sol was about the only place to buy outdoor-sports gear at reasonable prices. Here, you'll find two floors of tents, sleeping bags, backpacks, rugged boots, binoculars, and Swiss Army knives. For those affecting the paramilitary look, Sol stocks camouflage pants, army helmets, and Gurkha knives, as well as guns and ammo. Maybe that's taking fashion a bit too far.

HOME FURNISHINGS — NEW

87 **SMART FURNITURE**
360 Queen West, 596-8886

The home of funky '50s-inspired turquoise dinette suites and sexy sofas, Smart Furniture offers styles that won't break the bank. Closed Wednesday.

69 **URBAN MODE**
389 Queen West, 591-8834

A favourite with the money's-no-object bunch, Urban Mode retails decorous fittings that are decidedly deluxe. Leather or velour sofas, glass and steel dinettes, wrought-iron four-poster beds — all are showcased in this two-storey emporium. Not everything here requires a champagne budget: Mode carries the inexpensive Umbra and Smurf-inspired Koziol lines, too. If you ask, the staff will lead you out back to Urban Loft where their collection of even costlier furniture is kept.

HOME FURNISHINGS — USED

118 **DECADES DESIGN**
486-1/2 Queen West, 504-3121

Back in the good old days — 1984, for example — you'd be able to buy any of the wonderful stuff they sell here at the nearest Goodwill or Sally Ann for a fraction of the price. Decades' secondhand designer furniture — Eameses' molded-fiberglass chairs, Dodd's stacking plywood chairs, Herman Miller clocks — are priced to sell to the fashionable crowd. But as you admire the works' craftsmanship, you can't help thinking, "This once cost three dollars."

140 **RED INDIAN**
536 Queen West, 504-7706

With the city's largest selection of lava lamps,

this long-standing used-furniture shop specializes in '30s and '40s art deco furniture and kitschy fixtures from the '50s. Danish Modern dining-room sets, chromed airplane clocks, neon beer signs, transistor radios, and dial telephones fashion a look that defines retro. Closed Sunday.

41 **20TH CENTURY GALLERY**
23 Beverley, 598-2172

This small gallery and shop houses a collection of this century's designer furnishings, from art nouveau through Viennese art deco and modern Scandinavian to '70s futurism. Owner Ross Young has compiled a comprehensive collection of *objets d'art* that encompasses glassware, light fixtures, and elegant furniture. Canadian, American, and European designers are all represented. Look for Italian modernist Gaetano Pesce's flexible "spaghetti" light fixtures.

JUNK

51 **ACTIVE SURPLUS**
347 Queen West, 593-0909

After being ransomed from kidnappers — true! — the life-size gorilla robot has returned to guard the front door of this disorganized electronic-component store. Patronized by computer nerds and fans of the bizarre, Active sells such seemingly unconnected stuff as mirrored disco balls, reconditioned telephones, out-of-date computer software, and several sizes of fake eyeballs. Don't bother the staff with questions — they're too busy.

143 **QUEEN'S TRADE CENTRE**
635 Queen West, 504-6210

Never has the adage "one person's trash is another's treasure" been truer than at this curio shop. Collectible castoffs — broken-down Coke machines, accordions, wooden Indians, and kitsch bric-à-brac — litter the narrow aisles. Very few of the articles have a clearly marked price tag — haggling seems to be the rule here.

MEMORABILIA

14 **THE BEATLEMANIA SHOPPE**
71 McCaul, 368-4436

Publishers of the bi-monthly *Beatology* magazine,

and the only store in Toronto that specializes in official Beatles' merchandise, the Shoppe sells authorized reproductions of the Corgi Toy Yellow Submarine, as well as mugs, key chains, and T-shirts bearing the Beatles' logo. True fans will want to check out Astrid Kirchherr's book of Hamburg-era Beatle photos and the limited-edition lithographs by John Lennon and Yoko Ono's Bag One Productions. Closed Sunday.

MUSIC — CDS, RECORDS & TAPES

(121) BLACK PLANET
494 Queen West, 504-9261

This CD-and-vinyl emporium specializes in goth bands and progressive-rock combos from the '70s and '80s. Along with band T-shirts and videos, Black Planet carries a large selection of British and European large-format tour posters — Bowie, the Beasties, and Blue Note–period Miles Davis and John Coltrane. Cool.

(113) CD CAT
539 Queen West, 703-4797

(91) CD CHARACTERS
372A Queen West, 506-9229

(28) CD EXCHANGE
161 John, 977-6889

(128) COSMOS
607A Queen West, 603-0254

Wonder where all those rare-groove DJs find the Afro-funk vinyl they spin? The answer is Cosmos, a relative newcomer to the used-record scene. It's a very small storefront that specializes in the funk, y'all, the hippest of hop, and Latin soul. No tax, no refunds, and absolutely no exchanges — but they'll let you use their in-store turntable to listen to anything you're thinking of buying. Closed Monday.

(7) DRIFTWOOD MUSIC
247 Queen West, 598-0368

For 20 years, Driftwood has been Queen West's main used-vinyl emporium. The selection is mostly contemporary pop, but there are thorough jazz and classical sections, too. Local indie acts sell CDs and tapes on consignment here, and you can often pick up recent releases when T.O. rock critics bring in their review CDs to sell — still sealed!

(44) HMV
272 Queen West, 596-0333

See listing page 122.

(2) KOP'S KOLLECTIBLES
229 Queen West, 593-8523

This specialty shop upstairs from Vortex Records features CD reissues by rock 'n' roll greats from the '50s and '60s. Looking for that hard-to-find LP of Little Richard live in Germany? Kop's'll have it. It also carries a huge selection of rock, pop, and r 'n' b 7-inch singles from the '60s through the '90s — some in their original sleeves.

(96) METROPOLIS RECORDS
162 Spadina, 364-0230

Primarily a DJ specialists' shop, Metropolis caters to the public as well. New and used 12-inch vinyl singles share space with domestic and imported CDs in bins labelled "darkwave," "cinematic," and "experimental." Three turntable-and-headphone set-ups allow customers to test-spin discs before they buy. British clubbing bibles — *Mixmag, Muzik, DJ Times* — too.

(16) PENGUIN MUSIC
2 McCaul, 597-1687

See Hot Spot page 33.

(83) THE PIT
423 Queen West, 979-9415

Part record shop and part club-wear retailer, the Pit is a raver's paradise. Pre-release promo discs and dance-mix compilation cassettes share space with Homeboy Sistawear and Elektromotor Naugahyde shoulder bags. Two centrally located turntables provide a forum for jockey sluts in training.

(139) RECORD PEDDLER
619 Queen West, 504-3828

Toronto's oldest underground, punk, new wave, grunge, alternative — or whatever it's called these days — record store, the Peddler specializes in imported CDs and vinyl. Their large new and used stock covers drum 'n' bass, house, metal, hardcore, ska, and industrial — just about everything, really, including singles by local combos on impossibly obscure labels. T-shirts, concert flyers and tickets, and the latest UK magazines — airmailed weekly — are on sale, too.

17 SECOND VINYL
2 McCaul, 977-3737

This tiny shop carries mostly used classical, jazz, and movie soundtracks on vinyl, cassette, and CD. Closed Sunday.

88 SPEED
425 Queen West, 596-7609

1 VORTEX
229 Queen West, 598-4039

Downstairs from Kop's Kollectibles, Vortex features CDs — new and used, domestic and imported — by artists from the '60s to '90s. Their stock is clearly laid out and their prices for current releases are often lower than the Yonge Street superstores'.

Other location:
2209 Yonge (see page 228)

MUSICAL INSTRUMENTS

81 STEVE'S MUSIC
415 Queen West, 593-8888

One of Toronto's busiest and most comprehensive music stores, Steve's is also one of the most difficult to patronize. First, your bag or knapsack is pleasantly confiscated at the door. After you find what it is you came for, try to get the attention of staff members who always seem to be deeply engrossed in a Clapton-versus-Hendrix debate. Once they acknowledge your presence and fill out the bill, you line up at the Cage — a heavily secured cash station where you pay your money. Receipt in hand, you return to the counter to claim your purchase. And don't forget to pick up your knapsack before you leave. Closed Sunday.

PHOTOGRAPHY

129 WEST CAMERA
514 Queen West, 504-9432

This state-of-the-art camera shop for the professional and amateur alike sells frames, batteries, lights, refrigerated film, and processing supplies, as well as cameras. They also offer a one-hour in-house photo-processing service. Closed Sunday.

XX WEST LAB
516 Queen West, 504-9432

Next door to West Camera, this photo-supply shop offers darkrooms for rent by the hour.

16 PENGUIN MUSIC
2 McCaul, 597-1687

Though not the largest record store in the area, Penguin is certainly one of the most thorough. If your taste runs to electronica — illbient, trance, and trip-hop — as well as the more psychedelic genres of dance music, and you can't find what you want anywhere else, go here. Twice weekly, they receive shipments of limited-edition CDs and vinyl from the UK, including hard-to-find Britpop-single releases. And the knowledgeable staff will help you track down the most obscure of discs.

SEX

3 CONDOM SHACK
231 Queen West, 596-7515

Giggling pre-teens sans parental units are no longer admitted to this shop that openly sells — omigawd! — condoms. Foreplay board games, sex-ed videos, raunchy greeting cards, and a number of sexy potions and lotions complement a wide selection of flavoured and imported super-thin rubbers. If you're feeling shy, there are also sunglasses!

TATTOOS AND PIERCINGS

105 ABSTRACT TATTOO
452 Queen West, 504-8288

One of the strip's smaller piercing emporia, Abstract features a large fish tank for customers to stare at while they're having ink done. Unlike at most other parlours, tattoos here are applied to grimacing first-timers out in the open while their friends ask, "Does it hurt?"

21 NEW TRIBE
232 Queen West, 977-2786

Anyone expecting a grotty tattoo parlour will be surprised by the well-lit atmosphere at New Tribe. As well as wall displays of potential body embellishments, there are comfortable couches, a pool table, and complementary coffee. Tribe's tattoo designs include Celtic symbols, Japanese calligraphy, and good ol' U.S. of A. imperialist eagles.

132 STAINLESS STUDIOS BODY ART
609 Queen West, 504-1433

CITYTV: Bustin' out all over.

VIDEO

99 **QUEEN VIDEO**
412 Queen West, 504-3030

With over 20,000 VHS titles available — mainstream blockbusters, indie oddities, campy softcore porn — Queen Video is perfect for those who forget to return their rented videos on time: except for new releases, their $3 fee is good for five days.

137 **SUSPECT VIDEO**
619 Queen West, 504-7135

Quentin Tarantino's favourite source for the cultiest of the cultish, Suspect's Queen outlet houses over 10,000 titles of terror, exploitation, and auteur video. They also stock a wide selection of fanzines and obscurists' manifestos. Offbeat T-shirts and movie posters make this the perfect spot for cinema fanatics.

Other location:
605 Markham (see page 172).

Delux

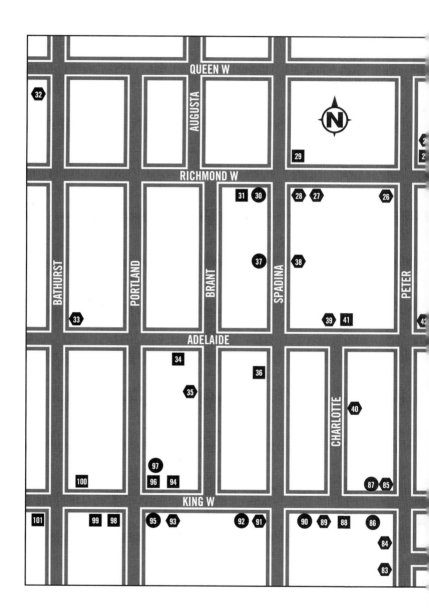

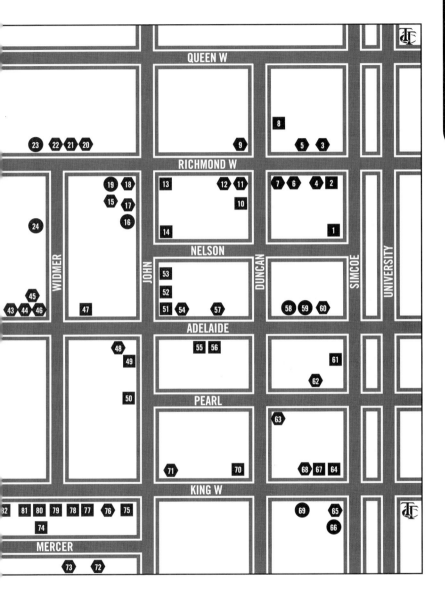

CLUBLAND

Love the nightlife? These inner-city blocks, officially dubbed the Theatre District, come alive after dark. Start your Big Night Out with dinner at one of the area's many swanky eateries, take in a Broadway-bound play, and then dance into the wee hours at any one of the zone's high-octane nightclubs.

FOOD & DINING

RESTAURANTS

25 ABRA CA DABRA
137 Peter, 593-1550

Don't be put off by the over-the-top decor of this upper-crust discotheque — imagine how Fred and Wilma Flintstone would redo their cave if they won the lottery. In the slightly more subdued second-storey dining room, superstar chef Elaina Asselin, a veteran of some of Canada's most acclaimed kitchens, dishes up *nouvelle* nouvelle cuisine. Close your eyes and let your other senses savour near-perfection. Closed Sunday to Tuesday.

Barrier-free, washrooms in basement. Fully licensed. Patio. $$$

50 ACME
86 John, 340-9700

A New York City–style burger-and-steak house, Acme also serves 15 types of draught, over 90 single-malt whiskies, and 3-ounce martinis. Saturday and Sunday brunch.

10 steps at door, washrooms on same floor. Fully licensed. Patio. $$

47 ALICE FAZOOLI'S
294 Adelaide West, 979-1910

Boisterous crab shack with a heavy suits-cutting-loose-after-work vibe.

One step at door, washrooms on same floor. Fully licensed. Patio. $$

98 INNOCENTI
587 King West, 203-0551

Very rarely, a restaurant bursts onto Toronto's dining scene perfectly formed — no finding its feet, spot-on from day one. One such is Innocenti, named after the Italian scooter manufacturer responsible for the Lambretta that greets customers in the eatery's entrance. The tastefully elegant space, with a tree (!) growing out of the floor and reaching up into a skylight overhead, is a perfect example of how to do a restaurant right: four seasoned pros at the helm, reasonably priced Cal-Ital contemporary mains at dinner, wallet-conscious sloppy sandwiches at lunch, and some of the hippest dinner music in town. Bravo Innocenti! Closed Sunday.

One step at door, washrooms on same floor. Fully licensed. Patio. $$

51 AVALON
270 Adelaide West, 979-9918

Considered by many foodies to be one of Canada's top restaurants, Avalon is also one of Toronto's most expensive eateries. Chef-owner Chris McDonald's constantly evolving menu goes beyond contemporary fusion fare but is rarely confused. Closed Sunday.

Nine steps at door, washrooms on same floor. Fully licensed. $$$

99 CICCONE'S
601 King West, 504-5037

Toronto's oldest restaurant hasn't changed since it opened in 1943. It's a textbook-perfect trattoria where Mary Ciccone's — yes, a distant relation to Madonna — cooking has remained true to its Italian roots. Foodies who find her cooking old hat will still dig the decor — red-and-white checked tablecloths, dripping wax candles in Chianti bottles, and soaring archways painted with murals of Venetian gondoliers. The look is so authentic, the restaurant has been used in many movies — notably *To Die For* with Nicole Kidman and Matt Dillon. Closed Sunday and holidays.

One step at door, washrooms on same floor. Fully licensed. $$

52 CLUB LUCKY
117 John, 977-8890

Sister eatery to Kit Kat on King West, Lucky features a similar contemporary Italian menu. This multi-level space also shares its sibling's eclectic clutter.

Nine steps at door, washrooms on same floor. Fully licensed. Patio. $$

80 FRED'S NOT HERE
321 King West, 971-9155

OK, so Fred's gone missing. This dramatic black room with contrasting red carpet and white-linen-clad tables serves up contemporary grub for the theatre crowd.

Five steps at door, washrooms in basement. Fully licensed. Patio. $$

56 HOUSTON'S
257 Adelaide West, 351-1601

Home of Texas prime beef, Houston's is an American-style steak house. Plush booths line the romantically lit room and a fireplace roars away year round. Private rooms can be booked for corporate affairs, and, after your meal, you can drift upstairs into Churchill's, the adjoining cigar bar (see listing page 42). Closed Sunday.

Barrier-free. Fully licensed. $$$

67 IL FORNELLO
214 King West, 977-2855

Decked out in unfinished brick, massive wood columns, and brown-paper-topped tables, each of Il Fornello's locations features a wood-burning pizza oven. Choose from four styles of thin crust — regular, multigrain, spelt, or gluten-free rice flour — and customize your pie from their long list of traditional and designer toppings.

11 steps at door, washrooms on same floor. Fully licensed. Patio. $$

Other locations:
576 Danforth (see page 188)
35 Elm (see page 117)
1968 Queen East (see page 200)
1560 Yonge (see page 224)

98 INNOCENTI
587 King West, 203-0551

See Hot Spot page 38.

MONSOON: Winner of the James Beard Award for best designed restaurant in North America.

64 JOE ROCKHEADS
212 King West, 977-8448

Seven steps at door, washrooms on same floor. Fully licensed. Patio. $$

75 KIT KAT
297 King West, 977-4461

To find this cool Italian restaurant, look for the halved fiberglass Guernsey cow sticking out of its King West facade. A favourite of Rolling Stone Keith Richards and Toronto-born comic Dan Aykroyd, this tchotchke-cluttered room dishes up old-school Ital fare like grilled Gorgonzola-topped polenta, rigatoni bolognese, and veal piccata. Insist on a booth in the glass-walled back room. Closed Sunday.

Barrier-free. Fully licensed. Patio. $$

79 LA FENICE
319 King West, 585-2377

This Milan-style study in sophistication features northern Italian fare-with-flare in upmarket digs.

Three steps at door, washrooms in basement. Fully licensed. $$$

78 LA FENICE PASTA BAR
317 King West, 585-2377

Downscale and downstairs, the Pasta Bar is the bargain basement of the chic La Fenice restaurant. Two-thirds the price of its glitzy upstairs neighbour, this popular room is often booked for private functions.

16 steps at door, washrooms on same floor. Fully licensed. $$

77 MARCEL'S BISTRO
315 King West, 591-8600

A bright second-storey bistro with a French accent, Marcel's provides a classic French menu that's spelled out on mirrors that line the pretty room.

23 steps at door, washrooms on same floor. Fully licensed. $$

74 MERCER STREET GRILL
36 Mercer, 599-3399

This is one eccentric-looking restaurant. From the street it resembles a corrugated tin shack with revolving stovepipe exhausts. Inside, the look is early-'90s industrial, and the grub Asian and

pricey. If the owners ever decide to redecorate, they'll only need an adjustable wrench to dismantle the joint.

Barrier-free. Fully licensed. Patio. $$$

82 MILANO
325 King West, 599-9909

Copper is the theme here, from the shiny metal sheets that cover the restaurant's facade to the hammered surface of the bar that dominates its sophisticated dining area. With its pool table and primo people-watching patio, Milano is understandably a haunt for the ultra-fashionable.

Barrier-free. Fully licensed. Patio. $$$

61 MONSOON
100 Simcoe, 979-7172

Winner of the prestigious James Beard Award for best restaurant design in North America, this Yabu Pushelberg creation evokes gasps. The tiki shtick's so thick, one almost expects Dorothy Lamour to jump into an erupting volcano. While the decor impresses and suits the retro funk of Barry White and the Reverend Al Green grooving on the sound system, the Pacific Rim fare is pricey and underwhelming. But, even if you don't have to go, the washrooms alone make a visit to Monsoon worthwhile. They're bigger than your apartment! Closed Sunday.

Nine steps at door, washrooms on same floor. Fully licensed. $$$

70 THE PEEL PUB
276 King West, 977-0003

Open for breakfast daily at 6:30 a.m., this barn of an eatery serves up pub grub till 2:30 a.m. 140-ounce pitchers, daily half-price food specials, and 9-cent Happy Hour chicken wings make the pub popular with theatre-goers on a budget. The muzak is dreadful '80s tunes, too — Big Country, not Frankie Goes to Hollywood.

Seven steps at door, washrooms on same floor. Fully licensed. $

81 RED TOMATO
321 King West, 971-6626

Downstairs from Fred's Not Here, the Tomato dishes up mains and starters that are surprisingly contemporary, given the traditional-sounding menu. Roughly stuccoed walls and large grey-flannel-upholstered booths add to the room's casual charm.

16 steps at door, washrooms on same floor. Fully licensed. $$

100 606
606 King West, 504-8740

After a quick look around 606, it's easy to see why this laid-back saloon is a popular site for hip corporate functions. Once through its alleyway entrance, you encounter a sunken restaurant area decked out in '50s kitchen furniture and fronted by a large glass garage door that opens to King West. Past the long stand-up bar and the open kitchen that dishes up a Thai-Cal-Carib menu is a rear room with the obligatory pool table and couch 'n' coffee-table combos. Every night except Monday, DJs spin acid jazz for a 30-something crowd. Closed Sunday.

One step at door, washrooms on same floor. Fully licensed. Patio. $$

88 SOLO
391 King West, 599-7000

Solo proves that there's more to takeout than pre-fab pizza and cheesy chicken wings. Although you're welcome to stay and dine in the fireplace-appointed space or on its curbside patio, all of Solo's *au courant* Cal-Ital fare is available to go. Surprise the gang back at the office with the likes of Provimi veal sweetbreads, jerk-glazed trout, or Kahlua-pecan pie. Or tell your dinner guests you made it yourself.

Three steps at door, washrooms in basement. Fully licensed. Patio. $$$

82 VERONA
335 King West, 593-7771

A combination of contemporary cuisine and upscale ambiance make Verona one of the choicest spots on the theatre strip.

One step at door, washrooms on same floor. Fully licensed. Patio. $$$

49 XANGO
106 John, 593-4407

This beautiful bright-yellow space features Cuban cuisine by way of Miami's South Beach. Start with seafood ceviche or empanadas with sliced pear and blue cheese before moving on to such Latin fare as grilled beef tenderloin with chimichurri and sweet beet relish or guava-glazed pork back ribs. Or go for the oysters, marinated in lime and chili and served as breaded croquettes with banana-lentil salad, or done deep-fried with plantain, spinach, bacon, and cheese 'n' horseradish cream. Afterwards, take in some live Latin jazz in the Mambo Lounge downstairs. Closed Monday.

16 steps at door, washrooms on same floor. Fully licensed. Patio. $$$

CAFES AND COFFEE HOUSES

36 IMAGINE
96 Spadina, 504-2379

Don't let the decor put you off — an etching of John Lennon staring at a ceiling painted with fluffy clouds, and a waterfall dribbling down a rock-covered grotto — because there's some pretty decent veggie cooking going on here. Service is cafeteria-style. Grab a tray and fill it with as much salad, soup, and casserole as you like, and have it weighed by the cashier. An extensive salad bar, chunky soups, and tofu-dominated mains make Imagine imaginative. Imagine that! Closed Saturday, Sunday and holidays.

Eight steps at door, washrooms on same floor. Unlicensed, smoke-free, cash only. $

29 SECOND CUP
147 Spadina, 591-1689

See listing page 17.

Barrier-free. Unlicensed. Patio. $

31 SUCRÉ
471 Richmond West, 703-8855

This stainless-steel-clad café is as stylish as the crowd that lounges on its wire-mesh Bertoia chairs. Open at 8 a.m. for power breakfasts, and serving fashionably late lunches to garment-industry workers till 6 p.m., Sucré has a menu that includes with-it salad-and-sandwich match-ups — baby field greens with balsamic vinaigrette teamed with a grilled-chicken club, for instance — as well as fruit salads and croissants baked in-house. Closed Saturday and Sunday.

One step at door, washrooms on same floor. Unlicensed. $$

DELIS AND DINERS

41 ZUPA'S
342-1/2 Adelaide West, 593-2775

Once Spadina's garment district was lined with delis — Shopsy's and United Dairy, most famously — but nearly all have either moved off the avenue or expired. Zupa's keeps chopped liver alive. Grab a tray and join the lunchtime lineup for first-rate thin-sliced Montreal smoked meat, pastrami, and corned beef. Sandwiches are twice as thick as need be — don't complain — and sides include industrial coleslaw and frozen fries with canned gravy — just the way it's always been. Closed Sunday and holidays.

Barrier-free, washrooms in basement. Unlicensed. $

TAKEOUT

45 THE PITA PIT
318 Adelaide West, 595-7181

Glaringly bright with screaming greens and reds, this falafel joint should come with sunglasses, especially after dark. There's nothing outstanding about its wares — pita pockets stuffed with veggie fixins and laced with spicy sauces — but the Pit stays open till 3 a.m. every night — 4 a.m. Fridays and Saturdays — which makes it one of the few refueling pit stops open late in the heart of Clubland. Bonus!

One step at door, no washrooms. Unlicensed. $
Other location:
235 College (see page 154)

BARS

14 AL FRISCO'S
133 John, 595-8201

Al Frisco's, which has one of downtown's largest patios — over 300 seats — also brews its own beer in an on-site microbrewery. Saturday and Sunday brunch.

Barrier-free. Fully licensed. Patio.

55 CHURCHILL'S
257 Adelaide West, 351-8857

This cigar lounge upstairs from Houston's is a library-like bar that attracts celebrities and big-business types alike. In fact, along one wall, $1,500 members keep their stogies behind brass plaques — cigar aficionados like hockey great Wayne Gretzky, baseball swinger Roger Clemens, and life-is-a-highway man Tom Cochrane. Although it has the feel of a private club, the hoi polloi is welcome to laze in leather chairs in front of the fireplace while listening to live jazz or DJs on weekends. Closed Sunday.

Barrier-free. Fully licensed.

1 THE DEVIL'S MARTINI
136 Simcoe, 591-7541

Closed Sunday to Wednesday.

Two steps at door, washrooms on same floor. Fully licensed. Patio.

10 EASY AND THE FIFTH
221 Richmond West, 979-3000

Don't look for the entrance to the Easy on Richmond West because it's around back in the alleyway off Duncan Street. You can't miss it — look for the walkie-talkie-toting doormen holding back the crowd on the other side of the velvet rope. Once they decide that you're suitably attired, you'll be ushered into a 700-person-capacity room that looks like a huge French country kitchen à la Martha Stewart. Music is anything but club — reggae, salsa, Latin jazz — and a pianist plays show tunes in the secluded cigar lounge. The Easy's super-exclusive and expensive restaurant, the Fifth, is a freight-elevator ride away on the fifth floor. Closed Sunday to Wednesday.

12 steps at door, washrooms on same floor. Fully licensed.

2 GARAGE PARADISE
175 Richmond West, 351-8101

Not to be confused with the legendary New York dance palace Paradise Garage, this Garage actually is a garage. Hubcaps and exotic license plates are nailed to the concrete-block walls and the rear end of a Pontiac props up the bar. Bumper sticker: "Party or bust." As frat-house rock wails, after-work suits hustle each other over the red-felt-topped pool table. Closed Sunday to Wednesday.

Barrier-free. Fully licensed.

94 THE MOCKINGBIRD
580 King West, 504-3081

Located in a former warehouse, the Mockingbird is all wood-plank flooring, exposed brick, and swagged gauze curtains. Chandeliers light the front restaurant — Mediterranean menu — and the roomy back room, which holds six pool tables surrounded by funky couches and coffee tables. Restage the World Cup to smooth r 'n' b on their foosball table. Closed Sunday to Tuesday.

10 steps at door, washrooms on same floor. Fully licensed. Patio.

13 MONTANA
145 John, 595-5949

Yee-haw! This two-storey Wild West roadhouse is decked out in enough barnboard and stuffed moose to fill a hunting lodge. Downstairs, there's a 200-seat restaurant serving up chuck-wagon chow like Buffalo chicken wings and Montana nacho pizza. Upstairs is more of a party space, full of pool tables, video games, and two 10-foot video screens broadcasting the game. Off the dining room is a cigar bar — the Big Smoke — decorated with dried tobacco leaves hanging from the rafters. But don't expect the Grand Ole Opry's greatest hits on the sound system. The soundtrack here is very mainstream — is that the Captain and Tennille's "Love Will Keep Us Together"? Yes'm. Celebrity cowpokes spotted here: diminutive comedian Danny DeVito, glamour girl Christina Applegate and — omigawd! — Brad Pitt.

Barrier-free. Fully licensed. Patio.

53 SMOKELESS JOE'S
125 John, 591-2221

Offering over 175 beers from around the world, the appropriately named Smokeless is Toronto's only nicotine-free bar. Those dying for a butt are allowed to smoke on the patio — local politicians have not banned the dreaded weed from being fired up out-of-doors. Yet.

Seven steps at door, washrooms on same floor. smoke-free. Patio.

8 SWINGERS
57 Duncan, 597-0202

Just because it's named after the movie that brought L.A.'s lounge and swing scenes back into

FLUID: An ultra-lounge with a high-tech dance area and an animal-print cocktail bar.

the mainstream doesn't mean they play swing music here, OK? Instead, expect silky-smooth quiet-storm r 'n' b from slick DJs most nights, and oddball film soundtracks and Broadway show tunes on Sunday evening. The elegantly appointed space boasts de rigueur velvet seating, a halogen-lit pool table, and a soothing aquarium. But no swing music. Closed Monday.

10 steps at door, washrooms on same floor.

101 THE WHEAT SHEAF TAVERN
667 King West, 504-9912

Opened in 1849 — yes, 150 years ago — the Wheat Sheaf is Toronto's oldest bar. Hell, it's almost the oldest anything! Recently tarted up, it still remains a classic watering hole — a jar of pickled eggs on the bar, a number of draught brews on tap, and a pair of pool tables. Off to the side, there's a semi-private room reserved for regulars arguing over last night's game.

Two steps at door, washrooms on same floor. Patio.

BREW PUBS

96 THE AMSTERDAM
600 King West, 504-1040

This microbrewery situated in a late-19th-century building ferments 10 types of beer in its glass-walled facility. Sit at the long wooden bar and sample Amsterdam's ales and lagers, or, weekends and holidays, take one of its guided tours. Upstairs, you'll find a retail outlet that sells, as well as beer, logo-emblazoned T-shirts, baseball caps, and shell suits. Even if you're not in the neighbourhood, you can still sample their suds — Amsterdam's beers are available at the Beer Store.

Barrier-free. Patio.

ENTERTAINMENT

LIVE MUSIC

48 MAMBO LOUNGE
106 John, 593-4407

A classy and beautifully appointed room fur-

nished with overstuffed leather couches and tall linen-covered tables, the Lounge attracts flocks of jazz fans for first-rate Latin sounds. Toronto-based saxophonist Jane Bunnett, balladeer Jon Secada, and Cuban flautist Nestor Torres have all appeared on the compact stage area that somehow manages to accommodate a grand piano. A favourite for private corporate affairs, and Miami sound machine Gloria Estefan recently celebrated her birthday here. Closed Sunday.

Four steps at door, washrooms in basement. Fully licensed. Patio.

76 N'AWLINS
299 King West, 595-1958

This New Orleans–style eatery features southern U.S. fare like Cajun catfish or alligator medallions, and showcases the best of Toronto's jazz musicians seven nights a week.

Barrier-free. Fully licensed. Patio. $$

COMEDY CLUBS

83 SECOND CITY
56 Blue Jays Way, 343-0011

Famous as the breeding ground for some of the biggest names in comedy — *Saturday Night Live* veterans Dan Aykroyd, Gilda Radner, and Mike Myers, as well as *SCTV*'s John Candy, Catherine O'Hara, and Martin Short got their start here — Second City is now in opulent digs in the heart of Clubland. With state-of-the-art sound and lighting and excellent sightlines, this 300-seat dinner theatre presents revues and sketch comedy as well as free late-night improv sets.

Barrier-free. Fully licensed. Patio.

85 SECOND CITY TRAINING CENTRE
388 King West, 340-7270

Offering various levels of study, from beginner's classes for students with limited theatrical experience, to courses for professional actors who want to improve their improv, the Centre is a school for those serious about comedy. Instructors include *SCTV* star Joe Flaherty, up-and-comer Shari Hollett, and Andrew Currie of the lampooning duo the Devil's Advocates. Free-admission improv sessions are held at the nearby Tim Sims Playhouse on Monday evenings.

Unlicensed.

TIM SIMS PLAYHOUSE
84
56 Blue Jays Way, 343-0022

Next door to Second City, the Playhouse is named in honour of a late and well-loved local comedian. An intimate cabaret-style space, the room features local fledgling stand-up comics, as well as established talent trying out new routines.

Barrier-free. Fully licensed. Patio.

DANCE CLUBS

ABRA CA DABRA
25
137 Peter, 593-1550

Toronto's glitziest nightclub, this two-storey space with a second-floor wraparound dining room is either the chicest spot du jour or a tasteless exercise in excess. Rococo wrought iron wraps around fiberglass columns, and faux stalactites menace from the ceiling. The glassed-in VIP room — so that the less fortunate can rubberneck — comes with its own humidor and smoke-ventilation system. A movie-set-like circular staircase leads to the rooftop patio, which overlooks the parking lot across the street. DJs spin adult-contemporary tunes mixed with Latin jazz and a smattering of club house. Closed Sunday to Tuesday.

Barrier-free. Fully licensed. Patio.

APOTHECARY
42
340 Adelaide West, 586-9858

Deep Plexiglas skylights set into the west wall of this jewel-like bar give the impression from the street that things are pretty warped inside — and that's how the rest of Toronto looks from the other side of the portholes. Sexy blond wood, chrome accents, and deeply funky beats render the front room conducive to canoodling. The backyard patio with corrugated steel walls makes dancing under the stars feel like a night in an enchanted — though industrial — forest. Closed Monday.

Barrier-free, washrooms in basement. Fully licensed. Patio.

AREA 51
93
577 King West, 977-4036

See Hot Spot this page.

ATMOSPHERE
60
214 Adelaide West, 595-5115

For a club purporting to have a vibe, Atmosphere

AREA 51
93
577 King West, 977-4036

Minimally decked out with black concrete-block walls sporting Day-Glo graphics, Area 51 — named for the restricted Nevada air force base where evidence of extraterrestials is said to be secreted — is an attitude-free room that focuses on the beats. Thursdays feature techno, Fridays industrial, and Saturdays blissed-out trance; occasionally, a weirded-out Sunday gets thrown in. It's a popular spot with touring DJs and bands, and the likes of John Aquaviva and Suede have been sighted lurking in the murk. Closed Sunday to Wednesday.

Eight steps at door, washrooms on same floor. Fully licensed.

lacks one. The split-level space is too squeaky clean — all electric-blue and sunshine-yellow, with asymmetrical benches and amoeba-shaped tables. Still, the crowd is attractive, and the house-via-r 'n' b grooves do their thing. Other than the dance floor, the action centres on a large, central bar inlaid with multicoloured mosaic tiles. A metaphor, perhaps? Closed Sunday to Thursday.

Three steps at door, washrooms in basement. Fully licensed.

BASSMINT
32
178 Bathurst, 362-6658

Downstairs from the restored elegance of the Paddock eatery and saloon, Bassmint is the kind of place 14-year-olds think is incredibly cool. A grotty subterranean grotto that oozes through three rooms, each with its own techno or drum 'n' bass DJ, this all-ages space rocks to non-stop hip hop from 10 p.m. Saturday till 10 a.m. Monday. Teenagers in baggy low-slung pants nod along to the beat while perched on dilapidated couches or behind the wheel of demolition-derby video games. Closed Monday and Tuesday.

16 steps at door, washrooms on same floor. Unlicensed.

BAUHAUS
73
31 Mercer, 977-9813

Located in an exquisite art deco building fronted

MONEY
199 Richmond West, 591-9000

Whenever the characters in the cult flick *Swingers* describe something as seriously cool, they use the word "money." Money, the place, is definitely money. And a lot of money was spent to refurbish this four-storey club housed in a former office building. After entering through an actual tent, you come into a lounge area with a see-through ceiling — the dance floor of the room upstairs, made of thick industrial glass. Surrounding the dance floor are walls of speakers placed directly on the floor so that the bass is guaranteed to be heavy-duty at all times. Watch that your fillings don't shake loose! Closed Sunday to Thursday.

10 steps at door, washrooms on same floor. Fully licensed. Patio.

with glass bricks, Bauhaus is a 300-seat-capacity club with a discriminating door policy — if you're not dressed to the nines, don't even think about getting in. Once past the doorman, you'll find a split-level room set up as much for dancing as preening. High-backed banquettes, a gas-fuelled fireplace, and two sculpted mahogany bars make Bauhaus the place to be scene — especially on Monday's Martini Night. Closed Sunday, Tuesday to Thursday.

Barrier-free. Fully licensed.

THE BEAT JUNKIE
306 Richmond West, 599-7055

As its name suggests, the Beat Junkie is serious about the tunes it plays. A remodelled neighbourhood house that doesn't play house, the Beat has two main areas — a first-floor lounge with deep-burgundy walls hung with Mayan masks, and a streamlined upper dance area draped in camouflage netting. Friday features drum 'n' bass DJs, Saturday rocks to hip hop, reggae, and r 'n' b, and Sunday showcases "interesting" live music. Chill in the JA-style covered shack out back. Closed Monday to Thursday.

10 steps at door, washrooms on same floor. Fully licensed. Patio.

CHA CHA CHA
11 Duncan, 598-3538

Until about 10 p.m., this formally appointed room

is an upscale nueva Cuban cantina serving such Island fare as conch fritters on sugar cane in a honey-rum drizzle, or smoked baby back ribs with south Miami barbeque sauce, corn pudding, and organic slaw. After dinner, stogies are lit and the mambo breaks out on the club's stainless-steel dance floor. '70s disco and '60s Motown, too. Closed Sunday to Wednesday.

35 steps at door, washrooms on same floor. Fully licensed. $$$

DELUX
322 Adelaide West, 596-2212

Reminiscent of the all-white Milk Bar in *A Clockwork Orange*, Delux is Toronto's most luxurious dance club. A message stencilled onto the full-length mirror that reflects the first-floor bar reads "Lack of charisma can be fatal" — not that anyone so lacking would ever be admitted. You can always count on a crowd outside waiting for someone to leave. Vertically mounted into the space's rear wall downstairs is a 10-foot airplane propeller that rotates, artfully fluffing the hair of the fashion victims who lounge on white vinyl chaises and animal-print ottomans. Upstairs, the dance floor — lined with shattered mirrors and oscillating electric fans — shakes to progressive house, old-school r 'n' b , and hot-buttered soul. The two floors' total capacity is only 150 partyers. Closed Sunday to Tuesday.

Five steps at door, washrooms on same floor. Fully licensed. Patio.

FLUID
217 Richmond West, 593-6116

Fluid is a very classy joint. A white circular staircase leads into the main dance room, a space lined with throne-like banquettes and a trio of go-go platforms. Walls, sofas, and the bar are all tufted with sparkly gold vinyl. This area is linked to a quieter lounge space with an equally striking decor — at centre stage is a mosaic-covered pool table. The third area — all animal prints and candlelight — turns, maze-like, back into the main dance room. Music runs from rare groove to disco and house. Sunday is Industrial Night — a party for workers from nearby clubs and restaurants who have the evening off. Celebrity spottings: Denzel Washington, LL Cool J, and wrestling superstar the Undertaker (but not all together). Closed Monday and Tuesday.

Six steps at door, washrooms on same floor. Fully licensed.

⑳ G-SPOT
296 Richmond West, 351-7768

G-Spot hits the groove-spot on weekends when over 1,000 party people fill the three-storey club, dancing to hip hop, r 'n' b, and club house. One side is dedicated to hard-core dance fiends, while the other draws a 30-something mob with smoother sounds. Check out the third-floor lounge complete with humidor, stuffed-alligator wall decoration, and chairs shaped like red, pouty lips. Closed Sunday to Wednesday.

10 steps at door, washrooms in basement. Fully licensed.

⑫ GLASS
150 Pearl, 593-4527

From its glass-brick entryway to its icy-blue frosted bar, Glass has a lot of, well, glass. Curved silvery walls, water curtains, and ice-sculpture-like lighting fixtures give this slick space the atmosphere of an ice cave. DJs spin commercial dance, house, and top-40 alternative for a well-dressed crowd. Summer nights, its patio allows a fabulous view of the downtown core's skyscrapers. Closed Sunday to Wednesday.

Five steps at door, washrooms on same floor. Fully licensed. Patio.

⑫ GRANITE
225 Richmond West, 979-3993

A basic basement beat room, Granite caters to a young crowd into hip hop and old-school r 'n' b. Closed Sunday to Thursday.

Six steps at door, washrooms on same floor. Fully licensed.

㊴ JET
360 Adelaide West, 408-2646

The converted first floor and basement of a Fashion District low-rise, Jet has two distinct faces. The main space is a large, glamourous room with several bars, a VIP lounge with bubbling water curtains, and curved canopies that vault over a spacious dance floor. The music? Progressive house, classic house, and plain old garden-variety house. The downstairs ravers' rec room has silver walls and a stripped-down techno look —

㊺ UP AND DOWN
270 Adelaide West, 977-4038

Although it doesn't have a dance floor, the music played in this two-storey townhouse makes Up and Down a very funky place. From after work till 3 a.m., DJs play drum 'n' bass, r 'n' b, jungle, trip-hop, rare groove, and up-beat jazz. It's tiny — licensed for a total of 40 clubbers — and furnished with leather wing-back chairs, afghan rugs, and fireplaces, so that it feels like you're visiting incredibly cool friends and listening to their amazing record collection. They make a great Caesar salad, as well. Closed Monday.

Six steps at door, washrooms on same floor. Fully licensed.

cinder blocks prop up the DJ's two turntables and microphone. Closed Sunday to Wednesday.

12 steps at door, washrooms on same floor. Fully licensed.

㉒ JOKER
318 Richmond West, 598-1313

From the street, the Joker resembles the cake that got left out in the rain in the song "MacArthur Park," with its dissolving ice-cream colours bleeding into each other. Inside, the look is more organic — spaces seem to blend together throughout the club's three floors. There are lots of pool tables, couches for those too pooped to party, and the rooftop patio offers a relaxing place to chill. Music ranges from alt-rock to progressive house, with Friday and Saturday night DJ-sets broadcasting on radio stations Energy 108 and Mix 99 respectively. Closed Sunday to Wednesday.

Eight steps at door, washrooms on same floor. Fully licensed. Patio.

㊾ KAJMERE
393 King West, 586-0990

A deep-crimson space decked out like something from *The Arabian Nights*, this 300-capacity club caters to an older crowd more intent on conversation than shaking their groove-things to club-house DJs. That doesn't stop the DJs, though. Closed Sunday to Thursday.

One step at door, washrooms on same floor. Fully licensed.

57 LIMELIGHT
250 Adelaide West, 593-6126

Limelight is one of the few monster dance clubs that are open during the week. A black bat-cave of a space, Limelight is a three-storey building dedicated to hardcore dancing. Wednesday, the club spotlights underground and progressive house, Thursday top-40 rock, Friday and Saturday house and retro '80s, and Sunday goth, industrial, and electronica. Expect over 1,100 club kids on weekends. Closed Tuesday.

12 steps at door, washrooms on same floor. Fully licensed. Patio.

43 THE LIVING ROOM
330 Adelaide West, 979-3168

Owned by the people responsible for the legendary but now-defunct Toronto club Twilight Zone — a then-unknown rap trio called the Beastie Boys played there in '86 to an audience of 10 unimpressed clubbers — the Living Room is a large rambling space. With three bars — one outfitted with a "last call" gong — the stylish space attracts an older group as interested in posing as in boogying to house and r 'n' b. A quieter lounge area overlooks busy Adelaide Street. Closed Monday and Tuesday.

Barrier-free, washrooms in basement. Fully licensed.

5 MAD BAR
230 Richmond West, 340-0089

Although it doesn't look big enough, this two-tiered club is legally licensed for 275 punters — they really pack 'em in here. Candlelit and chrome-accented, this functional party space caters to a hard-core dance crowd — Monday's jungle and drum 'n' bass, and the rest of the week is progressive house. Don't all race to the patio at once — it only seats eight. Closed Sunday, Tuesday and Wednesday.

Barrier-free. Fully licensed. Patio.

72 MINISTRY
19 Mercer, 977-8868

Ministry occupies a space that seems to change its name — and management — every couple of months. No matter what they call it, the club draws a mob mostly from the 'burbs, dressed to impress and score romantically while grooving to

hip-hop and house choons. In the centre of the cavernous black-on-purple club is a sunken conversation pit, but since it's located right in the middle of the dance floor, it's doubtful that much communication — verbal, that is — goes on there. Closed Sunday to Thursday.

One step at door, washrooms on same floor. Fully licensed.

6 MONEY
199 Richmond West, 591-9000

See Hot Spot page 46.

44 PICANTE
326 Adelaide West, 408-2958

At this South American–flavoured cantina that features dancing, DJs spin Latin jazz on Friday and Saturday nights. Free salsa lessons Saturday evenings at 10. Closed Sunday.

Four steps at door, washrooms on same floor. Fully licensed. Patio.

26 PLASTIQUE
128 Peter, 506-9481

This is where the beautiful people come to dance and show off, because there's nothing plastic about Plastique. Quite the contrary — it's a two-storey gilt palace decked out in plug-chain curtains, white vinyl wingback chairs, and a reproduction of Studio 54's man in the moon with coke spoon hanging over the dance floor. Friday is Ladies' Night — free admission if you're female — and Saturday evening is devoted to house music, freestyle, and r 'n' b. Celebrity sightings include heartthrobs "Marky Mark" Wahlberg, Antonio Sabatino Jr., and Antonio Banderas — unfortunately not at the same time — as well as pugilists Lennox Lewis and Naomi Campbell. Closed Sunday to Thursday.

Eight steps at door, washrooms on same floor. Fully licensed.

35 ROXY BLU
12 Brant, 504-3222

Situated slightly west of the main club area, Roxy Blu is decorated to resemble a very tacky '60s living room complete with luridly hued sectional sofas and plug-ugly swag lamps. The lower level — dubbed Grandma's Rec Room — is even more kitschy. Here, the couches all match! Despite the

CINECYCLE: Off the beaten track, cineaste Martin Heath screens classic and avant garde flicks.

campy decor, the room attracts a fashionable 30-something crowd that grooves to salsa Wednesday nights, house and trip-hop Fridays, and guest DJs Saturdays. Closed Monday and Tuesday.

10 steps at door, washrooms on same floor. Fully licensed.

54 UP AND DOWN
270 Adelaide West, 977-4038

See Hot Spot page 47.

3 VIBE
222 Richmond West, 599-8423

Behind the front window's heavy curtains, you'll find that Vibe is a small lounge where DJs spin serious beats and breaks. The playlist is eclectic — everything from house and old-school rap to classic r 'n' b and funk. Closed Monday to Wednesday.

Barrier-free, washrooms in basement. Fully licensed.

9 WHISKEY SAIGON
250 Richmond West, 593-4646

This four-storey funk funhouse attracts a mostly suburban crowd hell-bent on enjoying itself. To match their patrons' preference, DJs spin club house, alternative top 40, and '80s tunes in rooms painted with faux Lichtenstein pop-art murals and fake Warhol portraits of Mao Tse-tung. Whiskey is one of the few dance palaces in town with an ATM bank machine.

10 steps at door, washrooms in basement. Fully licensed. Patio.

POOL HALLS

40 CHARLOTTE ROOM
19 Charlotte, 598-2882

Named one of the top 10 pool rooms in North America by *Billiards Digest*, the Room resembles an olde English gentleman's club. With 10 tournament-quality tables and an upscale pub-grub menu, this inviting, carpeted space is a favourite with the media gang. For those without a cue, DJs spin laid-back grooves, and jazz groups occasionally play.

Seven steps at door, washrooms on same floor. Fully licensed.

7 THE COLOURED STONE
205 Richmond West, 351-8499

In this rustic pool parlour, canoes hang from the

ceiling and threadbare rugs are scattered over a
concrete floor embedded with cross-sections of
logs. Weekly Wednesday-night jazz performances
by the likes of Billy Newton Davis, and artwork by
Ojibway sculptor and painter Duke Redbird (who
creates and sells his wares in a space just off the
main entrance) make this subterranean hall jump
until 2 a.m.

10 steps at door, washrooms on same floor. Fully
licensed.

GALLERIES AND MUSEUMS

28 **A SPACE**
401 Richmond West, 979-9633

Canada's oldest artist-run gallery, A Space's current policy is to showcase highly political installations. A legendary Toronto institution — the Talking Heads played here in 1977 as a trio — the
centre celebrated its 25th anniversary recently by
plastering a piece designed by Head honcho
David Byrne on billboards across town. A four-
storey maze, this Richmond Street building also
houses galleries YYZ, Gallery 44, and Inter/Ac-
cess, among others.

91 **MERCER UNION**
439 King West, 977-1412

Mercer Union is an artist-run centre committed to
the presentation and examination of Canadian
and international contemporary visual art and re-
lated cultural conventions. Incorporating a wide
range of activities — exhibitions in its three
gallery spaces, lecture series, video screenings,
and artists' talks — Mercer also houses an
archive accessible to the public that contains information and slides from the gallery's 20-plus
years of shows. Closed Sunday and Monday.

27 **YYZ**
401 Richmond West, 598-4546

Another artist-run gallery, YYZ is a showcase both
for wall art and conceptual installations, and is
one of the few spaces to regularly feature work by
video artists.

CINEMAS — FIRST RUN

17 **IMAX 3D THEATRE AT THE PARAMOUNT**
Richmond West at John, 444-3456

Although the very first IMAX theatre anywhere was

opened in Toronto in 1971, the Paramount houses
the city's first 3D cinema. With over 400 stadium-
style seats — and eight wheelchair spaces —
the movie-house's patrons watch specially made
films projected on the eight-storey screen wearing
liquid-crystal shutter glasses. If they're showing
the Rolling Stones' IMAX concert flick, you won't
believe the size of Mick Jagger's lips!

Barrier-free. Beer and wine.

18 **THE PARAMOUNT**
Richmond West at John, 444-3456

The Paramount is a Famous Players multiplex
housing 13 separate cinemas. Each theatre features a wall-to-wall concave screen, state-of-the-
art projection, and digital sound equipment —
four are equipped with THX systems. All have
tiered, stadium-style seating and a total of 60
wheelchair spaces. A licensed café in the lobby,
too.

Barrier-free. Beer and wine.

CINEMAS — REVIVAL

38 **CINECYCLE**
129 Spadina, 971-4273

A warehouse with bicycle wheels and movie reels
hanging from the ceiling, Cinecycle is probably
the most unusual cinema in the city. But first you
have to find it — it's actually in the laneway behind the Spadina address. Projectionist Martin
Heath offers an irregular schedule of screenings
— often in cahoots with local cinephile groups
Pleasure Dome, LIFT (Liason of Independent Film-
makers of Toronto), and other outside-the-main-
stream organizations. Available for rent, Cinecycle is also the only facility in town capable of han-
dling 8 mm (Super and standard), 16mm, and
35mm prints. Best to check NOW's weekly movie
listings for information on upcoming flicks.
Closed most of the time.

One step at door, washrooms on same floor.

LIVE MUSIC — EXPERIMENTAL

4 **THE MUSIC GALLERY**
179 Richmond West, 204-1080

The Music Gallery is a 150-person-capacity performance space dedicated to the presentation of
new and unusual contemporary music. Started in

1976, the Gallery has presented concerts, dance festivals, performance-art spectacles, sound sculptures, and other multimedia works. Every event is recorded and is available to the public from the digital audio archive.

One step at door, washrooms on same floor. Fully licensed.

LIVE MUSIC — CLASSICAL

65 ROY THOMSON HALL
60 Simcoe, 872-4255

Designed by Vancouver architect Arthur Erickson and named for Toronto-born newspaper baron Lord Thomson of Fleet (the Conrad Black of his day), the Hall is home to the Toronto Symphony Orchestra and the Mendelssohn Choir. Hidden behind its mirrored-glass shell are a grand foyer — site of many Film Festival galas — and a 2,812-seat concert space complete with pipe organ. Performers who've trod the boards here include crooner Tony Bennett, Hendrix-inspired classical violinist Nigel Kennedy, and soul diva Aretha Franklin.

Barrier-free. Fully licensed.

THEATRE

33 FACTORY THEATRE
125 Bathurst, 504-9971

Since the early '70s, the Factory has been mounting productions that challenge Toronto theatregoers. Now located in a rambling Victorian manse — complete with café — the Factory is perhaps best known for its premiere productions of Canadian author George F. Walker's inventive plays — many of which have gone on to runs in New York City and London. Sunday matinees are pay-what-you-can.

Some areas barrier-free.

71 PRINCESS OF WALES
300 King West, 872-1212

Owned by the marvellous Mirvishes — father Honest Ed and son David — this theatre stages shows from Broadway and London's West End that these savvy producers bring to town. Specially built to present *Miss Saigon*, the theatre also sports a mural by pop abstractionist Frank Stella

on its rear wall.
Barrier-free.

68 ROYAL ALEXANDRA THEATRE
260 King West, 872-1212

As well as owning the nearby Princess of Wales theatre — named for Princess Diana — discount-store tycoon Honest Ed Mirvish and family also operate this opulent turn-of-the-century playhouse. Known to locals as the Royal Alex, the 1,500-seat theatre presents Broadway and West End touring productions like the perennially popular musical *Les Miserables*. Those afraid of heights should avoid sitting in the vertigo-inducing second balcony.

Some areas barrier-free.

ATTRACTION

15 FESTIVAL HALL
Richmond West at John, 864-1678

Festival Hall is a multi-format adult entertainment centre containing an IMAX 3D Theatre, the 13-screen Paramount cinema, the Playdium interactive gaming centre and a Chapters monster-bookstore.

Chapters (see page 52)
IMAX 3D Theatre (see page 50)
The Paramount (see page 50)
Playdium (see page 54)

SHOPPING

ART SUPPLIES

37 LOOMIS AND TOLES
130 Spadina, 703-4748

BEER STORES

97 THE AMSTERDAM BEER STORE
600 King West, 504-6882

On the same site as the microbrewery, this outlet is open every day of the year except Christmas and New Year's Day — and it's open longer hours than government-operated beer stores, too. Monday to Saturday 11 a.m. to 11 p.m. Sunday 11 a.m. to 6 p.m.

BICYCLES

59 THE BIKE RANCH
216 Adelaide West, 595-1576

If you've come in a hurry, you're in the wrong place. A minor adjustment that should take 20 minutes often becomes a two-day affair — the staff really like to talk bicycles. But where else can hard-core bike couriers tank up on granola bars while discussing bottom-bracket repacks? Check out the fanny packs, wallets, and kilts (!) made from recycled inner tubes and knobby tires — a rubber fetishist's fantasy come true. A number of reasonably priced secondhand clunkers are for sale, as well. Closed Sunday.

BOOKS AND MAGAZINES — NEW

19 CHAPTERS
Richmond West at John, 920-9299

A three-storey mega-bookstore, Chapters carries over 150,000 titles at their Festival Hall outlet. In-store readings and book-signings by authors are held regularly in the atrium lobby.

Other location:
110 Bloor West (see page 178)

DRUGS

92 CORRENTI CIGARS
443 King West, 596-6597

Hand-rolled on the premises, these Cuban stogies are the brand of choice for many corporate big-wigs. Correnti's is worth a trip even for non-smokers — in a dingy, tobacco-hued room that looks like a back-alley shop straight outta Havana circa 1954, workers fashion king-size smokes that fetch up to $30 a pop. Closed Sunday.

FASHION — VINTAGE CLOTHING

30 ZINC
471 Richmond West, 504-6013

Focusing on upscale retro threads for men and women, Zinc is a remarkably modern-looking store. Stock is neatly displayed and everything has been dry-cleaned. Of special note: Zinc is responsible for its own line of recycled and re-dyed look-like-new Levis. Closed Sunday.

FOOD

23 SUGAR MOUNTAIN
320 Richmond West, no phone

Looking for a sugar high? Satisfy your sweet tooth with candy cigarettes, cotton candy, caramel corn, or exotic American and British chocolate bars. Or buy in bulk — jelly beans, blackballs, peanut-caramel Turtles, Smarties, jawbreakers, and such licorice flavours as watermelon, piña colada, and blueberry. Don't miss the wall of Pez dispensers!

Other locations:
1920 Queen East (see page 206)
364 Danforth (see page 195)

34 VEGETABLE KINGDOM
443 Adelaide West, 703-6447

At this organic groceteria in the heart of the Fashion District, owner Anita Armstrong works to put healthy, preservative-free, earth-friendly food on the plates of both restaurant and home diners. Many big-name chefs shop here for some of the freshest veg in town. The Kingdom also prepares frozen dinners — saffron-infused eggplant soup, pumpkin-tomato quiche, and vegan lasagna. Closed Sunday.

HAIR — SALONS

95 JOHN STEINBERG AND ASSOCIATES
585 King West, 506-0268

John Steinberg and partner Russ Mackay are Toronto's kings of the coif. For over 20 years, they've been clipping the famous at this chic salon. Although they don't do lime-green mohawks, they know how to give their hip clientele — which includes skater Kurt Browning, torch singer Natalie Cole, and actor Marlee Matlin — cutting-edge cuts. Closed Sunday.

HIKING AND BACKPACKING

86 EUROPE BOUND OUTFITTERS
383 King West, 205-9992

Directly across the street from Mountain Equipment Co-Op, their main competitor offers much the same stuff — canoes, paddles, camping gear, Frisbees, and hacky sacks. Once through the street-side atrium, you'll find a surprisingly cavernous three-storey space, fashioned from three gutted row houses and filled with their own brand of knapsacks, travel books and maps, plus Tilley Endurable geek-wear for youthful fogies.

Other location:
49 Front East (see page 115)
69 Front East (see page 115)

87 MOUNTAIN EQUIPMENT CO-OP
430 King West, 363-0122

After you pay the $5 initiation fee, you're a lifetime member of this co-operative company that manufactures and sells must-have gear for fans of the great outdoors. Backpackers, hikers, canoeists, and bike riders will find a wide selection of quality goods at prices generally lower than elsewhere. Of special note, rock climbers will enjoy the indoor climber's wall. Everyone else can stay on the ground.

LIQUOR AND WINE STORES

69 LCBO
200 Wellington West, 977-0921

Monday to Friday 9:30 a.m. to 6 p.m.

Closed Saturday, Sunday and holidays.

MUSIC— CDS, RECORDS & TAPES

58 EASTERN BLOC
224 Adelaide West, 593-4355

This has to be the loudest store in the city! A DJ shop specializing in obscure dance music (pre-release white labels, compilation cassettes), when the tunes start blasting out of the humongous speakers here, you'll feel the earth move, literally. Sister to Manchester's Eastern Bloc, Europe's hippest record store, this place lets you stock up on the latest 12-inch vinyl singles, grab a T-shirt and a record bag, or check out the latest sounds at one of two turntable-equipped listening booths. Closed Sunday.

66 ROY THOMSON HALL MUSIC STORE
60 Simcoe, 593-4822 x358

Located just past the hall's ticket-sales area, this in-depth shop stocks classical orchestral and operatic works on CD, cassette, and video. Closed Sunday.

EASTERN BLOC: Dropping phat beats and old-school breaks for hard-core rhythm-heads.

SUGAR MOUNTAIN: Keeping the buzz alive at three in the morning.

SKATEBOARDING

95 **HOGTOWN**
401 King West, 598-4192

This totally rad board shop attracts not only thrashers, but all kinds of extreme-sports fanatics. As well as water skis, body boards, snowboards, and wetsuits, this graffiti-decorated, below-street-level store carries outerwear by Burton, Ballistik, Freshjive, and extremely cool camo-gear by Dub of Hong Kong. Later, skater. Closed Sunday.

Other location:
3246 Danforth (see page 230)

SEX

24 **THE BARRACKS**
56 Widmer, 593-0499

Launched in 1974 and situated in a townhouse on a quiet side street, the Barracks is Canada's oldest gay bathhouse. Open 24 hours every day, this dimly lit two-storey facility is described by the management as "an adventure in raunch." Fetish attire is encouraged — leather, denim, but no cross-dressing, please — in rooms dubbed "the sleazy shower," "the sling," and "officer's quarters." Wednesday is designated Naked Day and free condoms are available in the lounge. There's an in-house sex-toy store and a snack bar, too.

VIDEO

16 **PLAYDIUM**
Richmond West at John, 593-9703

Specializing in interactive video games and virtual simulators, Playdium is almost as good as the real thing. The four-storey electronic arcade houses over 250 total-immersion machines. Don't feel like playing Pong? Steady your nerves in the City Diner, a combination sports-bar and lounge. There's no admission fee, either — Playdium's strictly pay as you play. And play.

Other location:
99 Rathburn (see page 230)

Metro Retro

WEST QUEEN WEST

Queen Street grows funkier west of Bathurst, the cafés cooler, the boutiques freakier. Gone are the chains, and in their places are idiosyncratic eateries and one-of-a-kind shops selling everything from secondhand clothes to thirdhand junk.

FOOD & DINING

RESTAURANTS

37 **BLUE AGAVE**
783 Queen West, 504-3359

Remember the closing credits on TV's *The Flintstones* when Fred pulls up to a drive-in restaurant and a carhop serves him a rack of ribs so enormous that his prehistoric Pontiac tips over? That's why the beef ribs here are called Bedrock. Other selections include Santa Fe–inspired fare with unusual Asian tweaks — turkey corn chowder with coconut milk, or "drunken chicken" with tequila. Don't miss the fabulous desserts such as Key lime pie baked by the mom of one of the owners. Weekend brunch. Closed Monday.

One step at door, washrooms on same floor. Fully licensed. $$

62 **CITIES**
859 Queen West, 504-3762

Cities is not your average Queen West haunt. Rather it's a serious bistro decorated in gorgeous grey, with an ornate gold-leaf bar and kraft-paper-over-linen tables. Staff are accommodating and customers come here for the food, not the scene. They flock for swanky fare such as three-mushroom salad, snow-pea cakes with charred-pineapple salsa, and breast of muscovy duck glazed with Grand Marnier.

Barrier-free, washrooms in basement. Fully licensed. $$$

52 **CITRON**
813 Queen West, 504-2647

Super-chic with its dark mahogany wood and tortoiseshell accents, this bistro is one of the strip's coolest hangouts. You might expect attitude, but there isn't any. Citron pairs its authoritative wine list with mainly veggie mains and lots of heart-conscious seafood entrees with a slight Mediterranean bent. Weekend brunch and a hideaway backyard patio.

One step at door, washrooms in basement. Fully licensed. Patio. $$

54 **GYPSY CO-OP**
815 Queen West, 703-5069

Part candy store, part beanery, the Gypsy attracts a young crowd bent on unpretentious fun. Sofas surround a roaring gas fire and a pool table dominates the back space — but the grub's the main attraction here. Their eclectic menu features jerk chicken with homemade apple chutney, honey-

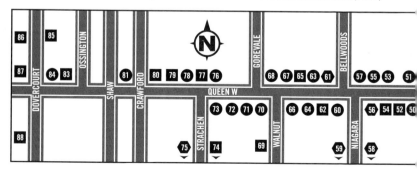

COME AS YOU ARE: Bringing it all out of the closet — a sex-toy shop minus the innuendo.

glazed calamari, and black-bean salsa. Nightly Tarot readings, too. Closed Sunday.

One step at door, washrooms in basement. Fully licensed. $$

86 JULIE'S
202 Dovercourt, 532-7397

Under tall shade trees on a quiet street, Julie's offers Cuban cuisine that's not as incendiary as its Caribbean counterparts. Among the best dishes served are grilled and pressed Cubano sandwiches — filled with marinated roast pork, Serrano ham, and cheese — and tapas-like papas

rellenas — deep-fried mashed-potato balls stuffed with shredded pork and olives. Both make excellent drinking buddies. Sunday brunch ranges from greasy-spoon bacon 'n' eggs to cantina-correct breakfast burritos and huevos rancheros. Closed Monday.

Two steps at door, washrooms in basement. Fully licensed, cash only. Patio. $$

88 MILDRED PIERCE
99 Sudbury, 588-5695

In an unlikely industrial space on the edge of the warehouse district, Mildred Pierce holds court in a

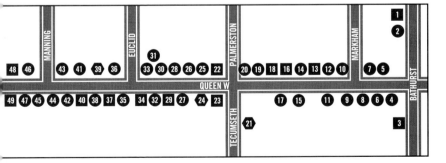

48 TERRONI
720 Queen West, 504-0320

Sure, everyone's got an opinion, but restaurant critics say this is Toronto's best pizza. It offers a super-thin crust that rivals a Carr's cracker, with artful toppings — carpaccio, arugula — casually sprinkled onto its lightly tomato-sauce-smeared surface. After a blasé toss of bocconcini cheese, it's thrown into a wood-burning oven and — presto! Perfect pizza. Eat indoors, where salamis swing from the ceiling, or seclude yourselves on the backyard patio with a bottle of vino.

Barrier-free. Fully licensed. Patio. $

Other location:
106 Victoria (see page 109).

room lined with medieval-looking murals and hung with gauzy swags. There's nothing old-fashioned about Mildred's thoroughly modern dinner menu, however — warm chèvre wrapped in vine leaves with red peppers and parchment bread, osso buco with creamy lemon polenta, Thai seafood hotpot — or her Sunday-brunch lineup of dishes honouring the characters in the 1945 Joan Crawford movie, *Mildred Pierce*. Joan would have approved of the coatroom's ban on wire hangers.

Barrier-free. Fully licensed. Patio. $$

29 MUNSTER HALL
751 Queen West, 603-7699

The Hall has nothing to do with TV's Munsters, although there are vampire posters on the wall; rather, it's a replica of an olde English pub. Every Sunday afternoon they show a two-hour tape of current episodes of the UK soap opera *Coronation Street* while dishing up authentic shepherd's pie, fish 'n' chips, roast beef suppers, and the like. There are pints of Bodingtons to sip and English tabloids to read, too.

Three steps at door, washrooms in basement. Fully licensed. $$

74 NOMADS
936 King West, 703-4942

Defying its location — it just seems like it's in the middle of nowhere — this friendly North African bistro mixes Eritrean, Egyptian, Sudanese, and Moroccan influences to produce a tasty modern

hybrid. Although the food here's not nearly as fiery as the stuff served back home, Nomads' flame-thrower-strength berbere hot sauce turns mild into wild. Couscous bases support veggie stews, meaty casseroles, and accompany unusual salad combinations.

One step at door, washrooms on same floor. Fully licensed. Patio. $$

3 THE PADDOCK
178 Bathurst, 504-9997

Although Queen and Bathurst is one of the grubbiest corners in town, the Paddock is remarkably swank. Built circa 1947, the saloon has been faithfully refurbished, restoring its original charm. Padded burgundy booths, dark wooden wainscotting, and a leather-tufted wraparound bar with a Bakelite counter make the perfect backdrop for cocktail swilling. Don't miss the food: mesquite-smoked steaks with potato gaufrettes and deeply flavoured shrimp bisque are a far cry from pub grub.

Three steps at door, washrooms on same floor. Fully licensed. $$

49 SQUIRLY'S
807A Queen West, 703-0574

Want to get away from it all? Try Squirly's year-round backyard patio with its ripped velvet banquettes and paint-splattered stacking chairs. The fare's fair — vaguely Thai noodle dishes and such — but it's the vibe that makes this place popular with the pierced-navel set. Squirly's anti-decor includes Naugahyde walls, a leopard-skin ceiling, and a mermaid caught in a fisherman's net over the bar. True grunge.

Barrier-free, washrooms in basement. Fully licensed. Patio. $$

79 SWAN
892 Queen West, 532-0452

This Swan is an ugly-duckling luncheonette that's shed its greasy-spoon past and emerged as a swanky joint du jour. Appetizers and mains combine comfort-food classics — grits and dumplings, slow-cooked ribs with corn on the cob — with upscale raw oysters on the half shell and blindingly hot horseradish. Warm service and cool tunes — Louis Prima, '60s Hammond-organ jazz — match the low-key restoration of the diner's

GYPSY CO-OP: Retro decor, contempo fare.

original furnishings, including its vinyl booths. Swan's extremely popular, so expect a lengthy lineup unless you've got a reservation.

Barrier-free, washrooms in basement. Fully licensed. $$

48 **TERRONI**
720 Queen West, 504-0320

See Hot Spot page 58.

○ BAKERIES

40 **DUFFLET PASTRIES**
787 Queen West, 504-2870

A stylish space serving up great cakes and pastries, Dufflet Rosenberg's bakery also supplies many of Toronto's top restaurants with her desserts. Along with her sensational treats, Dufflet markets a line of novelty birthday-cake decorations — marzipan beer cans, roller skates, golf balls — plus her own brand of truffles, coffee beans, and chocolate sauces, as well.

Barrier-free. Unlicensed. Patio. $

23 **FUTURE BAKERY**
739 Queen West, 504-8700

See listing page 165.

Barrier-free, washrooms in basement. Licensed. Patio. $.

13 **VIENNA HOME BAKERY**
626 Queen West, 703-7278

Though not as well known as her superstar-chef sibling Greg, Gay Couillard has an equally stellar pedigree. A consummate baker, she also turns out posh breakfast noshes and super south-of-France quiche-and-salad lunch combos. But it's her fruit-tastic pies and cassis-soaked cakes that cause the most fuss. Most mornings, and especially for weekend brunch, you'll find a group out front waiting for the narrow luncheonette to open. Closed Monday and Tuesday.

Barrier-free, washrooms in basement. Unlicensed, smoke-free, cash only. Patio. $

CAFES AND COFFEE HOUSES

83 CAFE BERNATE
1024 Queen West, 535-2835

This unpolished café on the frontier of Queen West has quickly become a neighbourhood favourite. Mornings, locals fill the narrow space for monstrous muffins, and at lunchtime for numerous soup, salad, and sandwich permutations. Saturday brunch leans towards Tex-Mex egg dishes like huevos rancheros with nippy salsa. The service, while mostly casual, is always amiable. Closed Sunday and holidays.

One step at door, washrooms in basement. Unlicensed, smoke-free, cash only. $

85 LUNA 181
181 Dovercourt, 588-3374

Housed in a converted corner store, Luna is open seven days a week but closes early — usually 6 p.m. The menu runs from grilled-veggie panini to goulash. This simple café is always full on weekends for brunches featuring poached-egg combos, scrambled-egg wraps, and St. Urbain bagels. Low-key chef Jackie Torres is an alumnus of the College Street bistro Ellipsis.

Two steps at door, washrooms in basement. Unlicensed. Patio. $

22 SECOND CUP
652 Queen West, 504-0433

See listing page 17.

Two steps at door, washrooms on same floor. Unlicensed. $

80 XXX
834 Queen West, 536-2822

The look of this chillin' café combines high-tech industrial fixtures with 19th-century butcher blocks, and boy is this place serious about caffeine. Next to the espresso machine, a coffee maker has been recycled into a deluxe plate warmer. The menu keeps things simple — vegan baked goods, jerk-chicken wraps, and three types of empanadas. Weekend brunch, too.

Barrier-free, washrooms in basement. Unlicensed, cash only. Patio. $

DELIS AND DINERS

87 THE ELVIS RESTAURANT
1136 Queen West, 535-9948

Are you lonesome and hungry tonight? Crave a

OCTOPUS: Deeply funky beats and a crowd that knows how to par-tay.

charbroiled cheeseburger made from a hunka-hunka frozen steakette, with a side of prefab fries slathered in canned gravy? This greasy spoon will satisfy any Hound Dog looking for Heartburn Hotel. Other than convenience-store busts of the King and an appalling mural of Elvis in Hawaii painted with distorted perspective, there's little here that would steal the King away from Graceland.

One step at door, washrooms in basement. Fully licensed, cash only. $

1 MIMI'S
218 Bathurst, 703-6464

Rock 'n' roll! Tiny Mimi's caters to Toronto's musical community. Just about any time of the day you'll find someone famous — or someone who used to be — in one of the three vinyl-upholstered booths or at one of the six stools that line the lunch counter. There's even a stack of *Mojo*s for flipping through while you down a stack o' flapjacks in this — did we mention tiny? — spoon festooned with Blue Rodeo platinum CDs. Go early if you expect to get a seat — and go often because Mimi's is one of the hottest meal tickets in town. Closed Tuesday and Wednesday.

One step at door, washrooms in basement. Unlicensed. $

77 NEW HARMONY
872A Queen West, 532-3266

Closed Sunday.

Barrier-free, washrooms in basement. Fully licensed. $

16 PRAGUE DELI
638 Queen West, 504-5787

Past the display cases crammed with takeout borscht, cabbage rolls, and veal lights in cream sauce, Prague Deli has a tiny lunch counter where they serve up homemade pierogi, goulash, Belgian waffles, and the like to budget-conscious diners. The shop's shelves, lined with boxes of apple strudel and jars of sauerkraut and rolled herring, are worth investigating as well. Closed Sunday.

One step at door, washrooms in basement. Unlicensed, smoke-free. $

34 THE RAGING SPOON
761 Queen West, 504-6128

Staffed by survivors of the psychiatric system, this friendly lunch counter serves a limited menu weekdays from 10 a.m. to 3 p.m. only. Spoon-style — but certainly not greasy — all-day breakfasts, salads 'n' sandwiches, and homemade soups such as curried-lentil and turkey-noodle make this modest spot a find. Closed Saturday and Sunday.

Barrier-free. Unlicensed. Patio. $

JUICE BARS

65 SMART BAR
754 Queen West, 504-0653

Decked out in holograms, this organic juice bar hosts impromptu conga-drum jam sessions. Liquid lunch elixirs include vitamin-charged Body Fuel, dairy-free grain-based shakes, and the liver-cleansing Toxic Avenger. Closed Sunday.

One step at door, washrooms in basement. Unlicensed, smoke-free, cash only. Patio. $

BARS

69 OCTOPUS
875 Queen West, 504-4798

The hottest of the haute spots when it opened a few years back, Octopus still has a certain cachet with Queen West's fringe crowd. Blood-red walls, lime-green-striped banquettes, and an out-there jazz-and-funk soundtrack make for a night of cool clubbing. On hot summer nights, the action moves to the outdoor rooftop littered with post office letter boxes. Open from 9 p.m. till — as their answering machine states — "you guys are ready to go home." Closed Sunday to Tuesday.

Barrier-free, washrooms in basement. Fully licensed.

61 SANCTUARY
732 Queen West, 504-1917

Calling itself a Vampire bar, this goth haunt's clientele throw themselves about the room to the sounds of Nine Inch Nails and their ilk. Scary! The decor consists of fake dungeon walls, a decrepit motorcycle (deceased), black-felt-topped pool tables, and a white wooden cross. The Catacombs — in the basement, natch — are even scarier. Compulsory cloak check.

One step at door, washrooms in basement.

⑦⑤ INDUSTRY
901 King West, 260-2660

A massive dance den with minimal decor, Industry concentrates on the groove. Open only on Friday and Saturday nights — and long-weekend Sundays — the club's music extends to soulful underground house on Fridays and, on Saturdays, nose-bleeding techno at rave-ups that don't end until 9 the following morning. Check out the safe-sex lounge — it's decked out with slippery wet-look vinyl sofas and a circular bed. Superstar-DJ visitors include New York's Danny Tenaglia and Victor Calderone — both Madonna cohorts — and Brit spinner Carl Cox. Occasional live shows from the likes of Roni Size and Meat Beat Manifesto, too. Closed Sunday to Thursday.

Barrier-free. Fully licensed.

ENTERTAINMENT

DANCE CLUBS

㊟ THE HOOCH
815 Queen West, 703-5069

Upstairs from the Gypsy Co-op, this funky fun palace features DJs spinning discs that vary from swing to trip-hop to jungle. The vibe is very down-to-earth — the crowd's here for the tunes, not the posing. Superstar DJ Denise Benson holds court at her Wednesday-evening "Glide" extravaganzas. Closed Sunday.

16 steps at door, washrooms on same floor. Fully licensed.

⑦⑤ INDUSTRY
901 King West, 260-2660

See Hot Spot listing this page.

POOL HALLS

㉔ RAQ N WAQ
739 Queen West, 504-9120

This warehouse-sized pool hall in a modified bread factory attracts upscale hustlers. With a dozen tables — two tournament-quality — three fireplaces, magnums of champagne, and a cigar humidor, this spot is especially hot with media

types. It's not hard to see why. DJs spin funkified acid jazz nightly.

20 steps at door, washrooms on same floor. Fully licensed. Patio.

GALLERIES AND MUSEUMS

㉗ ART METROPOLE
788 King West, 703-4400

Dedicated to the distribution of limited-edition multiples by artists both local and international, Art Metropole grew out of the archives of *File* magazine, a now-defunct publication by Canadian art stars General Idea. The gallery's mandate is to mix touring shows with rare items pulled from their own collection. Their bookshop is the only place in town where you can buy German art-terrorist Joseph Beuys' felt postcards.

㉑ COLD CITY GALLERY
686 Richmond West, 504-6681

Toronto's first commercial artists' collective, this gallery shows work by A-list members of the local and global art scenes. Just before his death, author William S. Burroughs came here to unveil his shotgun paintings — created by shooting paint from a modified firearm. Current stars include painters Brian Scott and Sandra Rachio, and sculptor Eldon Garnett.

㊴ STEPHEN BULGER GALLERY
700 Queen West, 504-0575

A gallery specializing in 20th-century Canadian and international social-commentary photography. The bookstore at the back carries a wide selection of current and out-of-print titles on photography. Appraising, framing, and archival-storage supplies, as well. Closed Sunday and Monday.

㉘ YDESSA HENDELES ART FOUNDATION
778 King West, 413-9400

Only open Saturday afternoons — or by appointments made way in advance — Hendeles's gallery regularly presents shows of work from the owner's exquisite private collection. Lauded by the international art community for shows by Jenny Holzer and Bill Viola, this gallery is not to be missed. Every installation is perfect — Hendeles ensures the room's walls are rebuilt for each exhibit to give the art proportionally correct settings.

SHOPPING

ART SUPPLIES

70 JAPANESE PAPER PLACE
887 Queen West, 703-0089

Not only does this serene shop sell the supplies for making Japanese paper — and the results of that process — but it also holds workshops that teach first-timers what to do. Origami kits, books on printmaking, and do-it-yourself calligraphy sets, too.

Other location:
210 Queen's Quay West (see page 212)

78 TERN
874 Queen West, 537-7338

Closed Sunday.

BEER STORES

7 THE BEER STORE
614 Queen West @ Bathurst, 504-4665

Monday to Wednesday 10 a.m. to 8 p.m.
Thursday and Friday 10 a.m. to 9 p.m.
Saturday 9:30 a.m. to 9 p.m.
Sunday 11 a.m. to 6 p.m.
Closed holidays.

BICYCLES

14 CYCLE SHOPPE
630A Queen West, 703-9990

Closed Sunday.

CRAFTS

28 THE ALGONQUIANS SWEET GRASS GALLERY
668 Queen West, 703-1336

Ojibway-owned and -operated, this indigenous-craft showcase is best known for its exquisitely executed moccasins and porcupine-quill pendants, chokers, and earrings. Native-inspired T-shirts, feathered-headdress-like wall hangings, and antique spearheads are also available.

32 PREZENTS OF MIND
761 Queen West, 703-8417

In a transformed church hall, this community-based not-for-profit shop showcases the work of

COMRAGS: Local designer superstars flog their frocks in deluxe digs.

more than 150 artisans, many of whom are survivors of the psychiatric system. Bargains scattered about the high-ceilinged room include hand-knit sweaters, stained-glass terrariums, and wonderful wooden rocking horses. Closed Monday.

FASHION — ACCESSORIES

33 J. ALFRED PRUFROCK
682 Queen West, 504-0706

Featuring intricate watches designed by owners Gisele Theriault and Daniel Thompson, this beautifully appointed shop represents the work of other up-and-coming artisans as well. Sproingy timepieces by Klokz, faux-alligator-hide attaché cases and clutches by Geranium, and wacky hats by Gwendolyne are just a few of the unique items they carry. Psst: Sarah McLachlan shops here.

67 RETRO-G
758 Queen West, 703-9025

Mad-for-it Manchester hatter Georgina creates one-of-a-kind *chapeaux* that start at whimsical and end up way out there, passing the Vegas-showgirl-headdress look en route. Now, after six years of concentrating on hats, she has begun to branch out with full-figured 17th-meets-21st-century frock coats. Closed Sunday.

FASHION — NEW CLOTHING

31 ANNIE THOMPSON
674 Queen West, 703-3843

Local fashion artist Thompson brings a touch of theatricality to this already image-conscious neighbourhood. Thompson plays with texture — her sensuous clothes are often made with the fabric reversed, giving them a subtle look that works with her hand-dyed palette. And it's not all girlie stuff. Her line of oversized men's shirts is called Snag, for Sensitive New Age Guy. Closed Sunday.

53 ANY DIRECT FLIGHT
724 Queen West, 504-0017

Featuring classic womenswear designed by owner Margot Allin, this shop decorated with draped linen offers clothes that can be worn straight from the office to the latest happening club. The look says glamour, the prices say not bad, really. Complementary accessories by local jeweller Myka.

25 COMRAGS
654 Queen West, 360-7249

Judy Gunhouse and Joyce Cornish have been a driving force in Canadian fashion for more than a decade. They sell in the U.S. and Europe now, but this shop was their first. Its cool blond-wood interior sets off the designing duo's duds' sleek lines, wild colours, and expert construction. During sales, the hands on the clock here move at 10 times normal speed, but Comrags' look is timeless.

43 DELPHIC
706 Queen West, 603-3334

Spot the scooter — Delphic's window display makes for the fourth Lambretta sighting downtown (the others: Aunties and Uncles, Innocenti, and X-Large). This hip menswear shop features UK haberdashers Hope and Glory — very Oasis — as well as New York City's Liquid Sky, and local designer Snug's club gear. Cool caps by the resurrected Guelph hatter Biltmore, too.

76 GRREAT STUFF
870 Queen West, 536-6770

Described by a local rag as stocking "casual hunkwear," Stuff handles men's end-of-the-line and sample merchandise from Canadian and international fashion houses. Among the deeply discounted designer labels spotted in the two-level store — Calvin Klein, Cinque, Big Star, and Timberland. Closed Monday.

35 LOWON POPE
692 Queen West, 504-8150

The last people to wear the sophisticated frocks of fashion artists Lana Lowon and Jim Pope are the goth and grunge kids who pass by their elegant shop en masse. But the cognoscenti flock here for the design duo's bias-cut, vintage-glamour dresses. Knockout wedding gowns, too.

27 NEARLY NAKED
749 Queen West, 703-7561

Almost naked, except for underwear. Here you'll uncover Triumph, Elita, Hanna Grenier, and Halston ladies' briefs, Filodoro stockings, and Mondor tights, as well as aromatherapy candles.

50 SAMUEL JACKSON
809 Queen West, 727-1402

Nothing to do with the Hollywood actor — that's

Samuel L. Jackson — the similarly named haberdasher creates one-of-a-kind outfits bound to impress. Funky streetwear, Jackson's Jesus jackets, and skimpy mohair sweaters make individual fashion statements.

FASHION — VINTAGE CLOTHING

30 **CABARET NOSTALGIA**
672 Queen West, 504-7126

With its slinky cocktail gowns, zoot suits, and stylish fedoras from the '30s and '40s, this compact boutique has all the duds you'll need to outfit yourself for Swing Night. Beat me, daddy, eight to the bar!

66 **WRAY'S RELICS**
867 Queen West, 603-1734

The pile on the curb out front hints at what's in store at this ragtag secondhand shop: furniture from the '40s and '50s, wrought-iron magazine racks, swag lamps, and black-velvet paintings compete for attention with old roller skates, used bowling shoes, and tons of costume jewellery. Closed Monday.

FASHION — SHOES

44 **AUSTRALIAN BOOT COMPANY**
791 Queen West, 504-2411

See Hot Spot listing next page.

FLORISTS AND PLANTS

71 **CUT AND DRY**
911 Queen West, 703-7370

Not a hair salon but a florists' supply shop featuring flowers, leaves, and herbs, both dried and alive. Closed Sunday.

FOOD

63 **APPLETREE NATURAL FOODS**
752 Queen West, 504-9677

A small neighbourhood operation with a general cross-section of supplements, herbaceous hair dyes, bulk seasonings, and organic veggies, they also have a takeout-only lunch stand that offers

44 **AUSTRALIAN BOOT COMPANY**
791 Queen West, 504-2411

Made famous by the film *The Adventures of Priscilla, Queen of the Desert*, these water-resistant slip-on boots by Blundstone have since become a fashion must-have. This shop has the best selection in town and also carries dressier shoes and leather jackets by R. M. Williams. And what goes better with Aussie stompers than New Zealand socks?

Other location:
2644 Yonge (see page 228)

vegetarian sushi, miso soup, smoothies, and herbal teas. Closed Sunday.

57 **SANKO**
730 Queen West, 703-4550

In the mood to make your own sushi? Sanko — a Japanese grocery — has all the supplies. You'll find sheets of nori seaweed for wrapping, bamboo mats for rolling, sticky rice, and tubes of hellishly hot wasabi horseradish. Closed Tuesday.

HAIR — SALONS

41 **COUPE BIZZARRE**
704 Queen West, 504-0783

46 **COUPE BIZZARRE**
710 Queen West, 367-8998

Closed Sunday to Wednesday.

68 **COUPE D'ART**
764 Queen West, 504-8606

26 **HARLOTS**
660 Queen West, 504-9551

51 **XTRAORDINAIRE**
722 Queen West, 504-1814

HOME FURNISHINGS — NEW

36 **INSIDE**
694 Queen West, 504-4919

With its white-on-white interior, Inside almost looks more like an art gallery than an outlet specializing in reproductions of classic '50s and '60s furniture. All the right names are represented:

funky fiberglass chairs and modern airport-lounge chairs by Charles and Ray Eames, as well as clever cardboard chairs by Toronto-born architect Frank Gehry. Expensive.

60 INTERIA
845 Queen West, 703-1658

Custom-designed and -manufactured, Interia's dramatic furniture looks like it belongs on a movie set — Buck Rogers sci-fi meets Malibu Madonna. The Toronto firm produces top-of-the-line velvet chaise longues, leopard-skin settees, and surprisingly affordable accent pieces.

84 STUDIO BRILLANTINE
1081-1/2 Queen West, 536-6521

Brillantine is a tiny studio overflowing with fabulously designed housewares. Each displayed *objet* comes with a label that lists the artist and a catalogue number — nothing as gauche as a price tag. Locally and internationally known artists represented include Toronto's Third Uncle, Star 69, and Euro stars Phillipe Starck and Alessi. Koziol's witty line of Smurf-inspired kitchen brushes are on sale, too.

72 THE TIN TAJ
913 Queen West, 703-755

Trained in Mexico, owner Carol Anne Castray is a tinsmith with a twist. Using sheet tin, some punches, and a pair of shears, she creates one-of-a-kind picture and mirror frames, lampshades, board games, and light-switch covers. She also carries tin ceiling panels and tin toys from around the world. Closed Sunday and Monday.

HOME FURNISHINGS — USED

12 AFTERGLOW
622 Queen West, 504-9923

Amidst the jumble of stuffed alligators, pre-transistor radios, and cocktail shakers, you'll find Queen West's largest selection of '50s table lamps. Glassware, salt-and-pepper sets, and a ventriloquist's dummy, too.

45 MAUVE DECADE
795 Queen West, 703-8500

15 METRO RETRO
715 Queen West, 504-1651

This store specializes in the kind of things that no

one else thought to collect — '60s Gucci-hued Princess phones, ugly coffee mugs, H.R. Pufnstuf records. It also has an impressive array of obsolete kitchenware. Of course, this stuff is incredibly hip again, so leave your gag reflex at the door. Not only does everything here look modish — '50s toasters, '60s blenders, '70s juicers — but it all still works.

38 MOSTLY MOVABLES
785 Queen West, 504-4455

The concept here is furniture that can be moved no matter how large from old apartment to new. The owners buy up container loads of furniture at estate sales in the UK and then sell it back in T.O. for ridiculously low prices. Not only sofa sets and afghan rugs but also armoires and dining-room sets with their original patinas. They'll strip the wooden pieces if you insist, but leave them as is — nothing betters a time-worn veneer.

9 ODDS AND ENDS
703A Queen West, 504-0579

42 QUASI-MODO
789 Queen West, 703-8300

Long before *Wallpaper* magazine appropriated the style, this almost-gallery space focused on the work of influential furniture designers like Ray and Charles Eames and George Nelson. Here, sleek modernist tables and sofas are complemented by origami-like lamps by Isamu Noguchi and postmodern French designer Phillipe Starck's wacky *objets*. Beautiful stuff. Closed Sunday.

5 SHOWCASE ANTIQUE MALL
610 Queen West, 703-6255

If your idea of heaven is aisle after aisle of display cases crammed with such collectibles as $100 Dinky toys, old cameras, cigarette lighters, and other items of dubious antiquity, you could spend hours in this place. The basement furniture department sells rickety stuff at ridiculously high prices.

6 THIRD TIME AROUND
677 Queen West, 703-7037

JUNK

17 INDOOR GARAGE SALE
721 Queen West

Closed Sunday.

MUSIC — CDS, RECORDS & TAPES

19 NEUROTICA
642 Queen West, 603—7796

10 ROTATE THIS
620 Queen West, 504-8447

Supermodel Helena Christiansen and starlet Claire Danes are just a couple of the celebrities who have shopped at this all-genre record shop. New and used CDs, lots of limited-edition vinyl LPs, and rare Viletones and Teenage Head singles make Rotate This a must for fans of cutting-edge music of all genres. Concert tickets, band T-shirts, and live performances (in the garage round back) are on offer, too.

11 SILVER DISCUS
703 Queen West, 703-8202

MUSICAL INSTRUMENTS

73 CAPSULE MUSIC
921 Queen West, 203-0202

The must-see spot that every musician — whether local or just passing through on tour — visits on a pilgrimage. Capsule's modest facade doesn't promise much, until you notice the mint-condition 1965 Rickenbacker 12-string guitar in the window. Inside, there are four rooms crammed with vintage guitars and amplifiers — Fender, Gibson, Mosrite, Danelectro — antique stomp boxes, bongos, analog synths, home organs, dulcimers, lap steel guitars, and cool-looking microphones. Rockabilly stage clothes, too. Closed Sunday and Monday.

20 NASH MUSIC
650 Queen West, 703-0019

47 SONG BIRD
801 Queen West, 504-7664

Looking for rare stomp boxes, vintage axes, and pre-digital synths? Song Bird's got 'em. Half the store is dedicated to used drum kits — retro transparent turquoise, anyone? — while the other features acoustic and electric guitars and pedals. By the door, you'll find what every aspiring musician's neighbour needs — earplugs.

PET SUPPLIES

81 FUZZY BELLY DELI
920 Queen West, 532-9478

Besides the usual bulk pet chow, Fuzzy features Stinkerware, Tina Cooper's hand-painted dinner bowls for cats. Other out-of-the-ordinary items include oatmeal-yucca shampoo for pets, organic catnip, and black vinyl fun-fur-lined doggie coats. Downstairs in the Peticure Lounge, staff will groom the family beast.

64 HELMUTT'S
863 Queen West, 504-1265

A friendly neighbourhood pet shop, Helmutt's delivers bulk bags of dog and/or cat food in the downtown core, and also has a pet-adoption registry. Locally made critter toys, natural-ingredient treats, and beastie beds, also.

SEX

8 COME AS YOU ARE
701 Queen West, 504-7934

Catering to people of all sexualities, Come As You Are sells sex toys made for safe, slippery fun. Whether you're looking for a silicone dildo, a powerful vibrator, or a leather restraint or harness, this is the place for the equipment to unleash any fantasy. All of the stock is openly displayed — in fact, you're encouraged to get hands-on. Workshops, discussion groups, readings, and performances are held as well. "Virgins" may want to take the introductory tour.

55 DOC'S LEATHERS
726 Queen West, 504-8888

This is one weird store. The first floor is full of used and new leather jackets and pants, motorcycle-cop helmets, bowie knives, antique duelling pistols, and Coca-Cola memorabilia. Past the bullet belts, human skulls, and New Age crystals (!), there's a sign saying that no one under the age of 18 is allowed to enter the Dungeon in the basement. There, among the whips, paddles, and fetish gear, consenting mannequins enact *tableaux vivants*, the kinkiest of which takes place in a dentist office. Another sign reads, "Don't be shy, Doc will gladly demonstrate." Thanks, but no thanks!

② **OAK LEAF STEAM BATHS**
216 Bathurst, 603-3434

An extremely down-at-the-heels bathhouse announced by a "For Men Only" sign stuck to the front door, the Fig Leaf — as habituees call it — features private rooms and men-in-towels round the clock, 24-7.

TATTOOS AND PIERCINGS

④ **WAY COOL TATTOOS**
679 Queen West, 603-0145

One of the city's favourite body-embellishment emporia, Way Cool has tattooed everyone from tongue-in-cheek metal-mongers Gwar to teen heartthrobs N'Sync. Though there's not much to look at other than panels of tattoos, Way Cool is staffed by knowledgable pros— you might recognize owner Ace Daniels as the biker in the Nokia cell-phone commercial.

Other locations:
604 Yonge (see page 158)
5203 Yonge (see page 228)

Il Gatto Nero

COLLEGE

Signs name the area Little Italy, but the action on this once exclusively Italian street is anything but small-time. Today, trendy trattorias rub shoulders with grungy swing lounges to create one of Toronto's more vital districts. *Utne Reader* rates this nabe one of North America's coolest.

FOOD & DINING

RESTAURANTS

21 **BAR ITALIA**
584 College, 535-3621

For more than 10 years, Bar Italia has been the place to see and be scene. Regulars include pretentious art pseuds, wannabes, and never-wills, but if you're reasonable, the extremely professional staff may take a shine to you. A small front patio offers optimum people-watching, and the quieter upstairs room swings with live jazz and DJs. Show up early to guarantee entry. Saturday and Sunday brunch from 9 a.m.

Barrier-free. Fully licensed. Patio. $$

55 **CAFE SOCIETA**
796 College, 588-7490

See Hot Spot page 73.

Barrier-free, washrooms in basement. Fully licensed. Patio. $$

18 **CAOBA**
571 College, 533-6195

A relative newcomer to the College strip, this all-over-the-map Latin-meets-Mediterranean-meets-Caribbean-meets-Thai eatery has something for everyone. In this pale-pink and black multi-level room, staff dish up such items as jerk-chicken Caesar salad, saffron–adobo-pepper steak with avocado-and-hard-boiled-egg salsa, and Asiatika pizza with stir-fried veg, mango, and mozzarella. Closed Sunday.

Barrier-free, washrooms in basement. Fully-licensed. Patio. $$

22 **CORSO ITALIA**
584 College, 532-6116

The former home of Bar Italia — which moved next door — Corso mimics Italia's recipe for success but somehow misses having the cachet of its neighbour. Yes, the marble-topped tables look familiar and the three-p menu — pizza, pasta, and panini — reads the same, but there's a far more informal vibe here. Walls are covered in graffiti— did Isabella Rossellini really add her autograph? — and most nights there's live music with a jazz, blues, or soul bent.

Barrier-free, washrooms in basement. Fully licensed. Patio. $$

57 **DIPAMO'S BARBEQUE**
838 College, 532-8161

Many do ribs, but few do them properly. Thank God for DiPamo's, a rather utilitarian-looking rib joint

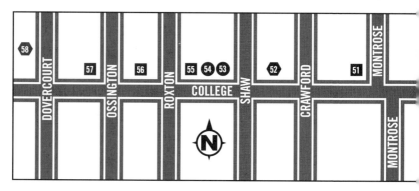

CIAO EDIE: Smoke trails and cocktails in a room named for a Warhol superstar (deceased).

just beyond the fashionable part of College. Slow-cooked for up to 10 hours on a trailer-mounted smoker capable of processing 250 pounds of pork at a time, the meat is fall-from-the-bone tender in true southern BBQ style. Try it with exceptional baked beans and you've got a major pig-out. Weekend brunch takes the barbecue on a Venezuelan holiday with Eggs Hector and Eggs Domino. Make sure to check out the smokin' smoker in the backyard!

One step at door, washrooms on same floor. Fully licensed. $$

37 DOLCE VITA
612 College, 531-0028

Classy pasta-and-panini parlour.

Barrier-free, two steps to washrooms. Fully licensed. Patio. $$$

9 EL BODEGON
537 College, 944-8297

Usually crowded — and justifiably so — this Peruvian cantina offers a strange mix of South American cuisine, wonton soups, and BLTs. True S.A. seafood stews and hefty grilled-meat platters

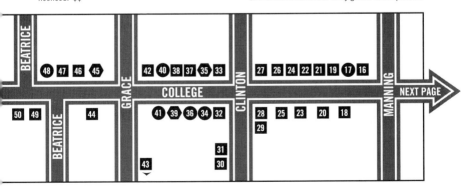

are served under a ceiling festooned with dried leaves and flowers.

One step at door, washrooms in basement. Fully licensed. Patio. $$

4 ELLIPSIS
503 College, 929-2892

Long a favourite with the culinary set, restaurateur Nancy Barone's eatery feels like a chic rural French inn. Warm off-white walls and whitewashed armoires give the room a sense of tranquility, while the astoundingly good grub — ricotta and arborio rice tart, couscous with chickpeas, figs, and eggplant, and calf's liver with spaetzle — makes first-timers instant fans for life. Weekend brunch causes lineups.

One step at door, washrooms on same floor. Fully licensed. Patio. $$

33 EMILIO'S
598 College, 531-7888

Modern Italian.

Barrier-free, washrooms in basement. Fully licensed. $$

56 IRIE
808 College, 531-4743

Most local Caribbean food is not known for its finesse. Firepower, sure, but not subtlety. Irie takes jerk pork tenderloin and rockets it into the stratosphere with subtle yet powerful spicings, and sides that venture beyond rice 'n' peas. Fresh salads of Island fruit and mesclun satisfy vegans. The place may look like a typical jerk shack, and the vibe is strictly old-school — '60s and '70s lovers' rock — but try the JA-style roti "pizza"

strewn with jerk chicken breast. Irie, indeed!

One step at door, washrooms in basement. Fully licensed. $$

25 JOHN'S CLASSIC PIZZA
591 College, 537-02794

Red-checked tablecloths, empty Chianti bottles holding dripping candles, and exposed brick walls signal a classic trattoria. Cousin to Baldwin Street's John's Italian Caffe, this extremely romantic spot doles out pizzas both old school and *nuova cucina*. From pepperoni and peppers to goat cheese with basil and artichoke hearts, John's thin-crust fare has made its reputation with pizza aficionados. Cue the accordion!

Barrier-free, washrooms in basement. Fully licensed, cash only. $

10 KALENDAR KOFFEE HOUSE
546 College, 923-4138

Maybe it's the dim candlelight that regularly causes Kalendar to win the NOW Readers' Poll for most romantic restaurant. An art-nouveau space where lovers linger over finger food and naan-based pizzas, Kalendar is the ideal place to pop the question. Or dump the jerk.

One step at door, washrooms in basement. Fully licensed. Patio. $$

7 LAVA
507 College, 966-5282

As lava lamps bubble, the late-night crowd at Lava lounge in comfy scalloped booths or bop to drum 'n' bass on the club's small dance floor. Few know that before the cocktail hour — which here is 11 p.m. — Lava is also a very good restaurant

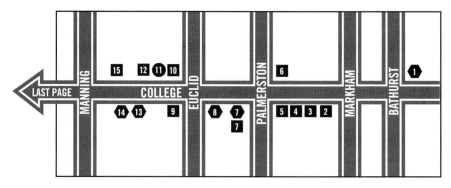

where global fusion fare holds sway and Asian and Mexican flavours tint Thai and Bengali mains. The less adventurous can opt for the Lava Burger with fries and slaw. Sundays host Swing Nights. Weekend brunch, too.

Barrier-free. Fully licensed. Patio. $$

15 MIDTOWN WEST
558 College, 966-6952

Farther west than its sister Midtown (see listing page 76), Midtown West doesn't have a sign either — it's the place with the green-and-white awning over its curbside patio. While the Midtown is more of a bar, its western counterpart is a fully realized restaurant with an Ital-Med menu that features pastas and grilled seafood with unusual salsas. Weekend brunch from 8 a.m.

Two steps at door, washrooms in basement. Fully licensed. $$

19 ORBIT ROOM
580A College, 535-0613

Although it's owned in part by Rush guitarist Alex Lifeson, the Orbit doesn't torture its patrons with prog rock. Instead, most evenings, house band The Dexters recreate the '60s soul-funk stew of Booker T. and the MGs. Better-than-average bar food ranges from Greek mezes to Montreal smoked-meat sandwiches and jerk free-range chicken.

16 steps at door, washrooms on same floor. Fully licensed. Patio. $$

28 SOTTOVOCE
595 College, 536-4564

The jet set haunt this jewel box of a wine bar on one of College's best people-watching corners. Superstar designer Yabu Pushelberg set new standards with this one; Sottovoce's washrooms are deluxe. Deftly executed panini and pasta, while quite good, pale to insignificance next to the beautiful people who pose at the Arborite bar and on the west-facing terrace. Sit back, sip the vino, and experience the buzz. You look fabulous, darling! Closed Sunday.

One step at door, washrooms on same floor. Fully licensed. Patio. $$

49 THE STANDARD CLUB
667 College, 588-8170

The name says it all.

55 CAFE SOCIETA
796 College, 588-7490

This thoroughly modern bistro serves contemporary cooking with a nouvelle French twist. The room is warm and unpretentious and attracts friendly locals looking for a fun night out. The appetizers are as innovative as the mains, mixing seasonal ingredients in combinations that sound unlikely but prove more than palatable. The patio's the perfect setting for languorous sangria seductions in the afternoon sun.

Barrier-free, washrooms in basement. Fully licensed. Patio. $$

Barrier-free, washrooms in basement. Fully licensed. Patio. $$

50 TAVOLA CALDA
671 College, 536-8328

Lineups are inevitable here at peak lunch and dinner times — and no wonder, there's room for only nine diners. In summer, when their curbside patio opens, the capacity triples. Many patrons opt to take out the ambrosial eggplant parmegiana, minted beet insalata, and rosemary roast chicken. Evidence of the owners' spell in Argentina surfaces in chimichurri, a gaucho hot sauce that makes a perfect addition to Tavola's grilled-meat panini.

Barrier-free, washrooms in basement. Unlicensed, smoke-free. Patio. $

29 TRATTORIA GIANCARLO
41 Clinton, 533-9619

Classy southern Italian restaurant — a favourite with visiting celebrities.

One step at door, washrooms in basement. Fully licensed. Patio. $$$

24 UTOPIA
585 College, 534-7751

One step at door, washrooms in basement. Fully licensed. Patio. $$

CAFES AND COFFEE HOUSES

27 CAFE DIPLOMATICO
594 College, 534-4637

Every day from eight in the morning till two the next, the Dip is a hub of activity. Regulars nurse cappuccinos and espressos to the tunes by Madonna, Queen, and the Village People that spin on the CD jukebox. Sun worshippers top up their tans on the crowded patio shown on the City-Guide's cover.

Barrier-free, washrooms in basement. Fully licensed. Patio. $

5 **ELLIPSIS 505**
505 College, 929-9745

Ellipsis owner Nancy Barone has expanded her business sideways into the space next door at 505 College. The result is a charming takeout-or-hangout café with extraordinary baked goods and such dynamite bistro fare as superb duck confit and steak bavette avec frites. It can be a bit of a mosh pit at lunch — only 20 seats indoors and another 30 on the sunny patio — and the near-perfect pastries are as expensive as the mains, but 505 offers food that warrants the crowd.

One step at door, washrooms in basement. Beer and wine, smoke-free. Patio. $

46 **GOLDEN WHEAT BAKERY**
652 College, 534-1107

A Portuguese bakery that never closes, Golden Wheat offers an array of European desserts and pastries. Sample an egg-custard tart, fish cake, or cornbread slice while taking in the game on the giant-screen TV.

One step at door, washrooms in basement. Fully licensed. Patio. $

47 **IL GATTO NERO**
656 College, 531-0543

This long terrazzo-floored den is dominated by a painting of a 20-foot feline prowling the bar's curbside patio — hence the name. Open daily from 7:30 a.m. for early-morning caffeine fixes, the counter is nearly always lined with sports fans gawking either at one of several ceiling-mounted TVs tuned to the sports channel or at a game of pool taking place in the room's smoky rear area.

Two steps at door, washrooms in basement. Fully licensed. Patio. $

51 **SICILIAN ICE CREAM COMPANY**
712 College, 531-7716

The Sicilian is an old-fashioned ice-cream parlour purveying Italian ices including stracciatella-, spumoni-, and tiramisú-flavoured gelatos. In warmer months, after dinner at one of the street's fancy

eateries, stop in for dessert on one of two patios watched over by a large bronze statue of an eagle.

One step at door, washrooms in basement. Unlicensed. Patio. $

JUICE BARS

6 **FRUITION**
492 College, 920-5428

Long ago, before the polyester era, juice bars like this were called health-food restaurants, but there's nothing retro-hippie about Fruition. Its sexy-sleek wooden flooring is also used on table-tops and echoed in molded plywood chairs. The place looks as great as some of the food tastes — sandwich-pressed chicken breast on focaccia, pulpy gazpacho, and healthful fruit and/or veggie drinks. However, it's not as serene as it seems — inside, the racket of streetcars rumbling past and juicers roaring like lawnmowers is alarming.

One step at door, washrooms in basement. Fully licensed, smoke-free, cash only. Patio. $

TAKEOUT

43 **CALIFORNIA SANDWICHES**
244 Claremont, 603-3317

Sloppy pounded-veal sandwiches swimming in tomato sauce with sweet onions and red peppers have made California an essential pit-stop — especially after the bars close.

Two steps at door, no washrooms. Unlicensed. $
Other location:
2197 Queen East (see page 203)

44 **PIZZA CATALINA**
661 College, 530-4300

Here's a textbook place for traditional pizza with a few concessions to contemporary palates. Try the Alla Patricia — roasted garlic cloves, mushrooms, mozzarella, spinach, onions, and feta. Five types of slices are always available, plus veal or grilled-eggplant sandwiches, too. Home delivery.

One step at door, no washrooms. Unlicensed. $

30 **SAN FRANCESCO**
10 Clinton, 534-7867

A neighbourhood favourite, this sandwich-shop standby sells messy tomato-sauce-slathered pounded-veal sandwiches that go down smoothly with Brio, the Coca-Cola of Italy.

One step at door, no washrooms. Unlicensed. $

BARS

14 **BARCODE**
549 College, 928-9941

Part of Ted's empire — along with Ted's Collision down the street and Ted's Wrecking Yard upstairs — Barcode is a very informal hang. Decor — what decor? Like its sister clubs, it looks like it's still under construction. Up front, you'll find a drinkin' 'n' dawdlin' space, while the massive back room, complete with grand piano, is home to regular gigs by Mean Steve Piano — think Jerry Lee Lewis — and '40s and '50s dance music from the Swing Gang.

Barrier-free. Patio.

26 **BOOM**
588 College, 535-6930

One step at door, washrooms in basement. Closed Tuesday. Patio.

21 **CAFFE BAR AZZURRI**
614 College, 532-9837

This old-world Portuguese and Italian sports bar features large TVs permanently tuned to soccer or hockey games.

One step at door, washrooms in basement.

32 **THE CAPITOL**
597 College, 534-2942

Local neighbourhood bar with typical pizza and pasta fare. Shady summertime patio.

Barrier-free, washrooms in basement. Patio.

3 **CIAO EDIE**
489 College, 927-7774

Throwback or throw up? Ciao Edie is certainly not to everyone's taste. Grotesquely ugly lamps with enormous mosaic-covered bases, repulsive shades, and red or green bulbs light this funky club which is also decked out in orange-vinyl banquettes, scarlet shag rugs, and lurid turquoise walls. The music policy is equally kitschy, with college-radio DJs spinning campy vinyl. Sunday is Womyn's Night, but cool confirmed bachelors are admitted as well.

Five steps at door, washrooms on same floor.

2 **CLEAR SPOT**
489 College, 921-7998

A barn of a room, Clear Spot is named for a Captain Beefheart album. With its well-worn wooden floors — especially around the eight pool tables — the Spot is the spot to shoot a few games while soaking up the sounds of Japanese King

EL CONVENTO RICO: Hands up everyone who wants to Macarena!

Crimson bootlegs.

Four steps at door, washrooms on same floor.

1 **COBALT**
426 College, 923-4456

A swanky cocktail bar with walls painted cobalt blue and a perfect-for-dancing wooden floor, Cobalt shakes up some unusual martinis. Try the Beef Jerky — spicy vodka, beef broth, and olive juice! Most nights there's some kind of music happening, from bossa nova DJs to jazzy combos, and occasional Swing Nights.

Barrier-free, washrooms in basement.

16 **COLLEGE STREET BAR**
574 College, 533-2417

Despite its name, the College Street Bar is far from being the strip's definitive watering hole. In this versatile room decorated with large Impressionist paintings, tables are pushed back on Sunday night to make room for dancing to local r 'n' b combo Soul Stew.

One step at door, washrooms in basement. Patio.

12 **MIDTOWN**
552 College, 920-4533

Don't bother looking for the sign that marks this popular hangout because there isn't one. Only the blue-and-white striped awning over its sidewalk patio lets you know you've found the Midtown. Although there is a small restaurant area at the front, the Midtown is more of a watering hole for film types and film-type wannabes. Three pool tables in the back are the centre of the meet-and-meat action.

One step at door, washrooms in basement. Patio.

31 **MONARCH TAVERN**
12 Clinton, 533-6373

A prehistoric two-storey hall perfect for student booze-ups.

Two steps at door, washrooms on same floor.

23 **SOUTHSIDE LOUIE'S**
583 College, 532-1250

A *Cheers*-style neighbourhood bar.

Barrier-free. Patio.

42 **SOUZ DAL**
636 College, 537-1883

Open only after dark, Souz Dal suggests a romantic rendezvous at the casbah. Tented ochre-pat-

terned walls sway as overhead fans churn the sheltering air. Middle Eastern–influenced finger foods — baba ghanouj, tzatziki, and grilled pita — encourage the most hard-to-get to become instantly available. The walled-in rear patio resembles a scene straight out of *West Side Story*.

One step at door, washrooms in basement. Patio.

20 **TED'S COLLISION**
573 College, 533-2430

Ted's was the first of College Street's anti-bars and the last place the BMW crowd would ever be caught dead in. Part Roman ruin — faux crumbling columns, decayed statuary — and part monument to Toronto's architectural past, Ted's features rootsy local entertainment, poetry slams, and mighty fine pizza.

One step at door, washrooms in basement. Patio.

13 **TED'S WRECKING YARD**
549 College, 928-5012

As its name suggests, the Wrecking Yard is a mess — countertops made from pipes and planks, floors covered in metal plates, and walls stapled with corrugated tin. In other words, the perfect joint to catch hard-rockin' shows from the Texas Dirt Fuckers and Dodge Fiasco. Bar Italia this ain't.

20 steps at door, washrooms on same floor.

39 **WILD INDIGO**
607 College, 536-8797

Looking like someone's incredibly groovy apartment, tiny Indigo is decorated with a few cast-off couches, coffee tables, and demonic masks that glow in the dark. Dark one-way glass in the street-side windows gives the intimate room a sense of mystery. Now you know what's behind it. Closed Sunday.

Barrier-free, washrooms in basement. Patio.

ENTERTAINMENT

LIVE MUSIC

58 **THE MATADOR**
466 Dovercourt, 533-9311

See Hot Spot page 77.

DANCE CLUBS

52 **EL CONVENTO RICO**
750 College, 588-7800

A subterranean cha-cha-teria that's as popular with cross-dressers as straights ready to rumba, the Rico is a scene that has to be experienced to be believed. Not at all decadent, it's actually charming in a down-at-the-heels-drag-queen kinda way. Even those with two left feet will find themselves on the end of a conga line. Early-evening dance lessons Sunday ensure that neo-phytes will be able to mambo when the night hits full swing after midnight. Drag shows start at 1 a.m. Closed Monday and Tuesday.

10 steps at door, washrooms on same floor. Fully licensed.

POOL HALLS

45 **BENITO'S BILLIARDS**
650 College, 537-9292

Long before College Street was cool, Benito's was the neighbourhood pool hall. It still is.

One step at door, washrooms in basement. Fully licensed.

8 **THE CORNER POCKET**
533 College, 928-3540

Resembling a loft in an overhauled warehouse, the Pocket sports 17 pool tables — and one foos-ball table. Standard pub grub like nachos, chicken wings, and pizza is on offer in the roped-off café complete with the ubiquitous big-screen TV tuned to the sports channel.

26 steps at door, washrooms on same floor. Fully licensed.

CINEMAS — REVIVAL

35 **THE ROYAL**
606 College, 516-4845

A member of the Festival Theatre chain, this reac-tivated repertory house sports the largest screen in downtown Toronto. Regular Sunday matinees.

58 **THE MATADOR**
466 Dovercourt, 533-9311

Toronto's only authentic honky-tonk, the Mata-dor has catered to a (very!) late-night crowd since 1964. Only open Friday and Saturday nights from 1:30 to 5:30 a.m., the speakeasy-style club has played host to shows by such musical legends as Blue Rodeo and Leonard Cohen — unannounced, of course. An after-hours club, the Matador is booze-free. Closed Sunday to Thursday.

Two steps at door, washrooms on same floor. Unlicensed.

SHOPPING

BOOKS AND MAGAZINES — USED

34 **BALFOUR BOOKS**
601 College, 531-9911

A well-stocked general-interest bookstore, Balfour also rents videos of art flicks.

COMIC BOOKS AND 'ZINES

41 **DRAGON LADY**
609 College, 536-7460

One of the city's more comprehensive shops for both new and collectible comic books, Dragon Lady also stocks *Life* and *Look* magazines from the '30s through '70s, as well as back issues of *Popular Mechanics*, *Time* and '70s proto fag mag *After Dark*.

FASHION — ACCESSORIES

54 **RAPP OPTICAL**
788 College, 537-6590

A longtime winner of the NOW Readers' Poll for best optician, Rapp not only represents such up-scale eyewear designers as LA Eyeworks, Alain Mikli, and Isaac Mizrahi, but it also makes its own one-of-a-kind frames and sunglasses. You can get an eye exam, too.

FASHION — NEW CLOTHING

48 **MOTHERSHIP**
670 College, 535-8618

The only shop on College to sell club clothes,

Mothership has a motherlode of such rave wear as Fiction Design's b-boy baggy jeans and Geek Boutique's form-fitting tops. This all-silver boutique with a grey Pirelli rubber floor also carries multicoloured hair extensions, ski goggles, and Gravedigga track suits, as well as clocks made from cans of Spam! Check out their own line — The People Have Spoken — of groovy catsuits.

36 WENCHES AND ROGUES
605 College, 536-9593

The sole mainland outlet of a St. John's, Newfoundland venture, Wenches mostly features sophisticated Canadian designers like Dubuc, Comrags, and Mimi Bizjak. With equal numbers of men's and women's outfits, Wenches and Rogues focuses on clothes that suit versatile lifestyles. Lots of discounted items, too.

FASHION — VINTAGE CLOTHING

11 GOODWILL
548 College, 967-0364

See listing page 114.

FOOD

17 CENTRO DEL FORMAGGIO
578 College, 531-4453

Among their many wonderful cheeses, you'll spot hard-to-find buffalo mozzarella — named for the beast, not the city — and other gourmet treats such as smoked Pacific salmon and homemade Italian sausage. Closed Sunday.

GIFTS

40 RED PEGASUS
626-628 College, 536-3872

Actually two separate storefronts, the furtherwest Red features trendy casual wear from Double XX and Spiewak, shoulder bags and vinyl purses from Snug and Kismit, as well as baggy jeans by Flygirl and Parasuco. Next door, off-the-wall gifts are the thing — one-of-a-kind Stinker the Cat ashtrays, teapots, and T-shirts, as well as candles, cards, and kiddies' rompers.

HOME FURNISHINGS — USED

 PHIL'Z
768 College, 536-3498

Specializing in Scandinavian furniture from the '50s, '60s, and '70s — the *Wallpaper* magazine look — Phil'z also carries a wide collection of art deco and modernist furniture. Funky reupholstered couches, teak redenzas, panther lamps, and reproductions of Marcel Breuer's classic chrome-and-steel Wassily chair are just a few of the finds here awaiting discerning homemakers.

Other location:
770 Queen East (see page 214).

COLLEGE

Coral Sea Fish Market

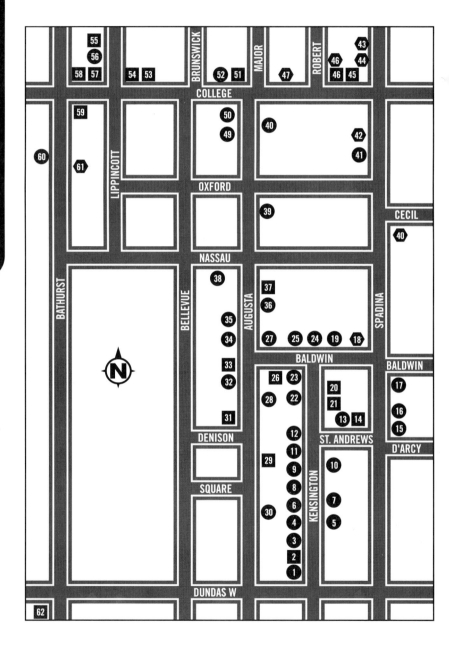

It is said that the breeze caused by the flutter of a butterfly's wings in China could affect weather patterns in New York. In essence, a very small occurrence could trigger a series of increasingly significant and monumental events. Just something to think about, the next time you open a book. Or quickly turn a page.

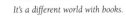

It's a different world with books.

Chapters

A Canadian Book Company

NOW

MUCH
new music

102.1
EDGE
Toronto's New Rock

VIRTUAL
no:se

3 day music festival & industry conferenc

northbynortheas

june 10 11 12, 1999 june 8 9 10, 2000 toronto www.nxne.co

KENSINGTON MARKET

Kensington Market is a microcosm of the city's vibrant multicultural scene. On its narrow, choatic streets, Portuguese fishmongers, Latin American bakers, and Jamaican patty peddlars rub shoulders with vintage-clothing shops, lively music clubs, and sidewalk vegetable stalls. The Market is an electric, eclectic, alive part of town.

FOOD & DINING

RESTAURANTS

31 **AMADEU'S**
184 Augusta, 591-1245

A Kensington Market landmark with a split personality, this Portuguese seafood palace serves up first-class formal dinners in the dining room, and bargain soup and grilled steak on a bun in its seedier watering hole. Daily specials sell out early — and are often oversalted — and the Revolution platter for two will satisfy up to four guerrillas. Seats on the laid-back patio are at a premium until the sun sinks behind the skyline.

One step at door, washrooms in basement. Fully licensed. Patio. $$

33 **CARLOS' PEPPER**
196 Augusta, 597-8462

Viewed through the front window, Carlos' Pepper's decor — warm-ochre stuccoed walls and dappled candlelight — suggests a room designed for romance. Open the door and be blown away by eardrum-popping acid jazz and Portuguese pop. The young crowd digs it, though, and jams the place when jazz trios perform. You may find it

hard to concentrate on the food — contemporary fare with a Portuguese twist, such as peppercorn steak with fabulous pimento-sauced frites — when there's a trumpet blaring three feet from your head.

Six steps at door, washrooms in basement. Fully licensed. Patio. $$

2 **THE LAST TEMPTATION**
12 Kensington, 599-2551

Whether you're on the shady patio or indoors in one of the two claustrophobically crowded rooms, the vibe is always relaxed at the Temptation. Yes, the bilious-green front room, with its '70s cocktail-lounge bar stools, and the bright-orange back room, with its two pool tables and Market mural by local artist Billy Askew, are meant to look this shlocky. Light lunches and bar food include grilled-veggie sandwiches and seasonal soups.

Two steps at door, washrooms in basement. Fully licensed. Patio. $

45 **OASIS**
294 College, 975-0845

Carnivores will find the odd red-meat dish, so it's not strictly vegetarian, but Oasis offers a diverse veggie-friendly tapas menu. While the room won't win any design awards — think shag carpeting, broken-down couches, and murals that wouldn't be out of place on the side of a '70s van — the home cooking's honest and down-to-earth. Assemble appetizer-sized portions of pasta e fagioli, spirited hummus, and market-fresh watercress with radicchio in a cider vinaigrette. The back room showcases earnest folkies, off-the-wall comics, and theatre workshops.

Barrier-free, washrooms in basement. Fully licensed, cash only. Patio. $

46 **RANCHO RELAXO**
300 College, 920-0366

Once a flamenco and salsa palace, the Rancho has changed into a Tex-Mex beanery that presents rockers both local and international on its upstairs Relaxo Lounge stage. Downstairs, dinners tend to be generous all-in-one taco 'n' burrito platters, but fancier mains such as blackened swordfish are also on the menu. Rancho's namesake nachos — chili con carne, jalapeños, guacamole, and refried beans over corn chips —

52 INC: A riot grrrl restaurant with a credo.

make super beer-drinkin' accompaniments.

One step at door, washrooms on same floor. Fully licensed. Patio. $$

59 SNEAKY DEE'S
431 College, 603-3090

Known by habitués as Sneaky Disease, this Tex-Mex cantina serves southern-style breakfasts well into the afternoon. Decorated with Fiona Smyth's psychedelic paintings, the cluttered space features graffiti-scrawled booths that encourage late-night lounging. On Monday nights, early-'90s rock blares — Fine Young Guns N' Roses — while large gangs of students play bingo.

Barrier-free, washrooms in basement. Fully licensed. $

62 TOMMY'S BACKYARD
771 Dundas West, 603-6161

Now you don't have to go to the Danforth when the urge for spanakopita strikes. This unassuming spoon on a dodgy strip of Dundas offers a different Greek specialty daily. Massive plates of broiled red snapper or steak are finished with roast potatoes, rice, garlic bread, and Greek salad. Sure, the classier joints on the Danforth offer more deluxe decor, but dinner at Tommy's

costs half as much. In the summer, enjoy great weekend bacon-and-egg breakfasts on the patio. Barrier-free. Fully licensed. Patio. $

10 VANIPHA
193 Augusta, 340-0491

Toronto's best pad thai — a spicy dish that's so ubiquitous it borders on clichéed — can be found in this subterranean grotto, a room that looks like an explosion at a jumble sale. Vanipha, sister restaurant to Eglinton West's Vanipha Lanna, was one of the first eateries in town to do Thai. Not everything here sets off fire alarms, but most dishes do. Still, the fiery fare's heat can be offset by cool cucumber salads and sweet coconut sauces. Closed Sunday.

Six steps at door, washrooms on same floor. Fully licensed. $$

Other location:
471 Eglinton West (see page 223)

CAFES AND COFFEE HOUSES

55 AUNTIES AND UNCLES
74 Lippincott, 324-1375

See Hot Spot page 83.

54 52 INC.
394 College, 960-0334

More than just a groovy hangout with a cool acid-jazz soundtrack, this café-cum-den of political subversives matches style with substance. It even has a manifesto! This women-friendly spot — its name refers to the 52 percent of the earth's population who are women — offers more than girlie food. Sandwiches are named for '60s art flicks (the Petulia features avocado, Swiss cheese, tomato, and sprouts), and one owner's mom bakes pulpy pumpkin and hand-picked blueberry pies. Closed Monday.

One step at door, two steps to washroom on same floor. Fully licensed. Patio. $$

18 KENSINGTON CAFE
73 Kensington, 971-5632

In a neighbourhood where the hungry aren't likely to be looking for tony dinners, owner K.K. dishes up light snacks and lunches. Making the most of its location in the heart of the Market, this stylish space is frequented by some of Toronto's top

55 **AUNTIES AND UNCLES**
74 Lippincott, 324-1375

Once a single-chair barber shop, this tiny cubbyhole now offers serious sandwiches and stylish breakfast specials. The room offers only nine chairs at three discarded kitchenette suites, so potential customers find getting a table at peak brunch and lunch hours means a wait on the street. But they know they'll be rewarded with ridiculously low-priced Belgian waffles, grilled croque monsieurs, and Caesar salad. Lotsa mod details — Jam LP covers, a Vespa scooter parked out front — add to the fun. Closed Monday.

Barrier-free, washrooms in basement. Unlicensed, smoke-free, cash only. $

chefs, and attracts locals as well as regulars on weekends, when long queues are inevitable. Try the grilled chicken breast with Korean kimchee on Portuguese bread. Closed Sunday.

Two steps at door, washrooms on same floor. Fully licensed, cash only. $

14 **MOONBEAN CAFE**
30 St Andrew, 595-0327

Perfect for a rejuvenating après-shopping cup of joe, this Tex-Mex-decorated coffee house roasts its own organic beans bought from fair-trade and in-dependent suppliers, not from exploitative multi-nationals. Under the morning sun on the patio or inside in the raised back room, the Bean dishes up all-day breakfasts. And coffee, of course.

Three steps at door, washrooms on same floor. Fully licensed, smoke-free. Patio. $

51 **SECOND CUP**
340 College, 323-3702

See listing page 17.
Barrier-free. Unlicensed. Patio. $

DELIS AND DINERS

58 **KOS**
434 College, 923-1868

Known as Chaos by regular customers, this grunge cafeteria started life as a luncheonette but has evolved over the last few years into the bitchin' kitchen it is today. Basic egg-and-bacon

breakfasts prevail in a casual room dominated by a painted portrait of Muhammad Ali. And unlike the deal at neighbouring diners, the breakfast special includes a cup of coffee.

Barrier-free, washrooms in basement. Fully licensed. $

57 **MARS**
432 College, 921-6332

The sign out front says the food's "out of this world," but really it couldn't be more down-to-earth. A long, narrow diner with tables for two and a stainless-steel lunch counter with vinyl stools for 20, Mars is truly timeless. Open normal hours, plus round the clock Thursdays to Saturdays, this Greece-y spoon — the owners are Greek — serves an all-day breakfast of eggs, bacon, home fries, and toast for those nostalgic for a nosh that never changes. "World famous" bran muffins and "lite" specials — French toast with maple syrup — complete the minimal menu.

One step at door, washrooms in basement. Unlicensed. $

TAKEOUT

53 **AMATO PIZZA**
380 College, 972-6286

See listing page 17.
One step at door, washrooms on same floor. Fully licensed. Patio. $$

37 **JUMBO EMPANADAS**
253-B Augusta, 977-0056

Until recently, Irene Morales manned her sidewalk stand year round. Now, she doles out empanadas, a South American version of a Cornish pasty, from her basement bakery. Usually fried doughy trian-gles stuffed with greasy shredded pork, Morales serves the ultimate rendition: twice the usual size and stuffed with beef or chicken, hard-boiled egg, black olives, and red pepper. Strange-sounding pastel de choclo makes a marvellous take-home breakfast: in this unlikely pie, beef, chicken, olives, raisins, and hard-boiled egg collide under a honey-glazed cornmeal crust. Pick up a jam jar of her hot sauce, an innocent-looking relish that packs a punch. Closed Sunday.

10 steps at door, washrooms on same floor. Unlicensed, smoke-free, cash only. $

WHO'S EMMA: Anarchy in the Ukraine! Punk's not dead — it's just having a nap.

21 **PIZZABILITIES R ENDLESS**
69 Kensington, 971-5521

If tramping around the Market eyeballing all the fruit and veg makes you hungry, head for this pizzaria for the perfect munchable on the go! Pizzabilities' square slices may have the traditional thick crust, but their toppings are completely contemporary: rapini and ricotta, Yukon Gold spud sections and kalamata olives, or mussels, shrimp, and marinara sauce. The shop resembles a walk-in pizza oven — all exposed brick and waves of delicious aromas.

Barrier-free. Unlicensed, smoke-free. $

BARS

26 **PLANET KENSINGTON**
197-1/2 Baldwin, 341-0310

Once the Market's raunchiest dive — a drunk tank known by all as "The Greek's" — this tiny diner now has a coat of black paint. The menu still offers burgers and all-day breakfasts, but the new chef has improved things greatly with fresh salads and health-conscious mains. Everything from blues bands and jazz trios to punk bands perform nightly on the postage-stamp-sized stage. Watch your head on your way to the downstairs washrooms; the low ceiling has knocked

customers unconscious.

One step at door, washrooms in basement.

ENTERTAINMENT

 **LIVE MUSIC**

42 **EL MOCAMBO**
464 Spadina, 961-2001

Some of the biggest names in rock 'n' roll have played this narrow two-storey tavern: the Rolling Stones, Elvis Costello, legendary punk rockers Bunchofuckingoofs.... The El Mo has closed and reopened so many times no one can keep count. Nowadays, mostly local fringe bands take to the two stages, as well as the occasional out-of-town act hoping for the big time. The Grand Ole Opry this ain't — the washrooms are particularly skanky. An often unruly crowd and burly bouncers have been known to tussle, too.

Barrier-free, washrooms in basement. Fully licensed.

47 **FREE TIMES CAFE AND BELLA'S BISTRO**
320 College, 967-1078

A leftover from when grunge was synonymous

with granola, Free Times has evolved from a hippie hangout to an upbeat bistro with live acoustic music every evening. To the accompaniment of klezmer music, weekend brunches dubbed Bella Did You Eat? are served in the café and its adjacent diner, Bella's Bistro. The menu includes such Jewish delicacies as latkes, blintzes, gefilte fish, and bagels with cream cheese.

One step at door, washrooms in basement. Fully licensed. Patio.

⑱ GRAFFITI'S
170 Baldwin, 506-6699

Chock full of Elvis Presley memorabilia, this cosy room offers live music — mainly acoustic — seven nights a week. When weather permits, the front garage door is opened to the street and the band and fans spill outside. The curbside patio — a stand-up bar, really — faces onto the street, so you can get a front-row view of the Market's anarchy. Between sets, pre-recorded sounds range from Springsteen to show tunes, and the open kitchen in the back churns out credible pizza slices.

One step at door, washrooms on same floor. Fully licensed. Patio.

⑳ GROSSMAN'S
379 Spadina, 977-7000

For longer than anyone admits to remembering, Grossman's has been a student booze-and-blooze hangout and general rogue's gallery. It's as if time stood still — actually, some nights it does. Steer clear of the hideous approximations of chow mein, egg rolls, and sweet-and-sour chicken bo-bo balls at the cafeteria-style kitchen. The entertainment's sometimes embarrassingly amateur, but you never know when you're going to stumble — excuse me! — across the next superstar, say, Amanda Marshall, who once trod this beer-soaked stage. Warning: subterranean washrooms.

One step at door, washrooms in basement. Fully licensed. Patio.

㊸ THE SILVER DOLLAR
486 Spadina, 975-0909

A showroom that harkens back to the '50s, the Dollar is the perfect space to take in local and international blues talent. Weekly no-cover jams welcome budding B.B. Kings to strut their stuff, while weekend concerts showcase legendary names from the American Midwest blues circuit.

The only downside to this joint is that because it has so much atmosphere, it's often closed for movie shoots.

One step at door, washrooms in basement. Fully licensed.

DANCE CLUBS

㊹ THE COMFORT ZONE
486 Spadina, 975-0909

In the dingy basement of the Waverley Hotel, this sweaty dive normally features a mix of live music and DJ-assisted rave-ups. The real action happens on Sundays at 9 a.m. — yes, in the morning — when the scene turns into the Devine Sunday Wakeup, an après-rave chill-out. All-nighter club kids find a haven here long after the last warehouse party has finished. And if you're up for it, the party continues until midnight.

12 steps at door, washrooms on same floor. Fully licensed.

CINEMAS — REVIVAL

㊶ CINEFORUM
463 Bathurst, 603-6643

Since the '60s, messianic cineaste Reg Hartt has been projecting the same six movies over and over again, or maybe it only feels that way. They're classics, though — Eisenstein's *Battleship Potemkin*, Kurosawa's *Seven Samurai*, Chuck Jones's Bugs Bunny cartoons — and the prints are pristine. In what's probably Toronto's smallest movie house, Hartt's living room, the screenings begin with long-winded lectures, and Hartt's publicity posters advise the audience to B.Y.O.F.&D.

SHOPPING

ART SUPPLIES

㊶ GWARTZMAN'S
448 Spadina, 922-5429

One of the remnants of Kensington's Jewish era, Gwartzman's has been a major supplier to Toronto's artistic scene since the early '50s. Under a high tin ceiling, well-worn wooden floors support shelves that hold the necessities for any budding artist: paints, pigments, canvas, stretchers, brushes, and easels. For those wanting to create their own masterpiece on a T-shirt, a wide range of fabric paints is available. And in a corner, you'll find autographed glossies signed by celebrity customers Burt Reynolds, Jerry Seinfeld, and *Married With Children*'s Al Bundy.

BEER STORES

60 THE BEER STORE
452 Bathurst @ College, 923-4535
Monday to Friday 10 a.m. to 9 p.m.
Saturday 9:30 a.m. to 9 p.m.
Sunday 11 a.m. to 6 p.m.
Closed holidays.

BICYCLES

48 BIKES ON WHEELS
309 Augusta, 966-2453
You could ride your bike through the wide double doors of this bright and breezy store and no one would say a thing. Here, the bicycle rules supreme. A co-op, though you don't have to belong to shop here, this all-things-cycling specialty shop sells new and overhauled used bikes, as well as parts and Pat Macmillan's cool PAC-brand courier bags. Artist Runt's bicycle sculpture hangs in the front window next to a bulletin board posted with pamphlets advocating cycling causes. Closed Sunday.

FASHION — ACCESSORIES

16 ROTMAN'S HAT SHOP AND HABERDASHER
345 Spadina, no phone
One of the last vestiges of Spadina's original Jewish community, Rotman's carries an amazing array of caps, fedoras and tam-o'-shanters. This small one-room shop is crammed with 10-gallon Stetsons and way-cool Kangols, many of which you won't find anywhere else. If you're not sure what you're looking for, don't even think of browsing. Unless you're here to buy, you're not welcome. Closed Saturday and Sunday.

FASHION — NEW CLOTHING

9 ATTENTION
28 Kensington, 599-5154
On a street that's famous for its secondhand —

sorry, vintage — clothing, this tiny, sparse shop sells voguish androgynous designer-label club wear. Slinky, barely-there tops and provocatively sheer dresses are displayed on tastefully minimal blond-wood fixtures. Asked who the designers are, the modish clerk replies, "People from New York and Los Angeles you've never heard of."

15 CHOCKY'S
327 Spadina, 977-1831
Chocky's is a great place to go to outfit the family with practical essentials, and everything's always discounted. Calvin Klein underwear, Hugo Boss socks, and Penman sweats are all sold for half what you'd pay elsewhere. Gore-Tex winter jackets, thermal long johns, and Thinsulate gloves keep customers warm all winter. Some stock in the basement is reduced even further.

49 FRESH BAKED GOODS
274 Augusta, 966-0123
Knitting fiend Laura-Jean is renowned for her made-to-order sweaters. Although her fuzzy cardigans are available at Queen West's Peach Berserk and Noise, the nimble knitter has set up her own factory outlet at the north end of the Market. Here, her colourful wares are displayed on a clothesline out front while the nimble knitwear designer whips up mohair turtlenecks and other one-of-a-kinds in the workshop. Pick up Laura-Jean's catalog and be dazzled by her combinations of colours and wools.

35 HARRY DAVID
220 Augusta, 593-9719
For anyone trying to affect the proletariat-chic look, this haberdashery for construction workers makes for one-stop shopping. Workboots, heavy-duty gloves, thermal underwear, fluorescent plastic vests, and classic Mackenzie Brothers plaid lumberjackets are all essential. Best of all, they carry the caramel-coloured super-thick Tough Duck line of work pants, overalls, coveralls and corduroy-collared coats. Never has functional been so fashionable. Closed Sunday.

FASHION — VINTAGE CLOTHING

11 ASYLUM
42 Kensington, 595-7199

3 COURAGE MY LOVE
14 Kensington, 979-1992

Courage has been selling retro fashions of the '30s, '40s and '50s since the '70s. With a long-established network of suppliers, it has the clothes that the hoi polloi will clamour for long before they're back in fashion. They also carry a line of inexpensive, stylish sunglasses, as well as *I Love Lucy*–era lamps and amoebic ashtrays. Nostalgia-wear ranges from crinkly crinolines to Hawaiian shirts. If the pros at Courage don't have it, you don't need it. Closed Sunday.

7 DANCING DAYS
17 Kensington, 599-9827

5 EGO
9 Kensington, 596-8282

6 EXILE
20 Kensington, 596-0827

The Market's largest vintage-apparel specialist, Exile — along with its sister shop, Asylum — showcases new fashions by PornStar and Lip Service, as well as the complete line of Manic Panic punky hair dyes and false eyelashes. The real finds are upstairs, but they're not for sale. These decades-old clothes, things that disappeared long ago from other retro shops — Vietnam War bomber jackets, leopard-skin pillbox hats, and swelegant flapper-era gowns — can be rented, though, for special occasions.

4 JAGGS
16 Kensington, 581-1423

Instead of the usual '70s clobber found elsewhere — polyester flares and ugly plaid jackets — Jaggs spotlights new-wave and punk-flavoured gear from the tail end of that decade. Unassuming from the outside, on the inside this boutique is striking — sheet-metal flooring and black-on-black walls. It's also chockablock with slinky shifts, pointy-collared shirts and skinny ties. Completing the effect, Blondie and the Sex Pistols play on the sound system.

1 PINEAPPLE ROOM
2 Kensington, 340-7859

With an old Louis Armstrong record setting the mood, fashion fanatics shop for frocks from the '30s and '40s. Actually two small rooms crammed

8 LE GOSSIP
38 Kensington, 979-9506

Attention, fashion-conscious shoe fetishists. Looking for that ultra-rare pair of antique Adidases, the type that kids in Japan pay thousands of dollars for? This is the place — a shoe lover's paradise. Mint-condition Converse running shoes, Nike and Reebok trainers, and Wallabies are piled to the ceiling in this small shop that also features '60s and '70s jeans and leather jackets. Don't miss the back room, where even more fabulous finds lurk.

with such ephemera as drum-majorette uniforms and matronly veiled hats, the Room appropriately smells of potpourri. Asked why his stock favours women's apparel, Pineapple's owner says, "Men throw things out. Old ladies keep clothes forever."

50 SHIRLEY YOU JEST
280 Augusta, 975-9712

TRIBAL RHYTHM
27 Kensington, 595-7278
See listing page 29.

FASHION — SHOES

8 LE GOSSIP
38 Kensington, 979-9506
See Hot Spot listing this page.

FOOD

34 ALVAND FOOD MART
214 Augusta, 597-2252

Subtitled the Middle Eastern Centre, this crowded shop offers foodstuffs from Persian to Lebanese. Freshly baked pitas and flatbreads vie for shelf space with pomegranates, quince, and dried limes. A refrigerator case displays hummus, baba ghanouj, and baklava, while bulk bins hold undyed Iranian pistachios, garlic pappadums, and Kellogg's Corn Flakes. Arabic music cassettes for sale and videotapes for rent are also on hand.

36 AUGUSTA EGG MARKET
251 Augusta, 593-9817

In John Waters's cult flick *Pink Flamingos*, Edie

COURAGE MY LOVE: Kensington Market's oldest vintage-clothing shop.

the Egg Lady lives in a playpen and pesters co-star Divine to feed her raw eggs, shell and all. Edie would be in heaven here. Laid out on flats, eggs of various sorts — even the seemingly impossible low-cholesterol version — are for sale in every size and colour. Pick up a dozen miniature quail eggs for $1.25 and experience what the gourmet set spend big bucks for at chi-chi up-town restaurants. Closed Sunday.

㉗ CASA ACOREANA
235 Augusta, 593-9717

Curbside bins holding every conceivable type of dried legume front this Portuguese emporium, whose marquee proclaims that "nuts make the world go round." Inside, jars filled with spices, herbs, tea leaves, coffee beans, dried pasta, and candied fruit fight for a foodie's attention. Linger over a fresh-brewed cup of Reunion Island java at the adjacent Louie's Cafe while listening to fla-menco or opera.

㉕ CHEESE MAGIC
182 Baldwin, 593-9531

Beware of Kensington Avenue's notorious cheese-mongers. What seem to be three separate shops are actually one, and if you ask a surly server for a

pound of cheddar, you end up with a pound and a half. At Cheese Magic, you get exactly the amount of cheese you ask for — and with a smile. Jars filled with marinated sun-dried tomatoes, arti-choke hearts, and kalamata olives entice. Tubs of additive-free peanut butter, sacks of coffee beans, and packages of fresh pasta are other fantastic finds.

㉘ EL BUEN PRECIO
227 Augusta, 597-8716

Selling everything from shrub-sized rosemary plants to piñatas, multicoloured lace hammocks, and imported crema fresca, this quirky Sal-vadorean groceteria also doubles as a community meeting-place. On the weekends, pupusas — cornmeal pancakes stuffed with spicy pork, re-fried beans, and stringy cheese — are prepared on an outdoor grill. Topped with some chili-spiked coleslaw, these street treats are perfect to munch while exploring the Market.

Cash only. $

㉔ EUROPEAN MEATS
176 Baldwin, 596-8691

Regular customers know the drill. Because this meat market is so busy, especially after 5 on weeknights or anytime Saturday, they grab a "now serving" number at the door, go and do the rest of their shopping, and return 15 minutes later to find that their number is about to be called. This insider's information used to work, but now that everyone knows it, at least half the customers whose numbers are called aren't in the store. So wait patiently while scarfing a great Debrecen sausage with sauerkraut, and you'll be served. Eventually. Closed Sunday.

⑫ FONG ON FOODS
46 Kensington, 598-7828

Ever wondered where tofu comes from? Find out at this tiny Kensington store that sells buckets of 12 pieces for less than $2. Soy-derived noodles, milk, and breads are available, too. Here's a tip when you buy tofu: drain the water from your pail before you leave the shop. That way, the tofu won't slosh around and break up on the way home. Refill with fresh water and refrigerate. Closed Sunday.

㉜ HOUSE OF SPICES
190 Augusta, 593-9724

The name says it all. Besides spices and herbs from around the world, this foodie paradise also stocks such items as Indian basmati rice, Ethiopian injera flatbread, and Thai hot sauces. With everything from frankincense to saffron, macadamia nuts to masalas, the House of Spices is the source for non-Eurocentric recipe ingredients. Closed Sunday.

㉚ LOBSTER ISLAND
169 Augusta, 591-6488

A secret known only by local seafood restaurants, Lobster Island is a supplier of all things crustacean. Open tanks of lobsters divided by weight line one wall; others hold live shrimp, mussels, oysters, and clams. It doesn't look as if it is, but the shop is open to the public.

⑲ MY MARKET BAKERY
172 Baldwin, 593-6772

The owners of Kensington's best *fromagerie* — nearby Cheese Magic — also own the area's best bakery. Here, shelves groan with a wide variety of breads: feta and rosemary focaccia, Italian Calabrese rings, potato-leek loaves. Those with a sweet tooth won't want to miss the strawberry-shortcake cheesecake or raspberry Linzertorte.

Traditionalists cherish My Market's classic Nanaimo bars.

㉔ PATTY KING
187 Baldwin, 977-3191

There's a lot more to the King than just Jamaican patties. Carrot and ginger cakes, hardo and corn breads, as well as jackass coconut biscuits fill the well-stocked shelves of this lively bakery and take-away. Salt-fish-and-ackee dinners and boneless chicken rotis get washed down with tropical slushies or homemade ginger beer. But it's the patties that this JA joint is famous for — curried beef, chicken, and all-veggie.

㉒ SANCI'S TROPICAL FOODS
66 Kensington, 593-9265

Opened in 1914, this cluttered fruit stall has been importing the bounty of the tropics from the time Torontonians thought bananas were exotic. Bushel baskets brimming with Scotch bonnet peppers, star fruit, papayas, mangos, plantains, and tamarind tempt the taste buds. And reigning over them all is an avocado so large it's dubbed Bahama Mama.

HAIR — SALONS

⑬ POISON IVY
32 St Andrew, 977-6666

Once a storage space for the fruit market next door, this slant-floored and slope-ceilinged space features two antique barber chairs where clients of all sexes get clipped and coiffed. Best of all, with weather permitting, the storefront garage door opens onto the ruckus of Kensington. Closed Sunday.

HOME FURNISHINGS — USED

㉟ KENSINGTON TRADING POST
281 Augusta, 217-0149

Talk about junk! The slogan on the sign out front says it all: "We sell the best and junk the rest." Used bikes, dilapidated display fixtures, falling-apart filing cabinets, trashed refrigeration units, shelves, lamps — they're all in here somewhere, but good luck finding them. The cast-off stuff is piled floor to ceiling in complete disarray and spills out the front door into a garbage heap on the street.

LIQUOR AND WINE STORES

(17) LCBO
335 Spadina, 597-0145

Monday to Wednesday 9:30 a.m. to 6 p.m.
Thursday to Saturday 9:30 a.m. to 9 p.m.
Sunday 11 a.m. to 6 p.m.
Closed holidays.

MUSIC — CDS, RECORDS & TAPES

(52) SHE SAID BOOM!
372 College, 944-3224

Part used-book store, part used-record emporium,
Boom! invites customers to come in and have a
look. Shelves stacked with hardcover and paper-
back volumes take up half of the well-lit space,
while the other half holds albums and CDs from
Abba to XTC. The CDs are organized into sections
marked ambient, mambo, and dub, among
others.

(38) WHO'S EMMA?
69-1/2 Nassau, 598-3354

A record store named for anarchist Emma Gold-
man, who died nearby in 1941, this collectively
run emporium features hand-printed fanzines,
limited-edition vinyl pressings by obscure hard-
core punkers, and, er, granola bars. These folks
take things seriously — and you're welcome to
attend their monthly consciousness-raising
forums. Closed Sunday.

SKATEBOARDING

(56) SPAZZ
72 Lippincott, 944-9368

On the street in front of this cubbyhole skate
shop, boarders fashion ramps from packing
crates and perform moves that scare passers-by.
Inside, among shabby-chic '70s sofas, Spazz carries mostly its own line of skateboards, snowboards, and ultra-cool skinny T-shirts. Co-owner
Heidi Wahl sums up the philosophy succinctly:
"The day we stop having fun is the day we close
our door for good." Closed Monday.

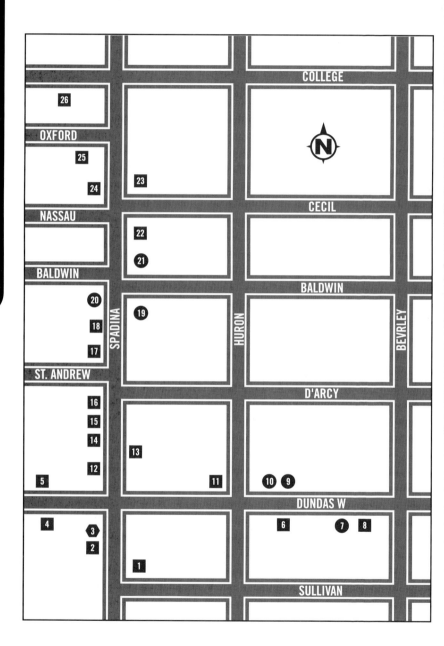

CHINATOWN

Traditionally a first stop for immigrants, this neighbourhood is in constant transition. Today, Spadina Avenue — the main drag — is home to shops and restaurants that reflect a mix of Asian cultures and cuisines — Chinese, East Indian, Vietnamese, and Thai.

FOOD & DINING

RESTAURANTS

23 **ANH DAO**
383 Spadina, 598-4514

Once a novelty, the meal-in-one soup called pho can now be found everywhere. One of the best pho spots, this split-level room with gaudy turquoise paint, plain tile flooring, and a flock of carved wooden ducks on the wall is not very inviting.

Ignore all that and focus on the fabulous pho. As well, there's the intriguingly named "Climbing Perch" and "Gunther's Walking Cat Fish." Other highlights include chicken watercress soup, green-papaya salad, and curried-coconut frogs' legs.

Barrier-free, washrooms in basement. Fully licensed. $

16 **BRIGHT PEARL**
346-348 Spadina, 979-3988

The largest restaurant in Chinatown, the Pearl is packed on weekends when suburbanites head downtown for a taste of the old neighbourhood. This bright and noisy banquet hall — kids love the place — isn't for those looking for a romantic rendezvous. Lunches offer the best meal deals. Traditional Cantonese cuisine still rules the menu and daily dim sum. Surly, cold-shoulder service doesn't exactly make you feel welcome.

10 steps at door, washrooms on same floor. Fully licensed. $$

6 **CHINATOWN INTERNATIONAL**
421-429 Dundas West, 593-0291

On Saturdays and Sundays, after an elevator ride to the third floor, you'll join a lunch lineup that of-

SWATOW: Their famous hot-and-sour soup causes lineups late into the night.

HOT SPOT

1. DAI NAM
221 Spadina, 598-3805

A squeaky-clean Vietnamese restaurant in Chinatown — a neighbourhood that's quickly becoming Little Saigon — Dai Nam dares to venture beyond pho noodle soups. Broiled oysters with coriander butter, shrimp in black-bean sauce, and rack of lamb with rice vermicelli are just some of their traditional-with-a-twist dishes. Rice-paper roll-ups wrap fresh bean sprouts, leaf lettuce, daikon, and carrot strips. Delicious dunked in sweet, vinegary peanut dip.

Barrier-free, washrooms in basement. Fully licensed. $

ten winds back down the stairs. Blandly spiced pork dumplings and other ho-hum steamed dim sum items won't excite the adventurous foodie, but loyal fans love this raucous room's fare. The more unusual items — deep-fried fish skin, and various gizzards — can be found on a buffet off to one side. A blank stare from staff is the answer to any question other than "Where's the washroom?"

Five steps at door, washrooms on same floor. Fully licensed. $$

1. DAI NAM
221 Spadina, 598-3805

See Hot Spot this page.

2. GOLDSTONE NOODLE HOUSE
266 Spadina, 596-9053

The atmosphere suggests a Hong Kong Burger King — food-court seating, families eating en masse, bright fluorescent lighting, and clean, clean, clean! — but there's nothing bland or disposable here. Soy-seasoned barbecued duck, pork, and chicken show up in multi-noodle formats, while mainstream chow mein and spring rolls arrive relatively grease-free. It's always crowded here (an excellent gauge for a Chinese restaurant), and the hearty oatmeal-like congee shouldn't be missed.

Barrier-free, washrooms in basement. Fully licensed. $$

18. HAPPY SEVEN
358 Spadina, 971-9820

This Cantonese seafood haven fills up once the bars close at 2 a.m. It stays open till 5 a.m., but it's more than the late hours that attracts the crowd. As regulars know, there are two separate menus. The first, a white multi-page laminated pamphlet, contains the usual chow mein and sweet-and-sour pork thingies. But the single-sheet pink menu is more adventurous. Fancy a hoisin-skinned fried pigeon? Deep-fried frogs' legs? Stir-fried chicken with apple?

Barrier-free, washrooms in basement. Beer and wine. $$

15. KIM HOA
332 Spadina, 971-9719

With a staff that verges on friendly, this brightly lit and stylish-for-Chinatown restaurant offers Cantonese favourites with a nod to Szechuan spicing. Barbecued meat from the window racks finds its way into first-rate noodle soups and chow mein mains. Their sweet-and-sour soup is the best on the Spadina strip — the chef once worked across the street at Swatow and has perfected its recipe. Mussels get a nip from Thai peanut sauce, while seared black cod comes with black beans, garlic, and soy. Closed Tuesday.

Barrier-free, washrooms in basement. Beer and wine. $$

12. KING'S NOODLE HOUSE
296 Spadina, 598-1817

During a noodle nosh, it's considered impolite not to slurp your dinner. And this pasta parlour in the heart of Chinatown fits the bill for anyone looking for cheap chow. Super soups brimming with bits of barbecued bird are efficiently served at communal polypropylene-topped tables. Not much on offer for vegetarians, but others will find a late-night King's Noodle refuelling filling.

Barrier-free, washrooms in basement. Unlicensed, cash only. $

22. LEE GARDEN
331 Spadina, 593-9524

Count on a half-hour wait at the door for a table at this beloved restaurant. For the area, Lee's is a rather formal joint — three rows of tables for four, and carpeting! As usual, order off the specials

LEE GARDEN: A glitzy favourite on Spadina.

listed on bristol-board placards: minced quail in a lettuce wrap, stir-fried sliced pickerel, sticky rice with Chinese sausage, garlic shrimp served in a hollowed-out pineapple. A neon sign in the window announces that there's no MSG in anything.

One step at door, washrooms in basement. Beer and wine, smoke-free. $$

8 LOTUS GARDEN
393 Dundas West, 598-1883

Here, Buddhist vegetarian cooking takes tofu and gluten and turns them into tasty, textured meat substitutes. But the best dishes happen when the talented chefs turn from mock meat and cook straight-ahead vegetarian Vietnamese fare. Rice-paper-wrapped spring rolls stuffed with crunchy jicama, lettuce, and mint come with a sweet peanut sauce made for dipping. Glutinous agar-agar salad with julienned carrot and daikon is dressed with imitation fish sauce. Finish off with an organic durian shake.

Barrier-free. Unlicensed, smoke-free, cash only. $

24 LUCKY DRAGON
418 Spadina, 598-7823

In typical digs — bright lights and blinding-white table tops — this mainstream diner doles out atypical fare. Your best bet is to start with shared dim sum and then move on to the deluxe seafood main courses. Also, unusual for this area, vegetarians aren't forgotten; there's plenty to choose from on the lengthy and diverse menu. If they're available, don't miss the meaty steamed oysters with soy and black-bean sauce.

Barrier-free, washrooms in basement. Fully licensed. $$

25 ON WOO
3 Oxford, 597-2087

The neighbourhood's cuisine evolves again as Japanese food finds its way to Spadina. Slightly off the main drag, this low-rent evocation of an upmarket Tokyo steak house serves super all-inclusive supper deals. Chefs man the table-side grills and cook your meal while you watch — true dinner theatre, minus the hokey antics found at Benihana (at the Royal York Hotel). The sushi's uncharacteristically cheap, but nothing to get excited about. Closed Sunday.

Barrier-free, washrooms in basement. Unlicensed. $

HOT SPOT

14 **CO YEN**
334 Spadina, 597-1573

Don't let the prospect of a Vietnamese submarine sandwich put you off — or the $1 price tag. These sweet French buns stuffed with "ham" (don't ask), fresh coriander sprigs, and daikon and cucumber julienne are fantastic! Subtle and spicy, there's also a veggie version made with tofu pâté, and say "Please" when asked if you want hot peppers. Strictly takeout, Co Yen also wraps up a superb vegetarian spring roll.

Barrier-free. Unlicensed, smoke-free, cash only. $

26 **PETER'S CHUNG KING**
281 College, 928-2936

Szechuan's gotten a bad rap and rep. When flame-thrower-strength Thai food swept through town 20 years ago, this garlic-heavy but not-too-hot regional Chinese cooking got labelled old hat. But taste has come full circle, as always, and Szechuan is now hotter than ever. Crispy beef on steamed green beans, orange chicken with large hunks of rind and whole chilies, and fiery tofu with oyster mushrooms are as good as ever at this spotless, if anonymous, spot. Dull fried-rice sides and a few veggie dishes accompany.

One step at door, washrooms in basement. Fully licensed. $$

17 **PHO HUNG**
350 Spadina, 593-4274

The Hung now has the only Vietnamese patio in Chinatown. Inside, they've tacked up wooden cutouts of Mickey and Minnie Mouse on one wall. Multiple variations of pho still draw a loyal following, while menu items such as snail vermicelli, beef fondue, and congee with heart, blood, and intestines will appeal to thrill-seekers.

Barrier-free, washrooms in basement. Unlicensed, cash only. Patio. $

4 **PHO PASTEUR**
525 Dundas West, 351-7188

Most Vietnamese pho houses are interchangeable — you'd have to be a klutz to mess up raw lettuce, carrot and cucumber julienne, bean sprouts, mint leaves, plain rice vermicelli, and a little grilled meat dusted with crushed peanuts. Here, the neon-lit doorway leads to tables for groups of six or more. Vietnamese pop music plays over the PA. Though not billed as such, the wrap-up combos make a feast for two or three. Very little for vegetarians is on offer, but carnivores can tuck into such dishes as duck salad and lemon-grass shrimp.

Barrier-free. Beer and wine, cash only. $

5 **SANG HO**
536 Dundas West, 596-1685

Don't even think of getting a dinnertime table on the weekend at this seafood stalwart. Regulars willingly endure lengthy waits on the steps outside. Crystal-clear aquariums hold live shrimp and tilapia waiting to be doused in garlic and black beans. And like elsewhere in Chinatown, the best stuff is advertised on the signs that announce the house specialties: razor clams, mussels, snails, and red snapper. Lunch bargains.

Seven steps at door, washrooms on same floor. Beer and wine. $$

13 **SWATOW**
309 Spadina, 977-0601

Featuring the fare of China's Fukien province, a coastal region northeast of Canton, Swatow's so popular that you're lucky if you can get a seat without waiting in line. It's worth the wait for the hot-and-sour soup, a sweet 'n' spicy explosion with shrimp, tomatoes, and crunchy veg. The special noodles are a must — wide rice noodles mixed with shrimp, shredded pork, green pepper, and crisp bean sprouts. Seating is communal and service informal. Ignore the decor and feast on great grub.

One step at door, washrooms in basement. Unlicensed, cash only. $

TAKEOUT

14 **CO YEN**
334 Spadina, 597-1573
See Hot Spot this page.

ENTERTAINMENT

CINEMAS — FIRST RUN

③ FAR EAST THEATRE
270 Spadina, 977-6339

Now that Hong Kong chop-socky action flicks are all the rage, world-cinema fans are flocking to Chinese movie-houses. The films are sometimes subtitled, but you don't need to speak Cantonese to follow the plots — car chases and martial-arts sequences communicate in a universal language. Now that Jackie Lee is mainstream, look for pictures starring Jet Li and Chui Man-Cheuk or directed by Ringo Lam.

20 steps at door, washrooms on same floor.

SHOPPING

FASHION — ACCESSORIES

㉑ GOLDEN SHINE TRADING
349 Spadina, 979-7755

There are a number of these variety store/wholesalers along Spadina, although many aren't open to the public. That's no great loss — their stock is mostly gaudy key chains and break-in-a-minute toys anyway. But Golden Shine sells surprisingly stylish sunglasses by the boxful. Sure, the plastic lenses scratch easily and the arms will fall off sooner or later, so who cares if they go missing?

FOOD

⑨ KIM MOON
438 Dundas West, 977-1933

In the front window, a miniature wedding party crosses from one multi-tiered wedding cake to another on a bridge of icing. Inside, display cases hold almond cookies, shrimp chips, Chinese chicken potpies, and western-style sponge cakes. Upstairs, dim sum buns, spring rolls, and deep-fried taro pastries are dished out in a boisterous cafeteria setting. Those with a sweet tooth can check out slices of chocolate layer cake and fruit-studded custard tarts.

Unlicensed. $

⑦ TAI SUN
407 Dundas West, 593-6964

Exceptionally fresh vegetables at better than usual prices, cheap chicken, and inexpensive noodles — it's impossible not to assemble the ingredients for a Chinese chow-down for less than five bucks here. Less cluttered than most food stores in the neighbourhood; even so, the narrow aisles are often impassable with customers just standing there. But listen to the truly off-the-wall muzak they broadcast — Argentine tangos, Sousa marches that recall the theme from Monty Python, and a tape that sounds like your dad playing Frankie Goes to Hollywood's "Relax" on the home organ. And none of the other shoppers thinks it's odd!

⑪ TEN REN'S TEA
454 Dundas West, 598-7872

One of Chinatown's poshest shops. If you didn't know they were selling tea, you'd think you were in a cigar store. Wooden boxes hold fine Chinese teas — hibiscus spice, black jasmine, oolong — and pamphlets describe their regenerative powers. One wall is lined with pricey packages of ginseng, the licorice-flavoured elixir the Chinese call "the human-shaped root." Once considered an aphrodisiac, ginseng is widely recognized as a tonic.

⑩ VIET HOA
434 Dundas West, 598-3767

On the outside, this subterranean store looks like a florist's — houseplants both real and plastic create a veritable forest at the entryway. But it's the treasure stashed at the back that gets foodies' knickers in a twist. There, in unmarked boxes covered with newspaper to keep them fresh, you'll discover a treasure trove of fresh herbs not to be found elsewhere: myriad strains of basil, mint, lemon grass, ginger-like galangal, and Kaffir lime leaves. And some other leaves no one seems to know the English word for! Closed Sunday.

HOME FURNISHINGS — KITCHEN

⑳ FORTUNE HOUSEWARES
388 Spadina, 593-6999

Although it's not the largest kitchen accessory store on the avenue, Fortune has the best-quality merchandise — everything any cook could want except the recipe and the food. Cookie cutters, spatulas, Henckel knives, cake forms, copper pots and pans, mortars and pestles, rolling pins, cast-iron cookware, glasses, chopping blocks, earthenware casseroles, teapots, coffee mills, and gadgets galore. Closed Sunday and holidays.

LIQUOR AND WINE STORES

19 **LCBO**
335 Spadina, 597-0145
Monday to Wednesday 9:30 a.m. to 6 p.m.
Thursday to Saturday 9:30 a.m. to 9 p.m.
Sunday 11 a.m. to 6 p.m.
Closed holidays.

Baldwin Street Grill

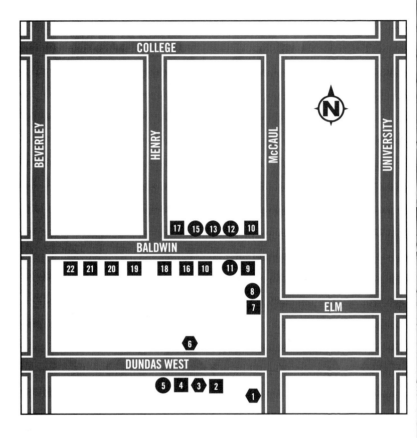

BALDWIN VILLAGE

A tiny enclave in the shadow of the Art Gallery of Ontario, this once-bohemian neighbourhood is rarely discovered by tourists. With its tree-shaded streets and summertime patios, Baldwin Village is home to true café society.

FOOD & DINING

RESTAURANTS

2 **AGORA AT THE AGO**
317 Dundas West, 979-6612

Located in the austere Tannenbaum classical sculpture gallery, Agora's fusion fare valiantly tries to upstage the room's vaulted ceiling. Chef Anne Yarymowich — late of the funky Mildred Pierce restaurant — offers stylish lunches and dinners as well as dazzling weekend brunches to gallery-goers (but AGO admission is not required to visit the restaurant). Lunch dishes include the artistry of Still Life with Pear, Pancetta and Fig, while dinner displays Mussels Monet. Weekend noshes feature grilled rainbow trout, vichyssoise à la Russe, and bucketfuls of Bloody Marys. Closed Monday.

Barrier-free. Fully licensed, smoke-free. $$$

19 BALDWIN STREET GRILL
35 Baldwin, 596-0278

Longtime iconoclast and chef Gaston Schwalb updates his *très chic* Parisian-perfect bistro, formerly known as Le Petit Gaston, for the new millennium. Romantic tables *à deux* sit amidst framed prints, and dim lighting and warm hospitality complement classic onion soup, garlic-buttered escargots — snails, to you — and mussels moulinière with frites. Not much here for vegans except a multi-veg Moroccan couscous, but carnivores get their fix from peppercorned filet mignon, braised 'n' deglazed duck, and veal tenderloin piccata. Closed Sunday.

One step at door, washrooms upstairs. Fully licensed. Patio. $$

7 CASSIS
168 McCaul, 979-0117

This charming Gucci-hued bistro keeps exhaustive hours, from 8:30 in the morning until 11 in the evening. The contemporary cuisine with a classical French twist is equally comprehensive — turkey schnitzel with potato rosti, and tamarind pork tenderloin with baked apple and Yukon Gold mash show innovation and flare. Cassis's only fault becomes apparent on occasions when service strains to keep up with the demands of a lunchtime full house. Since quality like this rarely comes at such low prices, occasional slip-ups are excusable.

One step at door, washrooms on same floor. Fully licensed, smoke-free. $$

16 JOHN'S ITALIAN CAFFE
27 Baldwin, 537-0598

See Hot Spot this page.

9 KOWLOON
5 Baldwin, 977-3773

Here's one of the few Chinese restaurants in town where you can dine outdoors — weather permitting, of course! There's nothing upscale or mondo here; this is good old-fashioned Cantonese sweet-

16 JOHN'S ITALIAN CAFFE
27 Baldwin, 537-0598

A cousin of the similarly named College Street pizzeria, this candle-in-a-Chianti-bottle old-school Ital eatery has an army of loyal followers who pack the place around the clock. Light insalata and panini lunches sate the nearby university crowd in the daytime, and after dark the Victorian double storefront is full of lovers of simple Italian food and others who are simply lovers. Pizzas come with either the traditional thick crust or *au courant* cracker-thin base, and toppings are always first-rate. They even deliver!

One step at door, washrooms upstairs. Fully licensed. Patio. $

and-sour-sauced fare. Daily dim sum deals (most under $2) such as chive pancakes, greasy veggie spring rolls, and wonton soup prove popular favourites, along with weekday $4.50 fried-rice-type lunch specials. The service tends to be agreeable if brusque, and weekend dim sum can be chaotic.

Barrier-free. Fully licensed. Patio. $

10 MARGARITA'S
14 Baldwin, 977-5525

A second-floor balcony doubles the al fresco dining — there's a vine-covered curbside patio, as well. Mammoth margaritas and the usual Mexican fare (tamales, burritos, and chimichangas decked out with rice and refried pinto beans) fight for attention in this tchotchke-riddled tacoteria decorated with serapes and macramé (!) wall hangings. Mariachi muzak sets the mood for after-work pig-outs. Killer jalapeño pickles!

One step at door, washrooms upstairs. Fully licensed. Patio. $$

20 MATA HARI
39 Baldwin, 596-2832

Named for the First World War spy and femme fatale, Mata Hari the restaurant is an upscale Malaysian dining room specializing in the sweet and spicy. Long, dark, and dominated by swags, gold halogen lamps, and mirrors that tilt over tables, the romantic room suggests mystery and intrigue — even if the only thing clandestine is your dinner date. A piquant sour soup laced with tamarind, skewered calamari satay with peanut sauce, and Casbah cashew chicken stir-fried with multicoloured peppers are typical dinner selections. Closed Monday.

Barrier-free. Fully licensed. Patio. $$

21 ROI DU COUSCOUS
45 Baldwin, 597-1366

Down a steep set of stairs lies this couscouserie serving searing Moroccan mains and North African vegetarian salads. While soothing Tunisian pop plays, enjoy icy milk-based fruit-syrup coolers as a starter. The tajine is a traditional casserole, a gently spiced lamb-and-sausage combo that at first seems mild-mannered but gains extra-strength heat from hellfire harissa hot sauce. Service is relaxed — the owners are rightly insulted if you eat and dash — so prepare to kick back and enjoy the hospitality. Closed Sunday, Monday.

10 steps at door, washrooms on same floor. Unlicensed, smoke-free. $$

14 SO SQUARE
19 Baldwin, 341-0777

Yet another bistro on a strip overflowing with them, So Square has something none of the others can claim — Hong Kong chef Mak Kam Kui, cousin of super chef Susur Lee. With its Tokyo hyper-kitsch decor — Hello Kitty inflatables, Chinese Coca-Cola bottles, and Asian Pez dispensers — and subtly spiced contemporary cuisine, there's incredible value here. Soups are superb, salads display pan-global aplomb, and pastas are plentiful. Did we mention the prices?

One step at door, washrooms upstairs. Fully licensed. $

22 WAH SING
47 Baldwin, 599-8822

Not to be confused with the nearby and nearly identically pronounced Hua Sing, Wah Sing offers the best two-for-one lobster deal in town. Yes, they're all chopped up and might be missing a claw or two, but who's counting? Smothered in black-bean sauce or elegantly turned out in garlic and butter, there are more crustaceans here than you could ever want. Bargain baby crab and mussels, too. All this in a space that verges on elegant — no cheesy discount furnishings or plastic sheets for tablecloths here!

Barrier-free. Fully licensed. $$

CAFES AND COFFEE HOUSES

4 CAFÉ AGO
317 Dundas West, 260-2482

Sleek and minimal, this snazzy cafeteria adjacent to the AGO's gift shop sells a selection of snacks, salads, and sandwiches. As it's overseen by Dinah Koo of Tiger Lily fame, don't expect the ordinary — Koo was one of the first to introduce haute pan-Asian cuisine to the city 20 years ago at Dinah's Cupboard in Yorkville. A large wraparound patio overlooks a neon sculpture by Michael Hayden.

Barrier-free. Beer and wine. Patio. $

18 KONICHIWA
31 Baldwin, 593-8538

Taking its name from the Japanese word for "thank you," Konichiwa offers several real-meal deals. Indoors under a rural mural or out front on the tree-lined street, the casual eatery dishes up budget-priced sushi such as California rolls, avocado maki, and inari tofu pouches. Tampopo ramen noodles — named for the Japanese cult movie — and donburi rice dishes piled with meat or veggies make up most of the modest menu. Buckwheat soba-noodle salad and miso soup will please the pickiest vegetarian. Closed Sunday, holidays.

Two steps at door, washrooms on same floor. Fully licensed, smoke-free. Patio. $

TAKEOUT

17 YUNG SING PASTRY
22 Baldwin, 979-2832

Regulars who line up here year after year know enough not to ask questions about the food at this Chinese bakery where stony-faced staff pretend they don't understand. Not that you need to — everything's cheap and tasty. Steamed barbecued-pork buns, vegetable chow mein, tempura chicken wings, and lotus-nut shortcake are also featured on their limited bill of fare. Closed Monday.

Barrier-free. Unlicensed, smoke-free, cash only. Patio. $

BARS

6 WEAVE
330 Dundas West, 598-1665

What started as a four-storey arts centre — a

gallery, restaurant, and nightclub complex — has been reduced to a late-night-only grungy grotto on the building's first floor and basement. Offering a full week's roster of alterna-entertainment from Obscurist's Cabaret to deep-house and trance sessions, it's the weekend lineup that draws the hipper-than-thou crowd. Drum 'n' bass, jungle, and illbient (or whatever name the current genre goes by) battle it out in a space that looks like a frat-house rec room. But then, it should. That's exactly what it is.

10 steps at door, washrooms on same floor. Fully licensed.

ENTERTAINMENT

GALLERIES AND MUSEUMS

3 ART GALLERY OF ONTARIO
317 Dundas West, 977-0414

Redesigned by internationally acclaimed Toronto architect Barton Myers, the AGO houses the world's largest public collection of Henry Moore sculptures and drawings — donated to the city by the artist himself. From paintings by old masters to installations by the art world's latest *enfants terribles*, the far-ranging permanent collection also includes key works by Warhol, Picasso, and Toronto trio General Idea. With the exception of touring exhibits, admission is pay-what-you-can.

Barrier-free.

CINEMAS — REVIVAL

1 CINEMATHEQUE ONTARIO
317 Dundas West (entrance off McCaul), 968-3456

An offshoot of the Toronto International Film Festival, the Cinematheque in Jackman Hall at the Art Gallery of Ontario shows over 350 cinema classics annually. Membership costs as little as $30 per year, giving members a 40 percent discount on single-ticket admission, but isn't required. Past programs have included retrospectives on Antonioni, Buñuel, Fassbinder, Orson Welles, and Atom Egoyan, and lectures have been delivered by the likes of auteur Bernardo Bertolucci, film theoretician Stan Brakhage, and essayist Susan Sontag.

THE AGO: Vaulted ceilings and naked ladies.

The glossy — and free — bimonthly catalogue is a must for movie-lovers.

Barrier-free.

SHOPPING

BEER-MAKING SUPPLIES

8 BREW-YOUR-OWN
168 McCaul, 977-2289

In a weather-beaten shop as dark and skunky as an ill-brewed ale, B.Y.O. sells supplies for setting up your own in-home brewery. Whether it's beer, wine, or cider that whets your thirst, this down-home outfitter sells startup kits, concentrates, stock pots, and pub glasses in cases for the real home-brew enthusiast. Scheduled seminars on such esoteric subjects as How to Mash Grain are followed by taste testings. Cookbooks and how-to guides mix with high-spirited personal anecdotes from the staff. Closed Sunday, Monday.

FASHION — NEW CLOTHING

12 COTTON BASICS
16 Baldwin, 977-1959

Walls lined with white wire baskets hold mountains of 100-percent cotton knitwear and separates. Nothing synthetic here at this Toronto-based manufacturer, whose credo is "all things au naturel." Warm, blond-wood floors and bright lighting put the focus on the duds, from funky, functional kids' wear to unisex sweaters and bike gear in sizes from newborn to extremely extra-large. Incredibly — though they do wholesale to other retailers — the Baldwin Street location is Cotton Basics' only outlet. Major find!

FOOD

15 BALDWIN NATURAL FOODS
20-1/2 Baldwin, 979-1777

Outside, a row of picnic tables welcomes customers who've just picked up a quick, healthy snack or those hoping to pass some time in the shade. It's that kind of place — almost a Whole Earther's community centre. A billboard announces found cats, wanted roommates, anarchist school, and les-bi-gay-friendly ballroom dance lessons. Indoors, the usual pills, potions, and hydroponic goods line the well-stocked shelves that crowd this multi-level store.

GIFTS

5 THE GIFT SHOP AT THE AGO
317 Dundas West, 979-6610

From catalogues and posters for current and past exhibits, to books, prints, and *objets* reflecting the AGO's collection, the gift shop sells more than curios and knick-knacks. Sure, there are greeting cards with naked people on them, but the shop also offers kids' stuff and a top-notch line of home accessories that are not only tasteful but artful, too.

MUSIC — CDS, RECORDS & TAPES

13 AROUND AGAIN
18 Baldwin, 979-2822

During the '60s, Baldwin was a tiny enclave of hippie head shops and tie-dye emporia. Fortunately, little of that past remains. Used-record depot Around Again wasn't around then, but it might as well have been. Lined with greying barnboard, lit by Japanese paper lanterns, and heated

by a furnace in the middle of the store, the decor alone can induce acid flashbacks. And the soundtrack's equally far out, man. Bins of rare vinyl line the walls, where you'll find righteous works by jazz masters, rhythm-and-blues belters, and protestin' singer-songwriters — but nothing contemporary. Trippin', fer sure. But hoppin'? No way! Closed Sunday, Monday.

VIDEO

11 LITTLE VIDEO SHOP
13 Baldwin, no phone

With its comfy overstuffed couches and handy monitor-and-VCR set-up, Little Video's modest selection is outweighed by its enthusiasm for film. Mainstream first-run releases rub cardboard covers with the more ephemeral — silents, Broadway musicals, foreign flicks — at this homey neighbourhood rent-all. Blockbuster Video this ain't — and we're grateful.

DOWNTOWN

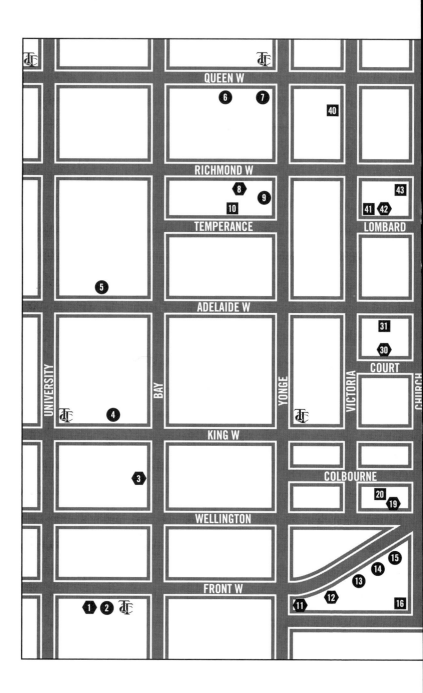

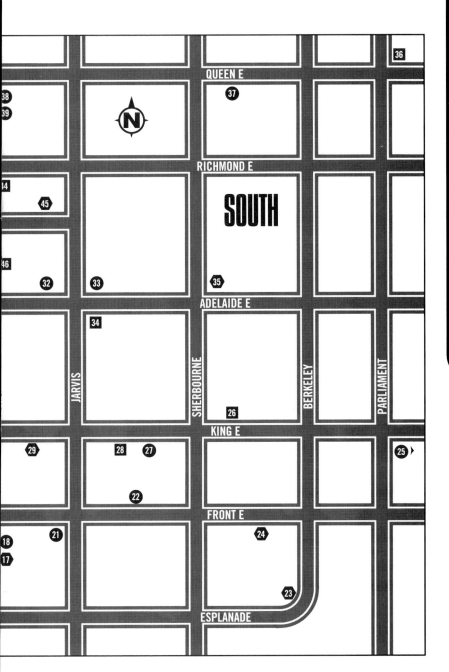

QUEEN E

36

38
39

N

37

RICHMOND E

14

45

SOUTH

46

32

33

35

34

JARVIS

SHERBOURNE

BERKELEY

PARLIAMENT

26

KING E

29

28

27

25

22

FRONT E

18
17

21

24

23

ESPLANADE

After the nine-to-five drudges evaporate from the core's canyon-like streets, downtown comes alive. A step away from the bright lights of Yonge Street — the longest street in the world — small joints jump with jazz, smart supper clubs start to swing, and even the Phantom of the Opera gets in on the action.

DOWNTOWN SOUTH

FOOD & DINING

RESTAURANTS

20 CAFÉ DU MARCHÉ
45 Colborne, 368-0371

Like a down-at-the-heels Parisian streetwalker, Café du Marché could do with a little tarting up — think of the decor as shabby-chic. Chow down on fine French fare that's perfect for downtown lunch takeout: classic onion soup topped with Gruyère, salade niçoise, or fancy fruit flans, which are proudly displayed in the front room. Eat-in diners fill the small back room from noon till 2 p.m. This foodies' secret spot provides some of the most luxe sandwiches in town. Closed Sunday and holidays.

Six steps at door, washrooms in basement. Beer and wine. $

31 THE COURT HOUSE
57 Adelaide East, 214-9379

Outfitted with chandeliers that Zorro could easily swing from, the Court House is located in Toronto's first judicial building circa 1850. Despite the rooms' elegance — several working fireplaces, and two-storey atriums — most of the business elite who frequent this basic surf 'n' turf steak house come casually dressed. Make sure you visit the washrooms in the basement — next to them are the original courthouse's jail cells, one of them occupied by a waxworks jailbird.

18 steps at door, washrooms in basement. Fully licensed. $$$

28 HIRO SUSHI
171 King East, 304-0550

Total dinner theatre happens when sushi-meister

THE COURT HOUSE: Swanky dining and clubbing in a 19th-century jail.

Hiro Yoshida slices and dices the freshest fish in town. The austere monochromatic room sets off spectacular raw delicacies dished out from the bar. Don't be afraid — let Hiro decide what's for dinner. While table service for tempura and yaki-tori bento boxes is unusually slow, no one's in a hurry here. Bay Street stockbrokers and advertising execs crowd in at lunchtime, but at dinner the pace is less frantic and more romantic.

One step at door, washrooms in basement. Fully licensed. Closed Sunday. $$

34 RODNEY'S OYSTER HOUSE
209 Adelaide East, 363-8105

Almost invisible from the street — look for a tiny sign on the building across from Goodwill — Rodney's is possibly Toronto's freshest restaurant for major seafood feasts. Lobsters, oysters, and mussels wait in aquariums or on crushed ice for the boisterous business crowd who hang out here to eat as much as they can before crying uncle. The basement space is decorated with the expected seafaring contraptions — nets, traps, and a framed clamshell autographed by Cape Breton chanteuse Rita MacNeil. Now that's a recommendation! Closed Sunday.

10 steps at door, washrooms on same floor. Fully licensed. $$$

44 SARKIS
67 Richmond East, 214-1337

Bad-boy chef Greg Couillard made his deserved tortured-genius reputation at a string of critically acclaimed and soon-closed bistros that included Queen West's Stelle and Rosedale's Notorious. Then Greg got serious and delivered the culinary knockout punch that is Sarkis — possibly Toronto's best restaurant. A former diner updated into a supper club for swells, Sarkis hits the bull's eye with fabulous ambience and so much spice-tacular fare there's no point in listing favourites. Expensive, yes, but a night out never to be duplicated. Closed Sunday.

One step at door, washrooms on same floor. Fully licensed. $$$

40 TERRONI
106 Victoria, 955-0258

See listing page 58.
Barrier-free. Fully licensed. $$

56 YOUNG THAILAND
81 Church, 368-1368

Owner and chef Wandee Young was one of the first to bring the chili fire of Thai food to Toronto 20 years ago. Now operating several outlets around the city, Young Thailand regularly wins NOW's Readers' Poll in its category. The bargain lunchtime buffet makes a good introduction to a cuisine that's not always overheated, and cooling salads offer some relief from the incendiary coconut- and peanut-sauced chicken and noodle mains.

Three steps at door, washrooms on same floor. Fully licensed. $$

Other locations:
111 Gerrard East (see page 118)
165 John (see page 16).

DELIS AND DINERS

5 MONTREAL'S DELICATESSEN
160 Adelaide West, 365-1212

See listing page 166.

Five steps at door, washrooms on same floor. Fully licensed. $$

TAKEOUT

36 PETER'S CAJUN CREOLE PIZZA
181 Parliament, 368-8099

Mixing things up, as its name implies, Peter's brings the spicy cuisine of New Orleans to southern Italian flatbread. The Seafood Creole pizza with shrimp, marinated mussels, and crawfish, and the Dixieland veggie version with broccoli and asparagus are just two of Peter's unorthodox pies.

Barrier-free, washrooms in basement. Fully licensed. $

BARS

26 BETTY'S
240 King East, 368-1300

See Hot Spot page 110.

30 THE COURT HOUSE
10 Court, 214-9379

Built in 1852, and the site of the last public execution in Toronto, the Court House today is a stunningly restored space that holds one of the city's

DOWNTOWN

HOT SPOT

BETTY'S
240 King East, 368-1300

When this east-side watering hole opened several years ago, it was amusingly called the Betty Ford Clinic, after the famous celebrity-rehab facility. Betty Ford's lawyers failed to see the humour and slapped a cease-and-desist order on the bar — you can see an enlargement of the paperwork hanging in the stairwell that leads to second floor, where the pool tables and foosball are. With its all-day breakfasts, its ploughman's lunch — cheese, pâté, pickle, and French stick — and 19 brands of beer on tap, Betty's is a favourite of nearby George Brown College students and members of the King Street tabloid press.

One step at door, washrooms on same floor. smoke-free. Patio.

most exclusive nightclubs. With its thirty-foot ceiling, grand piano, and four roaring fireplaces, the room attracts an older crowd from the financial district. Most are more intent on networking with each other than jiving to swing DJs on Thursdays or Latin salsa rhythms on Fridays and Saturdays. On Sundays, top-40 hits are simultaneously broadcast by radio station Mix 99. Closed Monday to Wednesday.

20 steps at door, washrooms downstairs.

MCVEIGH'S NEW WINDSOR HOUSE
124 Church, 364-9698

A popular spot with downtown office drudges, McVeigh's is a working-class pub proud of its Irish heritage. It's a small carpeted room with a stage in one corner — Celtic combos play nightly — and dartboards in the opposite corner, and you can be sure that the green Guinness flows like the Liffey River here every St. Patrick's Day.

Barrier-free, washrooms in basement.

THE STANDBY
4 Temperance, 364-3009

The Standby may seem like an unlikely name for a bar, but knowledge of courier lingo explains its origin. Whenever delivery service dispatchers have no work for their bicycle couriers, they bark into a walkie-talkie, telling the biker to "stand by." Three hours later, when the missing courier

emerges from this far-from-swank saloon and is asked, "Where the hell were you?" the road warrior answers innocently, "You told me to Standby." Closed Saturday and Sunday.

One step at door, washrooms on same floor. cash only. Patio.

BREW PUBS

DENISON'S
75 Victoria, 360-5877

Comprising three separate saloons — Louie's Brasserie, Conchy Joe's, and Growler's basement pub — Denison's also houses a microbrewery just inside its front doors. The in-house beers include wheat beer, Bavarian dark lager, and seasonal bock. All three eateries have similar seafood-and-pasta menus, but only Conchy Joe's has a neon-lit Raw and Nude Oyster Bar where you can eat all the mussels you desire for $7.49 on Tuesday nights.

Barrier-free, washrooms in basement. Patio.

ENTERTAINMENT

LIVE MUSIC

C'EST WHAT?
67 Front East, 867-9499

Split down the middle, this cosy basement with walls of exposed stone foundation houses a friendly neighbourhood pub and an intimate folkie venue. Under a very low ceiling, the bar side serves better-than-average pub grub like nachos, shepherd's pie, and steak and frites. The similarly decorated 100-seat performance space on the other side has hosted acts like the Barenaked Ladies and Jeff Buckley in their pre-fame days, and the then-completely-unknown Jewel.

10 steps at door, washrooms on same floor. Fully licensed.

FIONN MACCOOL'S IRISH PUB
70 The Esplanade, 362-2495

Fionn MacCool's couldn't be more authentically Irish if it tried. Why, they've got it all — dark, panelled room dividers pierced by leaded glass, Guinness on tap, glass-and-brass globe chandeliers, and soccer on the telly. Upscale pub grub makes up most of the menu — things like potato-leek soup, Donegal fisherman's chowder, and Yer Man's grilled salmon. Naturally, big-name Celtic combos such as Rollins Cross and Enter the Haggis beat the bodhran Wednesday through Saturday nights for a raucous crowd that usually gets into the spirit(s) of things.

One step at door, washrooms on same floor. Fully licensed. Patio.

🔵35 MONTREAL BISTRO
65 Sherbourne, 363-0179

Two places in one: half of Montreal houses a brightly lit bistro featuring such Quebecoise cuisine as pea soup, tourtière, and Montreal smoked-meat sandwiches, and the second half is an intimate 100-seat room lit by red-shaded lamps. Here, local jazz musicians and international legends take to the stage nightly — stellar artists like Oscar Peterson, Ray McShann, and Oliver Jones.

Three steps at door, washrooms on same floor. Fully licensed.

🔵19 RESERVOIR LOUNGE
44 Wellington East, 955-0887

Below street level, and reminiscent of a New York

City '50s-era jazz joint, the Reservoir presents a rotating roster of live jazz performers every night. Catch the New Orleans street sounds of the Funky Boot Brass on Mondays and the Harry Connick Jr.–like boogie-woogie and stride piano stylings of Tyler Yarema and his Rhythm pals on Tuesday evenings. Swing-era jazz takes over Wednesdays with Janice Hagan and continues on Thursdays when Alex Pangman and her Alleycats are joined by guitar god Jeff Healey. Fridays, Healey returns with his Dixieland Hot Six, while Jake and the Midnights knock out jump blues and swing boogie on Saturdays. Needless to say, reservations for this small 100-seat venue are mandatory. Closed Sunday.

Eight steps at door, washrooms on same floor. Fully licensed.

COMEDY CLUBS

🔵42 LAUGH RESORT
26 Lombard, 364-5233

In the third-floor space over Milwaukee's, the Laugh Resort looks just like the comedy clubs you see on TV — brick walls and little tables clustered around a small stage backed by brick. And

THE STANDBY: Wonder why your courier deliveries are always late? Bikers stop here to refuel.

THE FIREHALL: Comedy landmark.

the up-and-coming comedians who appear here look just like the ones on TV because they are the same ones as on TV — rising stars such as Ellen Degeneres, Adam Sandler, Gilbert Gottfried, and Paula Poundstone all gigged here before they hit it big on the tube. Closed Sunday.

35 steps at door, washrooms on same floor. Fully licensed.

GALLERIES AND MUSEUMS

③ THE DESIGN EXCHANGE (DX)
234 Bay, 363-6121

Located in a magnificent art deco building that once was home to the Toronto Stock Exchange, DX — as insiders call it — presents constantly changing shows featuring the work of Canadian and international industrial designers. Big names have included local housewares consortium Umbra and Parisian optician Alain Mikli. Not only a resource centre, the space also houses a bookstore, a café, and a gallery often used for fashion shows and Film Festival galas. Sundays are pay-what-you-can. Closed Monday.

LIVE MUSIC — OPERA

㉔ CANADIAN OPERA COMPANY
227 Front East, 363-8231

The C.O.C. presents its annual fall-to-spring program in the Hummingbird Centre, where simultaneous English translations of the presented work's libretto are projected above the stage so that neophytes can follow the plot. Recent cross-discipline film-and-opera productions include Robert Lepage's interpretation of Bartok's *Bluebeard's Castle*, Francois Girard's of Stravinsky's *Oedipus Rex*, and Atom Egoyan's of Richard Strauss's (via Oscar Wilde's) *Salome*.

THEATRE

㉓ CANADIAN STAGE COMPANY
26 Berkeley, 368-3110

Located in a towering converted warehouse, this not-for-profit company has presented such popular and acclaimed plays as Tony Kushner's *Angels in America*, David Mamet's *Oleana*, and Brad Fraser's *Poor Superman*. As well as producing an annual season of theatre in the St. Lawrence Centre's Bluma Appel theatre (see below), Canadian Stage mounts free performances of Shakespeare's works in west-end High Park every summer.

Barrier-free.

⑪ HUMMINGBIRD CENTRE
1 Front East, 393-7469

Although it changed its name a few years back, the Hummingbird will always been known to Torontonians as the O'Keefe Centre, the name it was given when it opened in 1960. With its excellent sightlines and acoustics, the 3,223-seat hall is home to both the Canadian Opera Company and the National Ballet of Canada. It's not all highbrow, though — performers like Céline Dion and Anne Murray appear regularly. Once a rock concert venue — David Bowie premiered his Diamond Dogs show here in the '70s — regular gigs were cancelled after the Clash encouraged their early-'80s punk-rock audience to rip up 28 of the theatre's plush front-row seats.

Barrier-free.

⑫ ST. LAWRENCE CENTRE FOR THE ARTS
27 Front East, 366-7723

Housing both the 900-seat Bluma Appel Theatre

and the smaller Jane Mallett Theatre, the Centre presents theatrical and musical productions by several local companies — most notably Canadian Stage (see listing page 112). Plays mounted here include *13 Hands* by Carol Shields and Michel Tremblay's English version of *Les Belles Soeurs*. Some areas barrier-free.

ATTRACTIONS

8 **CLOUD GARDEN**
Richmond West & Yonge, 392-1111
See Hot Spot this page.

45 **OLD FIRE HALL**
110 Lombard, 343-0011

Once the home to Toronto's famous *SCTV* gang, the comedy troupe has moved to new digs across town in Clubland (see listing page 44). But fans of the internationally popular cult TV comedy will want to see the building that prominently appeared in the program's closing credits. Now closed to the public, the building is a shrine to fans of the great late John Candy and Gilda Radner, performers who both trod the boards here early in their careers.

29 **TORONTO SCULPTURE GARDEN**
115 King East, 485-9658

Whenever streetcar riders on the King line pass this art parkette and spot the constantly changing unusual sculpture installations, many scratch their heads and wonder, "What the hell is that?" Mostly conceptual, the art displayed here is meant to prod and provoke. Chosen for the city-operated open-air gallery by a committee of local artists, the meaning of the three-dimensional work on display here is never as obvious as it appears.

1 **UNION STATION**
65 Front West

Toronto's train terminal, Union is the departure and arrival depot for VIA Rail, Amtrak, and the suburban GO Transit train service. No matter if you're coming or going, be sure to look up and marvel at the tiled ceiling that arches 88 feet above the Grand Hall.

GO Transit, 869-3200
VIA Rail, 366-8411
Amtrak, 800-872-7245

8 **CLOUD GARDEN**
Richmond West at Yonge, 392-1111

An oasis in the heart of Toronto's financial district, the Cloud Garden is a re-creation of a tropical rain forest. Your glasses fog up the moment you enter the atrium's 85 percent humidity. As birds twitter on tape, take to the park's catwalk and walk though the treetops — Florida royal palms, Tasmanian tree ferns, and Asian bamboo. Completing this miniature ecosystem, unseen bugs, not artificial insecticides, keep the plants healthy. Closed Saturday, Sunday, and holidays.

Barrier-free.

SHOPPING

BOOKS AND MAGAZINES — NEW

9 **LICHTMAN'S**
144 Yonge, 368-7390

Stocked with current bestsellers and trade paperbacks, Lichtman's also carries out-of-town newspapers and magazines that are received daily via airmail — essential reads like the *New York Times*, the *Village Voice*, and UK music mags *New Musical Express*, *Mojo*, and *The Wire*.

Other locations:
842 Yonge (see page 178)
1430 Yonge (see page 227)
2299 Yonge (see page 227)

13 **NICHOLAS HOARE**
45 Front East, 777-2665

Long before the mega-bookstores introduced comfy couches and latte bars to entice customers, Nicholas Hoare — a bookshop with a great selection of British titles and editions — offered customers a spot in front of the fireplace to relax with a good book. Furnished with high shelves made accessible by a ladder that rolls on a brass track, the room's decor is completed with a stuffed likeness of the beast from Maurice Sendak's *Where the Wild Things Are*. Knowledgeable staff, as well.

FASHION — NEW CLOTHING

6 **THE BAY**
176 Yonge, 861-9111

Mention the Bay to just about anyone and the '70s

PASQUALE BROTHERS: Now that's Italian!

come to mind — the 1670s. That's when the Hudson's Bay Company was founded as a fur-trading division of England's royal court. Four hundred years later, it still sells their distinctive striped blankets but also offers fashions by Perry Ellis, Tommy Hilfiger, and Wayne Gretzky. On the first floor of the company's flagship store, you'll find a Joe Boxer underwear boutique, and in the basement, a first-class food court.

Other locations:
2 Bloor East, (see page 179)
Hudson's Bay Company Outfitters (see page 121)

37 HE AND SHE
263 Queen East, 594-0171

See Hot Spot page 115.

25 REPP BIG & TALL
573 King East, 362-1882

Formerly home to haberdasher-to-the-big-boys George Richards, Repp is where stylin' b-boys come to get the baggiest clothes in town. And we mean really big — here, Wrangler jeans come sized up to a 68-inch waist. That's double the material of a normal-sized pair of pants, for the same price. Huge oversized Columbia and Ralph Lauren Chaps jackets and tops, too.

FASHION — VINTAGE CLOTHING

38 FRANKEL CLOTHING EXCHANGE
123 Church, 366-4221

In business since 1914, this old-school haberdasher deals in men's used formal wear and military uniforms. A carefully guarded secret amongst vintage clothing freaks and movie costumers, Frankel's is the place to find slightly used tuxedos, police uniforms, or so-hideous-they're-cool acid-washed denim jackets and plaid polyester sports jackets. Brand new way-cool porkpie hats, bowlers, and gaucho hats, too.

33 GOODWILL
234 Adelaide East, 366-2083

Two floors overflowing with recycled clothes and furniture, the Goodwill still holds great finds for the diligent who like to dig. The second floor houses beat-up couches and clunky '70s coffee tables — but again, if you go regularly, you can find some wonderful stuff. At the rear of the building is By the Pound, a warehouse where clothes are dumped randomly on tables and sold for $2 the pound.

Other locations:
306 Gerrard East (see page 130)
299 Coxwell (see page 214)
28 Roncesvalles (see page 216)
548 College (see page 78)

FOOD

27 PASQUALE BROTHERS
217 King East, 364-7397

By all rights, this well-worn cheese shop should be located in an Italian neighbourhood like College Street or St. Clair West. But Pasquale Brothers perseveres on King East, surrounded by high-end furniture designers. Shoppers come from across the city to browse over 50 types of imported cheese, as well as olives sold in brine, DeCecco pastas, and Paul Prudhomme's Cajun spice mixes. Ace Bakery breads, too. Closed Sunday and Monday.

21 ST. LAWRENCE MARKET
91 Front East, 392-7219

Although the merchants' stalls in the historic building that once was Toronto City Hall are open

Tuesday to Friday, the Market doesn't really rev up till Saturday morning when, from 5 a.m. on, local farmers hawk their fruit and veg in the modern hall across the street. The Saturday market attracts crowds of customers despite the fact that you can get anything on sale here in Kensington Market for half the price. Upstairs in the south market, the City of Toronto Archives uses the Market Gallery as its official exhibition space. Open only on Saturdays, the north market is rented out for events like the annual International Women's Day Dance and the regularly scheduled Old Paper Show and Sale. Closed Sunday and Monday.

HIKING AND BACKPACKING

14 **EUROPE BOUND OUTFITTERS**
49 Front East, 601-0854

See listing page 52.

18 **EUROPE BOUND OUTFITTERS**
69 Front East, 601-1990

See listing page 52.

15 **TRAILHEAD**
61 Front East, 862-0881

Trailhead supplies gear for outdoor enthusiasts, as well as for those who just want to look sporty. Along with Rockport and Simple brands of climbing shoes and other rugged stuff, the shop sells canoes, granola bars, and Tilley hats complete with an owner's manual on how to operate the silly things. In the stairwell leading to the basement, check out the photograph of former prime minister Pierre Trudeau in his shorts. Hiking ones, of course.

HOME FURNISHINGS — NEW

22 **HIGH TECH**
106 Front East, 861-1069

When the '80s revival gets under way in 2002, High Tech will be ready. Still selling modular chrome-wire shelving that assembles into kitchen and stereo units, the shop also carries most of the Umbra home-accessory line, as well as Smurf-inspired kitchenware by German firm Koziol. Stainless-steel Alessi teapots and kettles, and industrial ironing boards, too.

37 **HE AND SHE**
263 Queen East, 594-0171

Out front on the sidewalk, a provocatively attired mannequin models a revealing PVC get-up that constantly turns passing motorists' heads. Inside — to the appropriate Eartha Kitt soundtrack of "This Is My Life" — this double storefront sells naughty latex outfits that appeal to She-strippers and He-cross-dressers alike. Wigs, falsies, and fetish mags like *Boudoir Noir* and *Erotic Encounter* are available as well.

LIQUOR AND WINE STORES

4 **LCBO**
First Canadian Place Concourse, 594-9040

Monday to Saturday 9:30 a.m. to 6 p.m.
Closed Sunday and holidays.

7 **LCBO**
176 Yonge, 367-3567

Monday to Wednesday 9:30 a.m. to 7 p.m.
Thursday and Friday 9:30 a.m. to 9 p.m.
Saturday 9:30 a.m. to 6 p.m.
Sunday 11 a.m. to 5 p.m.
Closed holidays.

2 **LCBO**
61 Front West, 368-9644

Monday to Saturday 9:30 a.m. to 9 p.m.
Sunday 11 a.m. to 6 p.m.
Closed holidays.

PHOTOGRAPHY

29 **HENRY'S**
119 Church, 868-0872

One of downtown's largest camera stores, Henry's is a two-storey emporium dedicated to digital and analogue photography. The first floor has darkroom supplies, a photo-finishing service, and a rear area devoted to electronic equipment. Upstairs, Henry's offers a wide range of secondhand cameras and lenses. Closed Sunday.

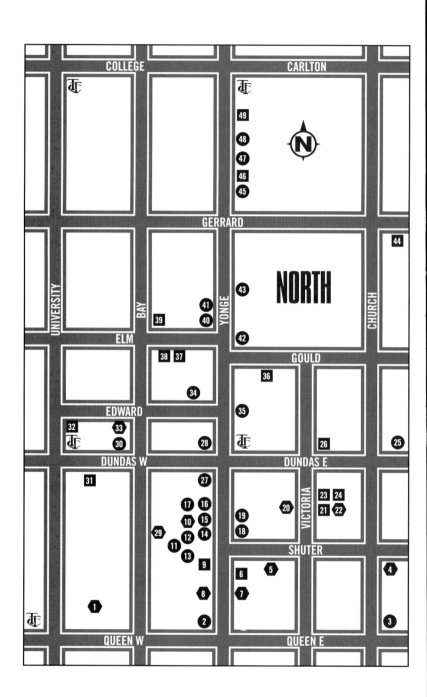

DOWNTOWN NORTH

FOOD & DINING

RESTAURANTS

6 **THE GREEN MANGO**
219 Yonge, 363-1615
See listing page 150.
Barrier-free. Unlicensed, smoke-free. $

37 **IL FORNELLO**
35 Elm, 598-1766
See listing page 39.
Five steps at door, washrooms upstairs. Fully
licensed. Patio. $$

39 **LE COMMENSAL**
655 Bay, 596-9364
The first Toronto location of a Montreal chain of
vegan cafeterias, Le Commensal sells everything
by weight. After a saunter through the salad bar,
a traipse through the tofu casseroles, and a visit
to the non-dairy desserts, your plate is placed on
a scale and priced accordingly. You can't go
wrong with the impressive fresh-veggie selection
— what can you do to a tomato? — but the pre-
pared dishes tend to be bland. A spicy selection of
salad dressings and homemade ketchup make
the mains more interesting.
Barrier-free. Beer and wine, smoke-free. Patio. $

38 **ORO**
45 Elm, 597-0155
See Hot Spot this page.

36 **SALAD KING**
335 Yonge, 971-7041
Think you can handle the heat? Salad King posts
a chili-pepper chart at its cafeteria-style lunch
counter that lets diners adjust the fire in their
Thai fare from a wimpy one-pepper grade to a
thermonuclear 20-pepper ("Can get stomach up-
set," cautions the sign). A modest five-pepper-
spiced Evil Jungle Prince — Asian veggies in gar-
lic-chili sauce — will satisfy most heat-seekers.
Extremely busy at lunch, Salad King is one of the

37 **ORO**
45 Elm, 597-0155
Some wag tagged Oro as one of Canada's top
10 restaurants. Imagine that — foodie snobs
deigning to recognize a Hogtown beanery! Oro
defies any pretentiousness a first-timer might
fear. A blazing fire welcomes, and the staff
couldn't be more continental — first helpful,
then out of your hair, and none of that hello-
my-name-is-Lamonte nonsense. Convention
combines with creativity in dishes like grilled
calamari drizzled with lemon and served in a
pappadum, and supernal sea bass with Asian
veggies. Swanky and swell. Closed Sunday
and holidays.
Three steps at door, washrooms in basement.
Fully licensed. $$$

few fast-food joints in town that takes reservations — they're essential. Closed Sunday and
holidays.
One step at door, washrooms on same floor. Beer
and wine, smoke-free. $

23 **THE SENATOR**
249 Victoria, 364-7517
Underneath Top o' the Senator, the Senator — not
the Senator Diner, that's next door — is one of
Toronto's oldest restaurants. The big attraction
here is seven semi-private wood-lined booths
with curtains that can be drawn to shelter the
space from prying eyes. Popular with the financial
set, the Senator's menu lives up to its turn-of-the-
20th-century steak-house decor — massive
aged-in-house prime USDA steaks served with
baked potatoes and sautéed mushrooms. Closed
Monday.
Barrier-free. Fully licensed. $$$

21 **THE SENATOR DINER**
249 Victoria, 364-7517
Open daily from 7 a.m., the Senator Diner is part
of the complex that also houses the Senator steak
house (see above), the Top o' the Senator jazz club
(see page 119), and the Victory 3B lounge (see
page 119). The diner is the least fancy of the
venues. A faithful recreation of a 1930s lun-
cheonette, it has a long counter with stools as
well as a row of wooden booths built for four. The

menu features such retro fare as liver and onions, and an all-day breakfast served till the 3 p.m. closing.
Barrier-free. Fully licensed. $$

44 **YOUNG THAILAND**
111 Gerrard East, 599-9099
See listing page 109.

See listing page 109.

CAFES AND COFFEE HOUSES

26 **SECOND CUP**
277 Victoria, 599-8286
See listing page 17.
Barrier-free. Unlicensed. Patio. $

46 **SECOND CUP**
419 Yonge, 595-6201
See listing page 17.
Barrier-free. Unlicensed. Patio. $

32 **SECOND CUP**
481 University, 596-8600
See listing page 17.

Barrier-free. Unlicensed. Patio. $

JUICE BARS

9 **PAPAYA HUT**
228 Yonge, 597-0602
See listing page 153.
Barrier-free. Unlicensed. Patio. $

TAKEOUT

49 **AMATO PIZZA**
429A Yonge, 977-8989
See listing page 17.
One step at door, washrooms on same floor. Beer and wine. $$

31 **COCONUT GROVE**
183 Dundas West, 348-8887
Newly located away from the crazy corner of Yonge and Dundas, things are still as spicy as ever at this tiny roti shop. Despite the move to a nicer area of town, the owners have kept their prices

ONTARIO SPECIALTY: A novelty shop specializing in rubber snakes, ray-guns, and X-ray specs.

DOWNTOWN

ridiculously low — $3 still gets you an wonderful eggplant wrap. Don't expect ambience — a ceiling fan and the glow from fluorescent tubes constitute the decor. Every Friday, the Grove cooks up Caribbean-style chow mein alongside its regular dinners of jerk chicken with rice 'n' peas. Closed Sunday.

One step at door, washrooms in basement. Unlicensed, smoke-free. $

BARS

26 **IMPERIAL PUBLIC LIBRARY**
58 Dundas East, 977-4667

See Hot Spot this page.

24 **VICTORY 3B LOUNGE**
249 Victoria, 364-7517

On top o' Top o' the Senator, the Victory is an informal cigar-and-martini lounge popular with the after-theatre crowd. Live jazz is piped in from downstairs, so even if the night's performance below is sold out, you can still dig the tunes while smoking a stogie and swilling a sidecar. Closed Monday.

40 steps at door, washrooms on same floor. Fully licensed.

ENTERTAINMENT
LIVE MUSIC

5 **MASSEY HALL**
178 Victoria, 363-7301

From almost any of Massey Hall's 2,800 seats, concert-goers get excellent sightlines — OK, the back row of the second balcony sucks. Built just after the turn of the last century, the theatre has witnessed many a memorable show over its near-100 years. In 1953, Charlie Parker, Dizzy Gillespie, Bud Powell, Max Roach, and Charles Mingus gave a performance here that is still today referred to by music critics as the "greatest jazz concert ever." More recent performers include Greek songbird Nana Mouskouri, Toronto folkie Gordon Lightfoot, and those ubiquitous Barenaked Ladies.

Some areas barrier-free. Unlicensed.

26 **IMPERIAL PUBLIC LIBRARY**
58 Dundas East, 977-4667

A popular after-class hangout for students of the nearby Ryerson Polytechnic, the Library — a bar with its own built-in excuse: "But darling, I really was at the library!" — features one of Toronto's best jukeboxes. In existence long before the current swing revival, this musical time machine is stocked with big-band-era hits by Benny Goodman, Glenn Miller, and Frank Sinatra.

One step at door, washrooms on same floor. Patio.

22 **TOP O' THE SENATOR**
249 Victoria, 364-7517

A long narrow club that recalls a smoky New York jazz joint, the Senator regularly features some of the best local and international names in the genre — people like singer Molly Johnson, saxophonist Jane Bunnett, and the legendary chanteuse Blossom Dearie. A standup bar snakes down one wall and a padded banquette down the opposite. In between them, black café tables and chairs face the raised stage at the end of the room. Closed Monday.

20 steps at door, washrooms on same floor. Fully licensed.

THEATRE

7 **ELGIN AND WINTER GARDEN THEATRE**
189 Yonge, 872-5555

Actually two theatres on top of each other, this exquisitely renovated complex was built in 1913 as a vaudeville house. Restored in the early '90s, the lower 1,500-seat Elgin has been home to runs of the Broadway production of the Who's rock opera *Tommy* and the outrageous Aussie danceathon *Stomp!* Oh, and far too many return engagements of Andrew Lloyd Webber's *Joseph and his Amazing Technicolor Dreamcoat,* starring former teen heartthrob Donny Osmond. The Winter Garden features smaller concerts and reviews like *Side by Side by Sondheim.*

Barrier-free.

20 **PANTAGES THEATRE**
244 Victoria, 872-2222

Home of Andrew Lloyd Webber's mega-musical

NOW MAGAZINE
189 Church, 461-0871

Wondering where you can score another copy of the NOW CityGuide? Come on down to our new headquarters in the downtown core in a building that over the years has — appropriately enough — housed a bingo hall, a booze can, and a punk-rock club. As well as picking up the CityGuide here, you can place classified ads in person, snag the latest issue of NOW magazine or blag official NOW merchandise — tasteful logo-decorated T-shirts, calendars, and baseball caps. In the mood to schmooze? Check out NOW's café-cum-nightclub where we present occasional literary, musical, and comedy performances.

Phantom of the Opera for over ten years, the Pantages is a restored vaudeville house reborn as a site for high-tech musicals. Lavishly refurbished, the theatre sports several ornate chandeliers — only one of which comes crashing down to the stage during each Phantom performance.

Some areas barrier-free.

THEATRE TICKETS

T.O. TIX
208 Yonge, no phone

T.O. Tix is Toronto's only outlet for half-price theatre tickets. Open at noon, the outlet does not sell over the phone — you have to show up in person and you're able to buy tickets only for shows taking place that day. While they do carry tickets for most local and southern Ontario theatre and musical performances, they do not handle ones for rock or pop concerts. Closed Monday.

ATTRACTIONS

CHURCH OF THE HOLY TRINITY
10 Trinity Square, 598-4521

In the late '80s, a band little known in their own hometown set up their equipment in this acoustically perfect church. The independent album the Cowboy Junkies recorded here, live in one take, came to the attention of international critics. Soon, Junkie vocalist Margo Timmins was named

one of the 50 sexiest people on the planet in *People* magazine. After selling millions of copies of *The Trinity Sessions* and other titles worldwide, the Cowboys still make their home in Toronto — and for fans making a pilgrimage to where it all started, a visit to Holy Trinity is a must.

CITY HALL
100 Queen West, 392-7341

Designed by Finnish architect Viljo Revell, Toronto's City Hall is a prime example of the late-'50s international style adored by *Wallpaper* magazine. Trekkies may remember its appearance as a building of the future in the classic *Star Trek* episode "The City on the Edge of Forever." Nathan Phillip Square out front has hosted some of the city's most memorable free music concerts, among them a hippie-era Jefferson Airplane– Grateful Dead double bill, and a performance by tartan terrors the Bay City Rollers. More recently, a relatively unknown Barenaked Ladies were not allowed to appear when Toronto's then-mayor took offence at their "sexist" name. Duh.

EATON CENTRE
250 Yonge, 598-2322

One of Toronto's biggest tourist traps — er, attractions — this three-storey atrium is a suburban mall plopped down in the centre of the city's core. Where you might expect to find a grocery or hardware store, you'll discover pricey boutiques that sell things to out-of-towners for showing to the folks back home. Among the better shops, Benetton, Roots, Brown's, Club Monaco, and Eddie Bauer have outlets here (see individual listings elsewhere).

NOW MAGAZINE
189 Church, 461-0871

See Hot Spot this page.

BUS TERMINAL

BUS TERMINAL
610 Bay, 393-7311

Located just north of Dundas Street West, Toronto's Bus Terminal is the arrival and departure station for Gray Coach, Greyhound, GO Transit, and all other out-of-town buses.

SHOPPING

BOOKS AND MAGAZINES — NEW

34 **WORLD'S BIGGEST BOOKSTORE**
20 Edward, 977-7009

Well sorta. It's not the biggest physically, nor does it carry the most titles — bookstores in New York and London hold the Guinness records for those categories — but World's Biggest is still pretty damn huge. The size of a two-storey football field — it was once Toronto's largest bowling alley — the store features discounted bestsellers, remaindered coffee-table books, and a large stock of paperbacks. As well, there's a big selection of magazines, and a multimedia room with CD ROMs and VHS or DVD tapes for sale.

FASHION — ACCESSORIES

3 **ONTARIO SPECIALTY**
133 Church, 366-9327

Since the '40s, this friendly toy shop has been selling wind-up toys, rubber snakes, and spark-shooting plastic ray-guns both wholesale and retail. But the real treasures here are vintage sunglasses from the '50s, '60s, and '70s, still displayed in their original packaging. A favourite spot with visiting celebs — check out the photos at the cash counter of Sean Lennon, Beck, Ashley MacIsaac, and Nicholas Cage wearing goofy glasses. Grandmotherly owner Libby Geller still gets a kick from demonstrating her stock. Closed Sunday.

FASHION — NEW CLOTHING

11 **CLUB MONACO**
Eaton Centre, 593-7299

See listing page 24.

16 **EATON'S**
290 Yonge, 343-2111

One of Canada's top department stores, Eaton's has the usual in-house designer boutiques — Roots, Calvin Klein, Tommy Hilfiger. But it also houses something no other store in North America has — a Jean-Paul Gaultier retail outlet. OK, it

doesn't carry the Parisian couturier's more outrageous creations, but it does sell his affordable accessory and jewellery lines. Check out the black leather shoulder bags that mimic the famous bustier that Madonna wore.

12 **EDDIE BAUER**
Eaton Centre, 586-0662

See listing page 180.

45 **FARSIDE**
399 Yonge, 971-8991

A rather sparsely appointed shop, Farside features essential b-boy gear by such designer labels as Reactor, MeccaDNM, Diesel, and Ecko Unltd. They also carry most of UK casual-wear company Kangol's line — not just the hats that you can find all over town, but its very cool and rarely-seen-elsewhere soccer shirts and anoraks, too.

15 **THE GAP**
260 Yonge, 599-8802

See listing page 25.

28 **THE GAP**
302 Yonge, 595-1306

See listing page 25.

18 **HUDSON'S BAY OUTFITTERS**
225 Yonge, 862-2663

Playing on tourists' fantasies about Canada — moose, maple syrup, and Mounties — Hudson's Bay has created the ultimate out-of-towners' mecca. As you enter, you're met by the recorded sounds of whooping loons and prop-planes buzzing overhead. From the ceiling, a two-thirds scale biplane appears to be coming right at you. A waterfall splashes down a wall. But what do they sell? Such Canadiana as snowshoes, miniature birch-bark canoes, and Hudson's Bay blankets. What, no Ookpiks?

40 **LE CHÂTEAU**
328 Yonge, 977-2559

See listing page 24.

14 **ROOTS**
250 Yonge, 593-9640

Started in Toronto in the early '70s as a manufacturer of negative-heeled shoes (don't ask), Roots now has shops around the world. Recently opened the Eaton Centre outlet is the company's flagship store. The tri-level space — with an in-house elevator — showcases Roots' line of sweats, leather bags, and shoes. Although most of Roots' high-quality gear is on offer, its line of home funishings is absent from this location. And so are those negative-heeled loafers.

Other locations:
356 Queen West (see page 27)
195 Avenue Rd. (see page 181)
95A Bloor West (see page 181)
1485 Yonge, (see page 227)

⑲ URBAN OUTFITTERS
235 Yonge, 214-1466

Think of Urban Outfitters as an alternative de-partment store, full of funky fashions and home furnishings. *Dharma and Greg*'s Jenna Elfman would be right at home here. Most of the clothes sold at U.O. can be easily classified as the raver-hippie-waif look — long batik-printed skirts paired with skinny little tops. To decorate your far-out pad, you'll find such essentials as inflatable furniture, lava lamps, and strings of Budweiser-bottle patio lanterns.

FASHION — SHOES

⑬ BROWN'S
Eaton Centre, 979-9270

HEALTH AND BEAUTY

⑰ THE BODY SHOP
220 Yonge, 977-7364
See listing page 30.

㊼ R. HISCOTT BEAUTY SUPPLY
425 Yonge, 977-5247

Offering more than the usual do-it-yourself hair-dye kits, Hiscott's also carries theatrical makeup and body paint. For the flamboyant, this friendly shop sells fluorescent wigs, hair extensions, glit-ter gel, Freak Streak lipstick, Nite Brite glow-in-the-dark hair mascara, and unavailable-any-where-else Dickson hair colour.

㉚ TORONTO BARBER AND BEAUTY SUPPLY
100 Dundas West, 977-2020

You're supposed to be a "professional" hair-

dresser to shop here, so if anyone asks, stare them straight in the eye and say, "Of course I am!" Not that it really makes any difference. Stock up on hair dye —Schwartzkopf, Wella, Manic Panic — as well as damaged-hair treat-ments by Kolestrol and Totally Fried. Mehendi henna and stencil kits, too.

LIQUOR AND WINE STORES

㉗ LCBO
1 Dundas West, 979-9978

Monday to Friday 9:30 a.m. to 9:30 p.m.
Saturday 9:30 a.m. to 8 p.m.
Sunday 11 a.m. to 6 p.m.
Closed holidays.

MUSIC — CDS, RECORDS & TAPES

㉟ HMV
333 Yonge, 596-0333

With outlets in London, Dublin, and Tokyo, HMV is Toronto's most cosmopolitan record store. And it's the flashiest — in-house DJs spin the latest re-leases over the store's sound system and there's a stage for live performances and autograph ses-sions with visiting stars. The first floor houses cur-rent-hit CDs and VHS and DVD videos, the second floor features back-catalogue and alternative ti-tles, and the third floor is home to jazz, world, and classical discs. In the "bassment," you'll find r 'n'b, soul, hip-hop, house, and electronica selections.

Other locations:
50 Bloor West (see page 183)
272 Queen West (see page 32)

㉕ HOOKED ON WAX
132 Dundas East, 504-8669

Hooked on Wax is an extremely specialized DJs' record store. A very sparse space, it carries about 200 CDs and records. Not 200 titles, 200 total! And a very essential 200 records they are. The choicest techno, lounge, trance, and rare-groove cuts are mixed by the owner on a pair of turn-tables on a raised platform in the front window. How funky can you get? Closed Sunday.

㊸ PLAY DE RECORD
357A Yonge, 586-0380

Dis mus' be de wrong place. The sign outside says Play De Record but it appears to be a typical

HMV: A temple of digital sound, video, and in-store autograph sessions.

Yonge Street convenience store complete with smutty videos for sale. But once past the sleaze, you'll find vinyl-junkie heaven. Play specializes in 12-inch singles that range from hard-hitting house and techno tracks to dance-hall reggae, deepest dub, and the latest hip-hop raps. They also sell compilation cassettes by top international DJs like Frankie Bones and Paul Oakenfield, and obscure-record-label T-shirts.

42 SAM THE RECORD MAN
347 Yonge, 977-4650

Sam's is Canada's largest chain of record stores, and its Yonge Street location is also the largest record store in the country. Sure, it's not as glitzy as HMV or Tower, but this shabby three-storey CD emporium has double the selection of its competitors — and artists get their own clearly marked sections. As well as current and catalogue titles, the first floor houses an extensive video area, a classical music department, and a magazine rack where you can find copies of mags like *Hendrix: The Official Jimi Hendrix Magazine*, the *Schwann Reference Guide*, and *Hot Press*, the cool Dublin equivalent of NOW magazine. The second floor's

jazz section is as extensive as you'll find on Yonge Street. And don't miss the third floor full of deeply discounted deleted vinyl and CDs.

Other locations:
1500 Yonge (see page 228)
2440 Yonge (seepage 228)
105 Danforth (see page 197)

41 SUNRISE
336 Yonge, 498-6601

Sunrise is a very mainstream record store that caters to the musical tastes of the general public — a little Alanis for the kids, some oldies for the boomers, and a second-floor dance section for the club kids. Ticketmaster has an outlet here. Nice glittery asphalt floor, though.

Other locations:
Bay-Bloor Centre (see page 183)
721 Yonge (see page 157)

2 TOWER RECORDS
2 Queen West, 593-2500

The first Toronto outlet of the USA's largest chain of record stores, Tower Records is a four-storey store loaded with CDs. On the first floor you'll find

current releases, as well as a thorough back catalogue with — not surprisingly — a lot of American imports, but a comprehensive selection of
British CD singles and a Ticketmaster outlet, too.
The upstairs floors are dedicated to classical music and jazz, but it's the basement that holds the
real finds. Tower's music-book and magazine selection is one of the most comprehensive in town
— titles like *Maximum Rock 'n' Roll, Ska-tastro-
phe,* and *Propaganda,* as well as *ZGB* (a Croatian
skateboard mag), *Bitch* ("a feminist response to
pop culture") and the bisexual bible *Anything
That Moves.*

48 **TRAXX**
427 Yonge, 977-4888

Carrying almost everything a happening DJ needs
— a hum eliminator, anyone? — Traxx has more
than just 12-inch singles. But much of the vinyl
on offer here is mostly unavailable elsewhere —
things like promo-only platters with special club
remixes released weeks before their official release. As well, they carry sound equipment, specially constructed flight cases, and bomber jackets embroidered with top dance-label logos.

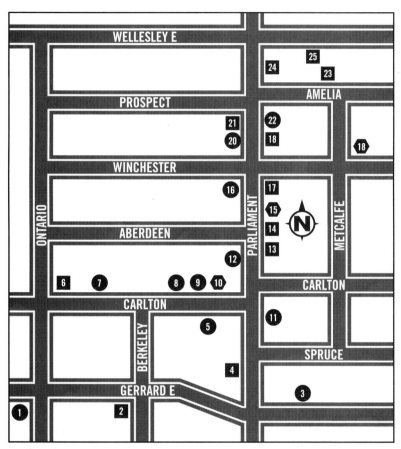

CABBAGETOWN

O nce a slum, Cabbagetown was one of Toronto's first neighbourhoods to be revitalized. Victorian row houses renovated to the nines cluster around its core at Carlton and Parliament streets. Here, specialty gourmet shops mix with funky coffee houses and bistros — and only minutes from downtown.

FOOD & DINING

RESTAURANTS

13 **PEARTREE**
507 Parliament, 962-8190

Exposed-brick walls, formally dressed linen-topped tables, and reasonable prices make the Peartree a favourite with area residents. Regulars perch on tall bentwood chairs round the central bar, waiting patiently for servers to deliver the likes of barbecued-chicken cashew salad, traditional tourtière, and classique

quiche. Weekend brunch.
Barrier-free. Fully licensed. $$

2 PIMBLETT'S
263 Gerrard East, 929-9525

Owner Geoffrey Pimblett is hard to miss. That's him in the Queen Victoria getup holding court over Sunday night's ultra-Brit roast beef and Yorkshire pudding dinner. He's not the only one in drag. Don't stare, but the diner at the next table just might be a graduate of Take a Walk on the Wild Side, the nearby cross-dressing school that uses the restaurant as a proving ground.

Four steps at door, washrooms on same floor. Fully licensed. Patio. $$

23 PROVENCE
12 Amelia, 924-9901

This *très chic bistro sur la rue* Parliament has been bringing a touch of the south of France to Cabbagetown since the late '70s. Lit by skylights by day and candles at night, Provence serves up such *cuisine française* as terrine de foie gras, granita of watermelon with gin, and confit of duck with walnut-semolina gâteau. For first-class foodies, there's a $70 *dîner gastronomique*. *Sacre bleu!*

One step at door, washrooms on same floor. Fully licensed. Patio. $$$

25 RASHNAA
307 Wellesley East, 929-2099

This unassuming bungalow might not look like the right setting for an Indian restaurant, but the seductive garlic and spice scents remove any doubts. Inside the cramped interior, south Indian dishes are served by a friendly staff. Mild mutton or veggie curries get added fire from atomic cashew chutney and sour anchar pickles. There's cooling mango lassi to drink, and for dessert, honey-and-cardamom crème caramel.

Barrier-free, washrooms upstairs. Fully licensed. Patio. $$

21 TIMOTHY'S CHICKENS
556 Parliament, 964-7583

The best thing about Timothy's is that they deliver. Sure, you can eat in the garish purple-on-pink dining room, but everything here tastes much bet-

ter at home. Tandoori-chicken dinners include fresh-from-the-clay-oven naan bread and a mixed garden salad. Separate sides such as cauliflower-potato aloo gobi, mixed-veg bartha and okra 'n' onion bhaji create an instant feast.

Barrier-free. Fully licensed. $$

CAFES AND COFFEE HOUSES

14 JET FUEL
519 Parliament, 968-9982

The rocket propellant here is caffeine, jolting cups of joe that'll kick-start anyone's day. A narrow space dominated by a stainless-steel kitchen — although, except for muffins, there's no food on offer here — Jet Fuel is a place to sit and procrastinate over $2 pints of latte when you should be doing the laundry. And, no, you're not paranoid; until the staff get to know you as a regular, you will be sneered at. To your face.

Barrier-free, washrooms in basement. Unlicensed, cash only. $

TAKE-OUT

6 JOEL'S GOURMET PIZZA
200 Carlton, 961-5635

From their bunker-like building in an alleyway

POPE JOAN: Every night is Ladies' Night.

just off Ontario Street, Joel and company whip up some mighty fancy pizza. *Au courant* ultra-thin crusts support such esoteric toppings as smoked salmon, Bermuda onion, zucchini medallions, and julienne of fennel. Traditionalists favour the veggie 'za with slivered snow peas, tomato concasse, and artichoke hearts.

Barrier-free. Unlicensed, smoke-free. $$

Other location:
1718 Avenue Road (see page 226)

24 **RADHIKA**
587 Parliament, 962-4888

This tiny takeout eatery features fiery Sri Lankan and south Indian dishes such as vegetarian or chicken biryani, bean-and-eggplant curries, and potato-stuffed samosas. Although the decor is garish, Radhika's subtlety shines through in signature veggie-heavy "string hopper" noodles and crispy crêpe-like masala dosai served with tangy chutneys.

Barrier-free. Unlicensed, smoke-free. $

BARS

4 **THE HOUSE ON PARLIAMENT STREET**
456 Parliament, 925-4074

Ye olde English pub, complete with draught and darts, the House holds regular Womyn's Nights.

Three steps at door, washrooms on same floor. Patio.

19 **POPE JOAN**
547 Parliament, 925-6662

Toronto's most popular gay bar for women — members of the lesser sex are admitted as well — features a varied schedule of DJs, live music, and livelier high jinx. During the summer, sand is trucked in to turn the outdoor patio into an oceanless beach complete with volleyball games and burger barbecues. Indoors, expect women-only strip shows or lip-sync spectaculars starring reverse drag queens The Drag Kings. Closed Sunday to Wednesday.

Eight steps at door, washrooms on same floor. Patio.

17 **WINCHESTER TAVERN**
537 Parliament, 929-1875

No matter how much the owners try to gentrify the

TORONTO DANCE THEATRE: Ready to rumba.

place, the Winchester will always be a down-at-the-heels working-class watering hole. Draft gets slung, country 'n' western blares from the jukebox, and the hours waste away. Some area homeowners think it ruins the tone of the neighbourhood, but as long as this rough-and-tumble tavern stands, a part of Toronto's history will endure that no amount of sandblasting can erase.

One step at door, washrooms on same floor.

ENTERTAINMENT

GALLERIES AND MUSEUMS

15 **HERE AND NOW**
527 Parliament, 923-7789

Ostensibly a picture-framing business, Here and Now uses its front room to exhibit work in all media by new and established local artists. A non-profit operation, the gallery favours pieces that upset expectations and transcend being mere framed pictures on the wall.

10 **TRIBAL EYE**
250 Carlton, 975-5566

Part gallery, part gift shop, this Afrocentric showroom spotlights artwork and crafts reflecting the

⊙ **Harbourfront** centre

Toronto's place by the lake.

School by the Water

Grupo Corpa   Photo: Jose Luiz Pederneiras

Roots Drummers

Proud to be the
National Partner
of Playdium

GENERATION**NEXT**

global diaspora experience. You'll find artifacts by local artisans, and *objets d'art* — sculpture, textiles, and jewellery — imported from Africa and Europe. Hard-to-find world music on CDs and cassettes, too. Closed Sunday.

DANCE THEATRE

18 **TORONTO DANCE THEATRE**
80 Winchester, 967-1365

Founded in the late '60s by choreographers David Earle, Patricia Beatty, and Peter Randazzo, TDT is one of Canada's leading dance companies. Its home base in the Winchester Street Theatre — once a church — includes a performance space and dance school. Director Christopher House also leads the troupe through performances at Premiere Dance Theatre. (See listing page xxx.)

SHOPPING

BEER STORES

1 **THE BEER STORE**
227 Gerrard East, 923-2122

Monday to Thursday 10 a.m. to 10 p.m.

Friday 10 a.m. to 11 p.m.
Saturday 9:30 a.m. to 11 p.m.
Sunday 11 a.m. to 6 p.m.
Closed holidays.

19 **THE BEER STORE**
534 Parliament, 925-1915

Monday to Wednesday 10 a.m. to 8 p.m.
Thursday and Friday 10 a.m. to 9 p.m.
Saturday 9:30 a.m. to 9 p.m.
Sunday 11 a.m. to 6 p.m.
Closed holidays.

BICYCLES

8 **SPINNING WHEELS**
240 Carlton, 923-4626

"Four wheels bad, two wheels good" could be the motto for Spinning Wheels, one of Toronto's finest cycling shops. Besides the customary spandex shorts, Gore-Tex shells, and clip-free shoes, they also stock top-of-the-line bikes from Specialized and Gary Fisher. Accessories include recycled-rubber knapsacks decorated with vintage licence plates, and Schwinn sparkly gold Naugahyde shoulder bags. In the split-level space's basement, you'll find state-of-the-art in-line skates, body padding, and helmets. Closed Sunday.

URBAN PRIMITIVE: To tattoo or not to tattoo?

FASHION — NEW CLOTHING

12 **MS. EMMA'S DESIGNS**
480 Parliament, 922-4518

See listing page 26.

FASHION — VINTAGE CLOTHING

3 **GOODWILL**
306 Gerrard East, 921-3396

See listing page 114.

FOOD

9 **DANIEL ET DANIEL**
248 Carlton, 968-9275

Two of the city's top caterers, the Daniels also sell their gastronomic riches to the general public from this delicacy-crammed storefront. Cater your own affair with the likes of beet-and-fennel salad, veggie lasagna, or tandoori salmon. From the in-house bakery, try a Parisian baguette, crusty French loaf, or raspberry–passion fruit mousse gâteau. *C'est magnifique!* Closed Sunday.

11 **LENNIE'S**
489 Parliament, 920-3777

Although he doesn't live here any more, all the customers of the Cabbagetown branch of the Health Service Centre know it by the former owner's name. So Lennie's it remains. In addition to a conventional lineup of natural, homeopathic products — rennet-free cheeses, organic sauerkraut — there are vitamins and supplements, too.

HEALTH AND BEAUTY

5 **M.A.C.**
233 Carlton, 924-3338

See Hot Spot listing this page.

LIQUOR AND WINE STORES

16 **LCBO**
512 Parliament, 923-6966

Monday to Wednesday 9:30 a.m. to 7 p.m.
Thursday to Saturday 9:30 a.m. to 9 p.m.
Sunday 11 a.m. to 6 p.m.
Closed holidays.

5 **M.A.C.**
233 Carlton, 924-3338

Known around the world for its glamorous spokesmodels RuPaul and k.d. lang, this Canadian cosmetic company's line of makeup was originally developed for fashion professionals. But when word of the products' excellence spread among supermodels and movie stars, public demand followed. The company uses cruelty-free manufacturing processes and eco-friendly packaging, and supports AIDS-related charities, so it's no wonder M.A.C. is the international sensation it is today. And it all started here in Cabbagetown. Viva glam!

Other locations:
89 Bloor West, 929-7555
176 Yonge, 861-4508
2 Bloor West, 972-3363

PET SUPPLIES

22 **MENAGERIE**
549 Parliament, 921-4966

Filling the combined first floors of three adjacent Victorian townhouses, this exotic beastie boutique retails more than regular pet foods in bulk — fancy some rat chow or monkey nuts? Aquariums hold snakes, fancy-finned goldfish, and hallucination-inducing cane toads, and a large walk-in aviary houses white doves, Java sparrows, and cockatiels. For those who like to take their lizards for walkies, the shop stocks adjustable iguana harnesses.

TATTOOS AND PIERCINGS

7 **URBAN PRIMITIVE**
216 Carlton, 966-9155

As its name suggests, this upmarket tattoo parlour caters to those who wish to connect with their pagan inner selves through the use of ancient body arts. Two types of tattooing — by hand or machine — are performed, as well as body piercing and scarification. For the undecided, there's temporary mehendi henna adornment, while the dedicated can opt for permanent makeup. Closed Monday.

BOYSTOWN

NEXT PAGE

Gay Pride weekend may take place during the last weekend of June, but the party goes year round in Boystown. From camp to raunch, there's something here for every perversion, er, persuasion.

FOOD & DINING

RESTAURANTS

67 **ALFRED'S**
634 Church, 925-0037

With its tall ceilings and romantic lighting, Alfred's oozes class. Customers sit at well-spaced linen-draped tables in two smart dining rooms divided by a stand-up bar. The menu focuses on contemporary Cal-Ital fare like Tijuana-authentic Caesar salad (one of the best in town), sake-mar-

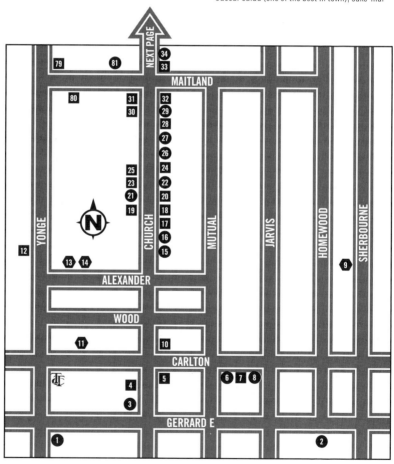

inated salmon, and flavour-intense chicken ballotine. Out front, the street-side summer patio starts the day in the sun and is shaded for evening dining. Sunday brunch.

Four steps at door, washrooms on second floor. Fully licensed. Patio. $$

43 **BYZANTIUM**
499 Church, 922-3859

Byzantium serves up some of the best food in the gay ghetto. Dried flowers spill from faux Grecian urns, and linen-covered chairs ring tables set with black china. The upscale menu features,

among other dishes, poached figs stuffed with goat cheese, Stilton and pear pizza, and pan-fried veal medallions with sweetbread-and-potato ragout in phyllo with purée of apple and roasted red pepper. The adjacent cocktail lounge has an early-'90s wire-mesh industrial look and could use an overhaul.

Barrier-free, washrooms in basement. Fully licensed. $$$

52 **DEVON**
556 Church, 921-4121

Anyone nostalgic for the times before the cata-

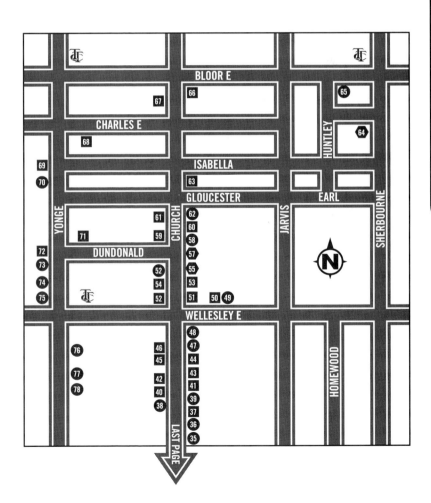

61 SPIRAL
582 Church, 964-1102

Housed in a Victorian townhouse, this modish and classy restaurant offers a menu unlike most of its cruisy competition's. Do try to get beyond the martini menu, 'cause the food's divine, darling. Mains tend toward seafood with Asian veggie sides or steak with Yukon Gold–garlic mash. Upstairs, the cocktail lounge makes the perfect place to show off your latest catch while the best of the local lounge scene perform on stage. Straights are welcome if they stick to the dress code — no Tilley hats — and refrain from public displays of affection. Puh-leeze — we're eating!

Six steps at door, washrooms in basement. Fully licensed. Patio. $$

clysmic gay-liberation movement that transformed the Church and Wellesley area in the late '60s should visit the Devon, a dreary Chinese restaurant that still dishes up '50s pseudo-Sino fare — sweet-and-sour spare ribs, moo goo guy pan, and chop suey. Some may find it hard to believe today, but the Devon used to be the major pick-up joint. Thank Goddess, the times — and food everywhere — have changed.

One step at door, washrooms in basement. Fully licensed. $$

19 GATSBY'S
504 Church, 925-4545

A throwback to the era when being gay meant having an encyclopedic knowledge of Broadway show tunes, Gatsby's still offers dinner-and-a-show packages under faux Tiffany lamps. Think roast beef, mashed potatoes, and — for dessert — a medley from *Mame*.

Barrier-free, washrooms in basement. Fully licensed. $$$

69 LIVING WELL
692 Yonge, 922-6770

The more sensible sister of Zelda (see listing page 139), the Living Well has an in-house bingo caller, Shirley. As well as bingo, the bare-brick and tchotchke-decorated eatery features tarot readings and live jazz combos. The menu is eclectic, too — seafood gumbo, veggie paella, and upscale Ital pastas. Upstairs, the music bar has a

very *Brady Bunch* vibe — '70s couches, swag lamps, and pool tables. Eggs B-B-Bennie and the Jets for weekend brunch.

Barrier-free, washrooms in basement. Fully licensed. Patio.

59 THE MANGO
580 Church, 922-6525

Sporting the largest patio in the ghetto — utter madness on Gay Pride weekend — the Mango serves contemporary cuisine in digs that are far more elegant than they look from the sidewalk. Inside, Mackintosh-style high-backed chairs surround tables topped with glass over linen. Add a pair of fireplaces, lots of mirrors, and Cal-Ital pastas 'n' pizzas and it's obvious why the Mango is a popular place to party. Weekend brunch.

Nine steps at door, washrooms on same floor. Fully licensed. Patio. $$

28 MARSHALL'S
471 Church, 925-0341

On a street where food usually means bar snacks, this friendly bistro is loaded with eccentric charm — from Marshall's front window, you can watch the furtive entrance and subsequent quick exit of the patrons of the straight (!) massage parlour upstairs. The menu's nearly illegible but, once deciphered, it rewards with nouvelle-tinged fare like rack of lamb, beef Wellington, and sea scallops swimming in a wine and saffron sauce. Chef Masaharu Mukai — Marshall to most — cooks his remarkable meals on a four-burner electric stove. House-made desserts excel as well. Quirky, but cute. Closed Monday.

Eight steps at door, washrooms on same floor. Fully licensed. $$

37 P. J. MELLON
489 Church, 966-3241

A New York City–style eatery — exposed brick walls, checkered tablecloths, apron-clad servers — Mellon's is a popular spot with those looking for a traditional nosh. The mussels may come with a teriyaki sauce, but almost everything else here is no-nonsense grub. Blackboards highlight specialties like smoked-salmon quiche, grilled loin of lamb, and — think *Mary Tyler Moore* — Happy Homemaker Sue Ann Nivens's favourite, veal Oscar.

One step at door, washrooms on same floor. Fully licensed. $$

61 SPIRAL
582 Church, 964-1102

See Hot Spot page 134.

31 WILDE OSCAR'S
518 Church, 921-8142

Ah, the love that dare not speak its name — that's Oscar's. The decor evokes Victorian opulence — chandeliers, wrought-iron accents, gas fires — and Wilde's menu is innuendo-laden. Bangkok chicken salad or Greek village salad, anyone? Oscar also whoops it up on Church's best patio. The non-tented area catches late afternoon rays and offers an unobstructed view of the comings and goings at the Spa On Maitland across the street.

Barrier-free, washrooms upstairs. Fully licensed. Patio. $$

71 YOUKI
4 Dundonald, 924-2925

Yummy Youki may be the best Chinese, Japanese, Vietnamese, Thai, Filipino, Indonesian, and Malaysian restaurant under one roof. Chef and co-owner Andrew Chase heads a crack team of cooks who aren't afraid to improve on cuisines whose recipes rarely change. Everything is served tapas-style and two plates soon become ten. Youki gets crazy on weekends — weeknights are less harried — so reservations are a good idea. Sunday brunch, too. Closed Sunday.

10 steps at door, washrooms in basement. Fully licensed. Patio. $$$

CAFES AND COFFEE HOUSES

53 CAWTHRA SQUARE CAFÉ
519 Church, 392-6878

Operated under the aegis of a local social-ser-

YOUKI: Pan-Asian eleganza and Toronto's best dim sum brunch.

vices program that promotes vocational rehab, the Café is a casual eatery offering light snacks and substantial lunches. On a mostly vegetarian menu, the restaurant dishes up hearty stews, healthful salads, and specialties like shepherd's pie. Closed Saturday and Sunday.

Barrier-free. Unlicensed, smoke-free, cash only. Patio. $

51 THE GARAGE SANDWICH COMPANY
509 Church, 929-7575

A funky little lunch shack decked out with auto erotica, the Garage serves up sandwiches with unusual names. Take the Little Red Corvette, a Prince-inspired combination of Montreal smoked meat and roasted red peppers on rye. Or the Police Cruiser — hot Black Forest ham and cheese on a kaiser, served and protected by a dill pickle. Comfort-food side dishes include a killer vegetarian chili and old-fashioned mashed potatoes slathered in gravy. For dessert, they offer Toronto's best ice cream — Greg's.

Barrier-free, no washrooms. Unlicensed, smoke-free. $

80 KUALI
7 Maitland, 923-0925

This tiny informal Malaysian eatery just off bustling Yonge Street offers $3.95 rice, veg, and chicken combos that will blow your socks off — or the top of your head, depending on how carried away you get with the killer hot sauce. Veggies and fruit — jicama, carrot, apples, and mushrooms — are mixed with shredded deep-fried tofu to create Vegetarian Delight. The sesame chicken comes with black-bean sauce or tart tamarind alongside homemade Singapore-style cucumber pickles. Closed Sunday.

Barrier-free. Fully licensed, smoke-free, cash only. Patio. $

5 MOCHA JOE'S
399 Church, 971-6356

Two steps at door, washrooms on same floor. Fully licensed. $

32 9 BELOW
473-1/2 Church, 923-5691

Located nine steps down from the street —

hence its name — this dark, smoky room is decorated with vaguely Egyptian hieroglyphics and black-and-red Pirelli rubber flooring. Strong coffee is brewed for those serious about their caffeine, and light snacks are served — homemade muffins, banana bread, waffles, and "size queen" cookies.

Nine steps at door, washrooms on same floor. Unlicensed, cash only. $

63 P.A.M.'S
585 Church, 923-7267

One step at door, washrooms on same floor. Unlicensed. Patio. $

66 SECOND CUP
175 Bloor East, 324-8936

See listing page 17.

Barrier-free. Unlicensed. Patio. $

46 SECOND CUP
546 Church, 964-2457

Home of the notorious "steps" — a half-block stepped veranda that locals like to think of as the neighbourhood front porch — this jam-packed coffee-teria is almost a community centre. At all hours of the day and night, the steps are lined with caffeine fiends checking out — and rating — every single person who walks by. And the pedestrians know it.

Four steps at door, washrooms on same floor. Unlicensed. Patio. $

68 2 CHEZ
3 Charles East, 968-9078

With its screaming lime-green walls and purple velvet French Provincial settees, 2 Chez — touché, geddit? — resembles a Marie Antoinette acid flashback. Food ranges from familiar soup-and-sandwich combos to early-morning muffin-and-java jump-starts. The cruisy front patio offers a prime view of Yonge Street — and overlooks the entrance to World Gym. Not that anyone would be caught staring, mind. Best of all, 2 Chez never closes.

Barrier-free. Fully licensed. Patio. $$

DELIS AND DINERS

7 **AUNTIE EMM'S**
105 Carlton, 260-6864

Just below street-level, this '60s-style lun-cheonette serves up massive all-day breakfasts in digs that are shockingly retro — appalling or-ange-vinyl-padded booths, and counters clad in wood-grain Arborite. In other words, it's perfect! While British Invasion and Motown hits play, cus-tomers tuck into classic diner fare like heftily por-tioned potato pancakes, chicken cacciatore, and roast lamb with scalloped potatoes.

Seven steps at door, washrooms on same floor. Fully licensed. $

33 **THE VILLAGE RAINBOW**
477 Church, 961-0616

With its prime people-watching terrace, the Vil-lage Rainbow is one of Church Street's busiest patios. Few come for the food.

Barrier-free. Fully licensed. Patio. $$

BARS

60 **BABYLON**
553 Church, 923-2626

Babylon is a three-tiered space with a triple per-sonality. The first floor is a comfortable room serving Mediterranean snacks and dinners. Up a flight is a martini lounge where bartenders mix up over 200 different cocktail concoctions for the swizzle-stick set. Fridays and Saturdays, the top floor opens for dancing to deep-house DJs.

Nine steps at door, washrooms on same floor.

44 **BAR 501**
501 Church, 944-3272

The Sunday-evening drag shows at Bar 501 liter-ally stop traffic. Held at 7 p.m. in the club's large front window that opens to the street, the action attracts crowds that spill off the sidewalk and of-ten block the neighbourhood's main drag. Inside is a rather garish turquoise space decked out with pinball machines and supermodel-style portraits of the queens. The room features two pool tables, and a large central bar. Friday nights, Georgie Girl presents Hags in Heels, and on Saturday evenings the Fabulous Freaks wig out. And don't forget Sat-

urday-afternoon bingo with Sister Bedelia, a nun with a bad habit.

One step at door, washrooms on same floor.

4 **THE BARN**
418 Church, 977-4702

Three floors of fun, the Barn — once a leather bar — caters to a young clientele that's into denim and subdued ranch-style raunch. Body Leather (see listing page 143) still operates a small sex-toy shop on the minimalist black premises, and there's a snack bar, too. Although most of the time there's no cover charge, at exactly 1:50 a.m. — yes, 10 minutes before last call — a $5 entry fee goes into effect. From then till closing time at 3 a.m., the place is a frenzy of so-far-unlucky bar-hoppers desperate to connect with anything that moves.

Barrier-free.

17 **THE BLACK EAGLE**
457 Church, 413-1219

As miniature sharks swim restlessly in an aquar-ium, the Eagle's leather-clad customers gaze blankly at the hard-core porn videos that are broadcast on several TVs in the very dark room. Upstairs is the camouflage-draped S & M play-room with posted and enforced rules — "Keep your hands off my slave." Unless you've been introduced, of course. True masochists will want to try the $2.50 Sunday brunch. And don't say we didn't warn you about the apple juice.

Seven steps at door, washrooms on same floor. Patio.

30 **BOSIE'S**
518 Church, 921-8142

A lounge upstairs from Wilde Oscar's (see listing page 135), Bosie's is a more contemporary-look-ing room than the Victorian-style restaurant be-low. Wednesday is open-mic night.

23 steps at door, washrooms on same floor.

72 **CARRINGTON'S SPORTS BAR**
618 Yonge, 944-0559

Located in two well-worn second-floor rooms overlooking Yonge, Carrington's professes to be a sports bar. Sure, there's the requisite pool table, and Alanis belts it out on the CD jukebox, but there's not much of a sporting nature going on here. The decor consists of '70s-era sectional couches clustered around an out-of-order fire-place, and a TV set tuned to the soaps. Dire.

20 steps at door, washrooms on same floor. Patio.

25 ## CREWS
508 Church, 972-1662

The main attraction of this straightforward bar-room, complete with neon beer signs, is the week-end drag shows. Local celebutante Chris Edwards and those friggin' Freaks take to the tiny corner stage on Friday and Saturday nights respectively — and respectfully. With one patio out back and a second tiny one overlooking Church Street, Crews is designed for cruising.

Seven steps at door, washrooms on same floor. Patio.

POPE JOAN
547 Parliament, 925-6662

See listing page 128.

18 ### THE RED SPOT
459 Church, 967-7768

A second-floor lounge with a Latin twist, the Red Spot is one of the newest bars on Church. Open

seven nights a week, the club features an eclectic mix of entertainment. Tuesday is Jazz Night, Wednesday spotlights David Maclean's Comedy Handbag stand-up sessions, and reggae and bhangra DJs spin on Friday and Saturday evenings.

16 steps at door, washrooms on same floor. Fully licensed.

20 ### SAILOR
465 Church, 972-0887

Get hammered in a bar with a hammerhead shark hanging from the ceiling. The more seaworthy mate of next-door Woody's, Sailor sports a naugh-tical motif — lots of frigate paintings and a dis-play case of G.I. Joes dressed in naughty uni-forms. Special events include regular Bad Boy Nights Thursdays and naval-gazing drag extrava-ganzas on Sunday evenings.

Six steps at door, washrooms on same floor.

54 ### SLACK ALICE
562 Church, 969-8742

Holder of more NOW Readers' Poll awards than any other establishment — best bartender, best gay bar and restaurant, best place to drink alone,

WOODY'S: Hanging out by the pool table — "White ball, corner pocket? No, that can't be right . . ."

best place to pick up a lesbian, best ashtray (we just made that one up) — Slack Alice's is a postmodern playground that combines a comfort-food menu with major martini guzzling. The front windows open onto a tiny curbside deck, and DJs spin club house on Friday and Saturday evenings. Weekend brunch, too.

Barrier-free.

12 SNEAKERS
502A Yonge, 961-5808

The specialty of the house at this darkly lit emerald-green saloon is chicken — and we aren't talking about Buffalo wings. The main thing that attracts the middle-aged clientele is that supposedly teenaged hustlers from the nearby Breadalbane and Grosvenor track hang out here — despite the sign on the door saying that anyone under 19 will not be admitted. It's all somewhat desperate and tawdry. No wonder it's Toronto bad-boy cineaste Bruce LaBruce's favourite bar.

Barrier-free.

23 TANGO
508 Church, 972-1662

Primarily a women's space, Tango is part of the Crews complex. A stripped-down, minimally decorated club, the action here takes place on two floors. Perfect your Anne Murray or Courtney Love impression, 'cause Tuesday and Sunday evenings are Karaoke Nights. Other evenings, DJs spin dance hits in the intimate upstairs area. Closed Sunday and Monday.

Six steps at door, washrooms in basement. Patio.

79 TRAX V
529 Yonge, 963-5196

See listing page 140.

24 WOODY'S
467 Church, 972-0887

Horny? Then stand under the stuffed rhinoceros head that protrudes over the bar at Woody's, one of Church Street's favourite bars. A small lounge area overlooks the street while the large back space holds a pool table. Soft-core pornos — mind-numblingly boring flicks featuring racy stuff like nude volleyball — play over several video monitors. House DJs most evenings.

Six steps at door, washrooms in basement.

50 ZELDA'S
76 Wellesley East, 922-2526

Owner Zelda Angelfire is trailer trash and proud of it. The bespeckled host of her namesake restaurant is one of Boystown's biggest characters. She holds court over this campy eatery that features regular toga nights, pyjama parties, and taped reruns of Jerry Springer's slugfests. Every week she comes up with yet another idea for a theme night — howzabout Lumberjack Ladies, or Nuns on the Run? Oh, and weekend brunch, too.

Barrier-free, washrooms in basement. Patio.

50 ZELDA'S
76 Wellesley East, 922-2526

See Hot Spot this page.

10 ZIPPERZ
72 Carlton, 921-0066

Once a pre-game watering hole for Maple Leafs fans, since the team moved to new digs downtown so did this bar's patrons — thank God. With a new name and management, the club is now divided down the middle by a glass wall. In the front, a cocktail pianist tinkles while some of the cutest bartenders in town sling martinis. On the other side of the glass, DJs spin house for a crowd bent on dancing amidst pool tables on Fridays and Saturdays. Sunday nights they host drag shows, and Wednesday evenings, talent shows.

Two steps at door, washrooms on same floor.

ENTERTAINMENT

9 THE PHOENIX
410 Sherbourne, 323-1251

When it's not a dance club, the Phoenix is a 1,000-capacity concert venue. An intimate room with good sound and sightlines, it's the perfect place to see up close acts like Kiss, David Bowie, and Men Without Hats. Closed Tuesday to Thursday.

Barrier-free. Fully licensed.

79 TRAX V
529 Yonge, 963-5196

One of Toronto's oldest gay bars, Trax has two entrances — a low-profile entry off Yonge and an even more discreet doorway off the alleyway at the back. Not that there's anything out-of-the-ordinary going on. A two-level sports bar — upstairs is a pool hall — Trax showcases local roots-rock bands Thursday through Saturday evenings, as well as swing musicians on Mondays, and country combos Wednesdays. Regular Talent Nights, euchre tournaments, and daily bingo.

Barrier-free. Fully licensed. Patio.

COMMUNITY CENTRES

57 THE 519 CHURCH STREET COMMUNITY CENTRE
519 Church, 392-6874

Located in Cawthra Park — known to locals as the Beach because of its legions of skimpily attired summertime sunbathers — the centre is home to more than 350 activist and community groups. Among those sharing the space, you'll find organizations as diverse as AIDS Action Now, Sex and Love Addicts Anonymous, and Queer Tories.

DANCE CLUBS

64 BOOTS WAREHOUSE
592 Sherbourne, 921-0665

Situated in a cavernous warehouse space attached to the historic Selby Hotel, Boots has several dance areas — one done up as a glittery dungeon and another as a white-tiled hospital operating room. While the mostly under-25 crowd groove to house DJs — except on Sundays when retro sounds from the '80s rule — things quiet down in the adjacent Selby Lounge complete with leather wingbacked chairs, a fireplace, and a pool table. Closed Monday to Thursday.

One step at door, washrooms on same floor. Fully licensed. Patio.

9 THE PHOENIX
410 Sherbourne, 323-1251

One of Toronto's oldest dance halls, the Phoenix attracts a very mixed crowd — pan-sexual, multiracial, and omni-generational. Its in-house art department constantly changes the 1,000-capacity club's look to keep it fresh. Friday is '80s Night, Saturday's Club 102 is broadcast live on CFNY, and Sunday's Planet Vibe goes out over the airwaves on Energy 108. On Mondays, it hosts Toronto's longest-running club night, Strange Paradise, when headbangers boogie to everything from Led Zeppelin to Monster Magnet. Closed Tuesday to Thursday.

Barrier-free. Fully licensed.

14 TALLULAH'S CABARET
12 Alexander, 975-8555

Nominally a cabaret space, Tallulah's becomes an alternative dance hall late on Friday and Saturday evenings. Friday's club night is called Wet Spot and attracts a straight-gay-lesbian-whatever crowd that dances and poses to goth and industrial sounds. Saturday the space becomes Sissy, *Xtra* gossip columnist Daniel Paquette's tribute to the inner nerd hidden within every Muscle Mary. Expect everything from Abba to Zamfir.

Barrier-free. Fully licensed.

IN MEMORIAM

55 AIDS MEMORIAL
519 Church, 392-6878, ext. 102

Erected in 1993 and funded by private donation, the AIDS Memorial in Cawthra Park stands as a symbol of the fight against the disease. A place for grieving, healing, and remembering, the series of engraved monoliths standing in the park is the focus of the annual Candlelight Vigil held on Thursday evening of Pride Week.

POOL HALLS

41 PEGASUS
491 Church, 927-8832

First-timers and fans of Miss Piggy will want to check out the Shrine of Swine, a display case by the entryway that holds a collection of stuffed toy pigs. This second-storey room — accessible by elevator — features five pool tables, as well as a number of video and pinball games.

Barrier-free. Fully licensed.

CINEMAS — FIRST RUN

11 THE CARLTON
20 Carlton, 598-2309

An 11-screen multiplex, the Carlton screens art flicks, critics' favourites, and indie features.

THEATRE

13 BUDDIES IN BAD TIMES
12 Alexander, 975-8555

North America's largest lesbian and gay theatre, Buddies has been controversial since its formation in the late '70s. In 1994, the company took over its current location — once the home of the pioneering Toronto Workshop Productions — in the heart of Boystown. Every year the 300-seat main stage mounts a 13-week season of radical new Canadian theatre by playwrights like Brad Fraser and Sky Gilbert. In the second space, Tallulah's Cabaret presents more intimate performances (see listing below) and weekend club nights (see listing page 140).

14 TALLULAH'S CABARET
12 Alexander, 975-8555

The second space at Buddies In Bad Times (see listing above), Tallulah's has showcased singers Carole Pope and Holly Cole, comedian Sandra Shamas, and writers Quentin Crisp, Timothy Findley, and Ann-Marie MacDonald. Weekends, the room becomes a late-night dance club (see listing page 140).

Barrier-free. Fully licensed.

SHOPPING

BEER STORES

56 THE BEER STORE
572 Church, 921-6036

Monday to Friday 10 a.m. to 10 p.m.
Saturday 9:30 a.m. to 10 p.m.
Sunday 11 a.m. to 6 p.m.
Closed holidays.

AIDS MEMORIAL: A quiet spot to reflect and remember.

BOOKS AND MAGAZINES — NEW

73 GLAD DAY BOOKSHOP
598A Yonge, 961-4161

Despite lengthy battles with Canada Customs, Glad Day endures. Since the early '70s, this shop has offered publications on sexual politics and theory as well as heavy-duty gay and lesbian "erotica" — that's the intellectual name for porn. The second-floor shop is stacked with fiction and poetry, and, on the magazine rack, copies of the *London Review of Books* rub shoulders with raunchy mags with titles like *Girlfriends, Slurp, Curve,* and *Handjobs.*

16 THIS AIN'T THE ROSEDALE LIBRARY
483 Church, 929-9912

Boystown's favourite bookseller, This Ain't is a local institution. Topics range from new fiction to gender studies and spiritual travel. At the back of the shop, there's a separate children's reading room furnished with an adult-size comfy chair and a smaller one for kids to curl up on.

BOOKS AND MAGAZINES — USED

75 ELIOT'S
584 Yonge, 925-0268

A three-storey shop selling used and rare books — the first floor contains mostly paperbacks, the second historical hardcovers, and the third theatre and women's titles.

FASHION — NEW CLOTHING

27 BODY BODY
471 Church, 929-2639

Underwear designer Stephen Sandler's clothing empire began in this chic space a couple of steps below street level. Now sold in over 26 countries — there are Body Body boutiques in South Miami Beach, the United Arab Emirates, New York City, and Beverly Hills, and chi-chi department stores like Bloomingdale's and Neiman Marcus — San-

BODY BODY: Non-stop videos of runway models strutting their stuff in skimpy undies and T-shirts.

dler's body-conscious clothes are the ultimate decoration for a gym-buffed bod. Jean-Claude Van Damme, Jason Priestley, and Jackie Chan agree.

58 OUT ON THE STREET
551 Church, 967-2759

You'll find everything under the rainbow at Out on the Street — all of it decorated with a gay-and-lesbian diversity rainbow. There are candles and clocks and licence-plate holders and beanies and . . . Upstairs, the shop carries Calvin Klein underwear, Guess sweats, and Storm watches. They also stock those Gay Pride Week T-shirts everyone seems to wear with slogans like "Recovering Catholic" and "I Can't Even Think Straight."

22 PRIAPE
465 Church, 586-9914

Knowing Priape's reputation as a leading light in the leather scene, it comes as a surprise, after mounting steps painted with the words "dildos" and "harnesses," to find a wholesome boutique selling Calvin Klein underwear. Sure, raunchy custom-made stuff can be found at the rear of the store — along with videos and toys — but the front room features Kangol baggy pants and jackets, as well as glittery disco tops and Priape's own brand of jeans.

70 SHKANK
672 Yonge, 515-0959

See Hot Spot this page.

2 TAKE A WALK ON THE WILD SIDE
161 Gerrard East, 921-6112

Wild Side is the focal point of Toronto's cross-dressing scene. Not only does it carry large-size lingerie, stockings, and stilettos, as well as foam and silicone padding, but the store also offers complete transformations. Here, a burly fireman can become the girl next door. Saturday nights, the shop holds B.Y.O.B. suppers in the lounge upstairs — wives welcome — and there's a bed-and-breakfast facility for out-of-towners, too. Thanks to its discreet location in a townhouse, no one will notice your entry or exit — the crowd you'll likely see on the sidewalk out front is there to protest the nearby abortion clinic.

70 SHKANK
672 Yonge, 515-0959

When this glitzy dress shop is closed, a drag-queen-proof security fence protects the awe-inspiring frocks by the Shkank design duo. Think Joan Crawford on acid — ultra-slinky figure-fitting gowns, faux monkey-fur bolero jackets, and skin-tight catsuits in moire fabrics with names like "liquid hologram." The store's red-glitter floor and swinging chandeliers perfectly match the futuristic glam fashions available here exclusively. Shoulder pads live! Closed Sunday.

FASHION — VINTAGE CLOTHING

34 WAYNE'S GREAT USED BOOTS AND CLOTHING
481-1/2 Church, 924-4545

Housed in a converted alleyway between two buildings, Wayne's has one of the best selections of clone wear in the city. Under its translucent ceiling, you'll find used patent-leather cop boots, Doc Martens, and riding boots, as well as flight jackets, plaid lumberjack shirts, Levi's 501 jeans, and kilts. And for anyone attempting the Monica Lewinsky look, Wayne's got a basketful of berets and baseball caps. Closed Monday.

FASHION — LEATHER

21 BODY LEATHER
508 Church, 924-2639

Originally located in the Toolbox — and still operating a stall at the Barn — Body Leather is Canada's oldest gay-owned leather store. From fetish to fashion, Body Leather carries everything from chaps, jackets, and jocks, to custom-fit harnesses and other toys for boys.

74 NORTHBOUND LEATHER
586 Yonge, 924-5018

Now that fetish gear has gone mainstream, Northbound's low-profile rear entrance on St. Nicholas Street isn't used much anymore. Its Yonge Street location attracts a more mainstream kinky group than its counterpart on Church. Here, the emphasis is on shiny PVC naughty-nurse outfits and French-maid get-ups. In the back, find plastic-wrapped magazines

BOYSTOWN

such as *Skin Two*, *Goddess*, and *Taste of Latex*, and a $5 bargain bin.

FOOD

35 CUMBRAE
481 Church, 923-5600

Foodies flock to what many consider Toronto's choicest butcher. Along with such unusual meats as ostrich, venison, and buffalo, the shop also carries Ace Bakery's fabulous breads. Those looking to impress dinner guests need only look as far as Cumbrae's display cases of prepared foods — quiche, lasagna, garlic mashed potatoes, and pre-fab appetizers like bruschetta moderna and Bombay chicken salad.

38 REITHER'S FINE FOODS
530 Church, 961-3892

This German deli's lunch counter comes with a stern warning: "15 minute time limit." Regulars know that a quick bite can be easily and inexpensively assembled from the contents of the display cases — whole BBQ chickens, veggie samosas, pickled herring. As well as stocking bulk jellybeans and Pita Break's great flatbreads, they also carry *Stern* magazine. Of course.

HEALTH AND BEAUTY

48 THE BODY SHOP
71 Wellesley East, 323-1878

See listing page 30.

29 PLANET EARTH
473 Church, 929-2007

See listing page 196.

LIQUOR AND WINE STORES

65 LCBO
345 Bloor East, 923-9054

Monday to Wednesday 9:30 a.m. to 6 p.m.
Thursday and Friday 9:30 a.m. to 9 p.m.
Saturday 9:30 a.m. to 6 p.m.
Closed Sunday and holidays.

76 LCBO
545 Yonge, 923-8498

Monday to Wednesday 9:30 a.m. to 6 p.m.
Thursday to Saturday 9:30 a.m. to 9 p.m.
Sunday 11 a.m. to 6 p.m.
Closed holidays.

NATURAL REMEDIES

16 OTTWAY HERBALIST
453 Church, 967-9222

See listing page 197.

15 SUPPLEMENTS PLUS
451 Church, 962-8269

PET SUPPLIES

62 VILLAGE PET FOODS
557 Church, 413-1928

Overflowing with some of Church Street's perviest kinky gear, this shop brazenly displays chain leashes, leather harnesses, and studded dog collars, as well as velvet-covered cat chokers, gerbil exercise balls, and . . . wait a minute, this is a pet store!

SEX

77 BARBWIRE XXX THEATRE
543 Yonge, 934-1359

Open till 4 a.m. to those over the age of 18, Barbwire is a sex-toy, stroke-book, all-male-porn-video shop with private "viewing" booths.

THE BARRACKS
56 Widmer, 593-0499

See listing page 54.

3 THE BIJOU
64 Gerrard East, 971-9985

Situated at the end of an alleyway is the Bijou, Canada's only porno bar. Scattered throughout several catacomb-like lounges, TV monitors show hard-core flicks to patrons guzzling cheap (for Boystown) shots and beer chasers. Even more action takes place offscreen than on.

16 steps at door, washrooms on same floor. Fully
licensed.

THE CELLAR
78 Wellesley East, 944-3779

Oops. Excuse me. Sorry . . . boy, is this place dark!
The lighting in the Cellar — a bathhouse marked
only by an unmarked black door next to Pizza Pizza
— is virtually nonexistent, and the clientele likes
it that way. A maze of black rooms, this subterranean sex grotto is perfect for those who don't
like to be recognized. Not that anyone could be,
mind you.

CLUB TORONTO
231 Mutual, 977-4629

Part of the international Club chain, the Toronto
outlet is more like a health club than an oasis for
sex. The compulsory $45 annual membership —
which includes a free first-time visit — presum-
ably keeps out the riff-raff. Facilities include a
fully equipped workout room, whirlpool, and
sauna, as well as a swimming pool. Half-price
specials on Mondays and Tuesdays.

OAK LEAF STEAM BATHS
216 Bathurst, 603-3434

See listing page 68.

REMINGTON'S
379 Yonge, 977-2160

A little south of the gay village is Remington's, a
seven-days-a-week male-strip club in the middle
of Yonge Street's decidedly hetero sleaze zone.
With almost as many celebrities off-stage as on
— drag chanteuse extraordinaire Bitch Diva
waits tables between belting out torch songs on
stage — Remington's and its Men of Steel
dancers create an atmosphere that's a lot less
uptight than the surrounding straight burlesque
clubs. Fridays, the club hosts Virgin Night — the
dancers, not the audience.

Barrier-free. Fully licensed.

SPA EXCESS
105 Carlton, 260-2363

The only thing shocking about Spa Excess,
Toronto's newest bathhouse, is its shocking pink
lockers — that, and the fact that the motorcycle
in one of the fantasy rooms is a Honda. Four floors

PASSAGE BODY PIERCING
473 Church, 929-7330

Passage has a reputation throughout the city as
being one of the Toronto's leading practitioners
of body arts — tattooing, body piercing, scarification, branding, and temporary henna body
painting. With a staff comprising some of the
most respected names in the field, Passage is
an unusually friendly space with the ambience
of a dentist's office. A very hip and happening
dentist, of course.

of squeaky-clean frolicking, the Spa features a
satellite-TV lounge and a snack bar. The fourth-
floor Cell Block — they call it a "leather Disney-
land" — houses a dungeon, bunkroom, and the
aforementioned wimpy motorcycle.

Fully licensed. Patio.

THE SPA ON MAITLAND
66 Maitland, 925-1571

At over 18,000 square feet, this spa is Toronto's
largest. Comprising the second floor of a low-rise
commercial building, the facility houses a steam
room, sauna, and fully licensed video lounge
showing "group film festivals of an adult nature."
We should hope so. Pool tables and pinball machines, as well.

Fully licensed.

ST. MARC SPA
543 Yonge, 927-0210

St. Marc Spa — part of a Quebec chain of bath-
houses — is a utilitarian space complete with
single and double rooms. As well as a steam
room, a jacuzzi, a tanning bed, and a porn-video
lounge, there's a "vending machine."

THE TOOLBOX
508 Eastern, 466-8616

See listing page 214.

TATTOOS AND PIERCINGS

PASSAGE BODY PIERCING
473 Church, 929-7330

See Hot Spot this page.

VIDEO

47 **NEW RELEASE VIDEO**
489 Church, 966-9815

As you descend the stairway that leads to this video-porn arcade, you're met by the smell of the bleach that's used to hose down the private viewing booths. Yuck! Most of the titles for sale in this blank-walled basement are male-male action, but there are a few lesbian flicks as well. Most tapes come minus their official packaging but are priced as low as $6.99. A few used magazines and videos for rent, as well.

39 **7-24**
501A Church, 924-0724

Though not open around the clock as its name suggests, this comprehensive video store does stay open most nights till 4 a.m. As well as Hollywood blockbusters and indie features and documentaries, the shop has the largest selection of lesbian and gay titles for rent in the city.

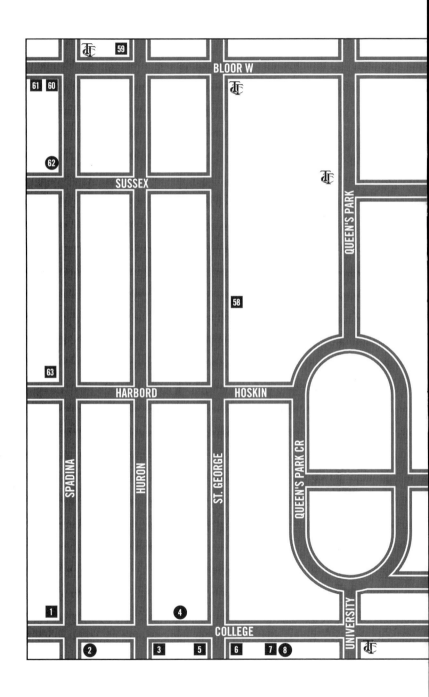

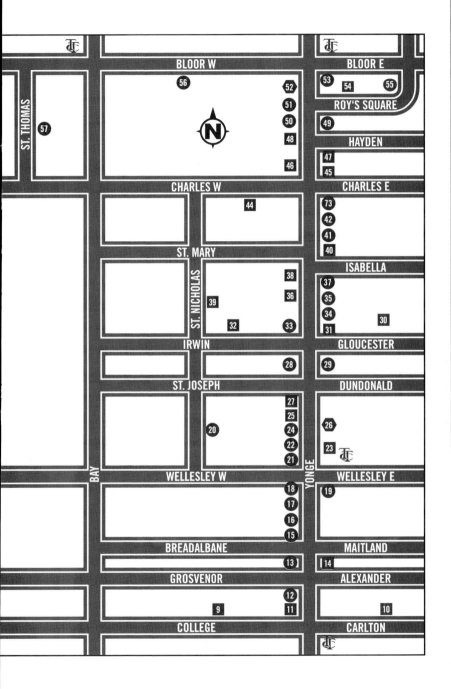

U OF T

The streets surrounding the University of Toronto — U of T to locals — reflect the student life. College Street is lined with copy shops and beer halls, Yonge Street with dollar stores and beer halls, and Bloor West with cheap restaurants and, well, beer halls.

FOOD & DINING

RESTAURANTS

60 THE BLUE CELLAR ROOM
469 Bloor West, 921-6269

Down a long, cavernous hallway carpeted in well-worn blue shag, the Cellar awaits. This leftover from the '50s features an ancient jukebox and a selection of schnitzels and strudels that, while not exactly cordon bleu, fill the starving students who flock here. Cheap beer, checkered tablecloths, and dim blue lighting.

Barrier-free. Fully licensed. $$

32 ETHIOPIAN HOUSE
4 Irwin, 923-5438

See Hot Spot page 151.

48 FORKCHOPS
730 Yonge, 964-8410

You have to use your noodle at Forkchops, an Asian eatery where customers build their own dinners from a list of basic ingredients. Broth? Tokyo bonito, Peking chicken, Bangkok beef, or vegetarian miso-shiitake. Noodles? Ramen, udon, soba, or rice vermicelli. Toppings? Beef, chicken, or tofu, all with Chinese greens. For a casual spot, Forkchops is actually rather elegant.

Barrier-free. Fully licensed, smoke-free. $$

Other locations:
1440 Yonge (see page 223)
2311 Yonge (see page 223)

47 THE GREEN MANGO
707 Yonge, 928-0021

This Thai takeout joint consistently wins NOW's Readers' Poll in the fast-food category. Well,

THE BRUNSWICK HOUSE: Every first-year university student's initiation into academe.

maybe not that fast. At lunchtime, lineups snake out the front door, and getting one of the few tables is next to impossible. But the queue moves quickly, and soon you'll be brown-bagging it to one of the nearby parks or malls. Mostly noodle dishes with fiery toppings — many veggie-friendly — combined with cooling salads and shakes make a great nosh at any time of the day.

Barrier-free. Unlicensed, smoke-free. $

Other locations:
219 Yonge (see page 117)
3006 Bloor West (see page 229).

36 INDONESIA
678 Yonge, 967-0697

The cooking of Indonesia — which incorporates the fare of the Spice Islands — also assimilates the cuisines of neighbouring Southeast Asian lands. Fiery Thai chilies, Chinese noodles, and colonial Dutch influences combine to create a cuisine that's sometimes subtle and always tasty. This humble eatery won't win design awards, but who cares when what's on the plate is so engaging? Highlights include tofu stuffed with minced spice-spiked shrimp, and sweet-soy bami goreng noodles studded with bean sprouts. Inexpensive lunch specials draw a weekday crowd.

Barrier-free, washrooms in basement. Fully licensed. $$

39 MATIGNON
51 St. Nicholas, 921-9226

A charming French bistro on a street slightly off the beaten track, Matignon offers prix fixe lunches and dinners in an intimate country-inn-like space. Even the simplest dinner sounds refined when labeled potage du jour, salade de saison, et terrine du chef. Expect such traditional fare as mussels marinière, steak et frites, and tiger shrimp in pesto cream over spaghettini.

Six steps at door, washrooms on second floor. Fully licensed. $$

25 NICE AND NUFF
606 Yonge, 515-9289

Nice and Nuff is an unpretentious Jamaican-fast-food eatery with a great people-watching table in the front window. Walls are painted a bilious yellow, tables are covered in emerald-green vinyl, and the restaurant's front is screaming red — the

32 ETHIOPIAN HOUSE
4 Irwin, 923-5438

Some like it hot, and some like it thermo-nuclear! This fiery fare gets eaten without cutlery; just tear off pieces of the injera (unleavened bread) the spicy stews are served on and use them as scoops. Meat dishes are either raw or so overcooked they resemble a pair of Imelda Marcos's Gucci slingbacks. Your best bets are the vegetarian combos that offer some (some!) relief from the heat. Since all the portions are big enough to share, you can't find a better bargain than this down-home — if East Africa's your 'hood — eatery.

Four steps at door, washrooms on second floor. Fully licensed, smoke-free. Patio. $

colours of Jamaica's flag. Jerk chicken and pork are on sale by the pound and as dinners with all-spiced rice 'n' peas. Veggie patties, pumpkin fritters, and a tonic called Stud, too.

Barrier-free, washrooms upstairs. Fully licensed. $

30 OLYMPIC '76 PIZZA
8 Gloucester, 960-0092

Two steps at door, washrooms in basement. Fully licensed. Patio. $

11 PASTA PERFECTION
462 Yonge, 964-0929

Pasta Perfection knows how to use its noodle. Customers choose the type of pasta they'd like — penne, fettucine, linguine, fusilli, or whole-wheat spaghetti — then select from a number of low-fat Cal-Ital sauces to top it. As well, the kitchen prepares internationally influenced dishes like Mexican-style meatless lasagne and Thai-twisted lemon-grass peanut-chicken salad. Marvellous takeout, too.

Fully licensed, smoke-free. $

45 SPRING ROLLS
687 Yonge, 972-7655

Just what Yonge Street needs — another noodle house. But Spring Rolls is different from its competitors. Instead of being in grungy digs, this Thai-meets-Szechwan-meets-Vietnamese eatery is remarkably stylish for the neighbourhood. The style of the room — exposed-brick walls decorated

HART HOUSE: Hitting the books at U of T.

with colourful prints, and copper-coloured tables and moulded-plywood chairs — evokes that magazine that starts with a W and ends with an asterisk. Particularly good, the pho soups here — though pricier than on Spadina — have far superior ingredients than those cooked on the avenue.

One step at door, washrooms upstairs. Fully licensed. $$

CAFES AND COFFEE HOUSES

40 **KILO**
601 Yonge, 920-6288

Toronto's only outlet of a chain of popular Montreal cafés, Kilo is a pair of bright, high-ceilinged, mosaic-tiled rooms that overlook Yonge Street's constant cavalcade of crazies. Whether you're here for a quick cuppa java, or for a lingering lunch, Kilo's sandwich, salad, and croque — that's Monsieur to you — menu will fill the bill.

Barrier-free, washrooms in basement. Unlicensed. Patio.

58 **SECOND CUP**
105 St. George, 598-1921

See listing page 17.
Barrier-free. Unlicensed. Patio. $

7 **SECOND CUP**
179 College, 595-0244

See listing page 17.

Five steps at door, washrooms in basement. Unlicensed. Patio. $

6 **SECOND CUP**
217 College, 593-4834

See listing page 17.
Barrier-free. Unlicensed. Patio. $

10 **SECOND CUP**
30 Carlton, 593-0058

See listing page 17.

Nine steps at door, washrooms on same floor. Unlicensed. Patio. $

46 **SECOND CUP**
730 Yonge, 923-6866

See listing page 17.

Barrier-free, washrooms upstairs. Unlicensed. Patio. $

27 **7 WEST**
7 Charles West, 928-9041

See Hot Spot page 153.

28 **TIMOTHY'S**
618 Yonge, 929-1432

Barrier-free, washrooms in basement. Unlicensed. Patio. $

DELIS AND DINERS

38 **BROTHERS**
698 Yonge, 924-5084

Run, oddly enough, by two very friendly brothers, their namesake lunch counter serves timeless greasy-spoon grub. Seat yourself in one of the drab olive-vinyl booths and savour immemorial fare like liver and onions — gravy on the fries? — or chicken-salad sandwiches on toasted brown. Those on a budget can take out the Brothers' special salads — combos of potato salad, coleslaw, and dill pickles — that come with so many slices of pastrami, Montreal smoked meat, and cheddar cheese, that, with the addition of a dozen kaisers, starving students can feast for a week. Closed Sunday.

Barrier-free, washrooms in basement. Fully
licensed. $

9 FRAN'S
20 College, 923-9867

An institution on Toronto's dining scene since the
1940s, Fran's hasn't closed once since the day it
opened — it operates round the clock every day of
the year. The menu has changed only marginally
since WWII, too — it still features the retro Fran-
burger, and iceberg-lettuce salad topped with
founder Fran Deck's raspberry dressing. Popular
in the middle of the night with bleary-eyed club
kids, Fran's slightly updated menu offers veggie
burgers and wraps alongside more traditional
dishes like macaroni and cheese.

One step at door, washrooms in basement. Fully
licensed. $$

Other locations:
21 St. Clair West (see page 228)
45 Eglinton East (see page 228)

JUICE BARS

14 PAPAYA HUT
513A Yonge, 960-0821

Ponce De León — ask your parents — once said
that papaya is the golden tree of life. He'd have
loved Papaya Hut — a narrow luncheonette de-
voted to healthy living. As well as freshly pulped
papaya and mango juices, the Hut serves such
nutritious vegetarian dishes as veggie lasagna,
meatless chili, and sugar- and dairy-free carrot
cake. The campy space is decked out with fake
grass, phony palm leaves, and signs painted with
motivational slogans.

Barrier-free. Unlicensed, smoke-free.

Other location:
228 Yonge (see page 118)

TAKEOUT

54 BIRYANI HOUSE
6 Roy's Square, 927-9340

A meal in itself, a biryani is an Indian casserole of
yellow-tinted rice mixed with curried meat or veg
and topped with hard-boiled-egg quarters,
chopped coriander, and sultanas. The House's
version is quite good — and better still, only
$4.95 at lunchtime. Even more economic, its veg-

44 7 WEST
7 Charles West, 928-9041

Just off Yonge's main drag, this three-storey
converted Victorian house has several incar-
nations: a bright and cheerful lunch stop, a
more formal dining room complete with fire-
place and doors that lead to the street-side
terrace, and a late-night club-kid refuelling
pit stop. It's all very dark and subdued — ex-
cept at 5 in the morning, when the pasta,
panini, and insalata menu served in the top
floor café is more than passable, considering
the hour.

Five steps at door, washrooms in basement.
Fully licensed. Patio. $$

etarian thali lunch special — two veggie curries,
basmati rice, raita, salad, and pappadum — will
gladden the frugal since it's only $4.25. Although
technically a fast-food eatery, service can be
snail-paced but the food is worth the wait. Closed
Sunday.

Three steps at door, no washrooms. Unlicensed,
smoke-free. $

63 CORA PIZZA
656A Spadina, 922-1188

The corner of Harbord and Spadina streets has
several pizza parlours, but the best by far is Cora.
Modestly decorated, the focus is on slices, the
tastiest of which is the Texas — spicy ground
beef, mushrooms, and mozzarella on an old-
school thick crust.

One step at door, no washrooms. Unlicensed,
smoke-free. $

1 MASSIMO
302 College, 967-0527

Long a favourite with pizza fiends, Massimo
bakes a trad pie with standard toppings — you'll
find no smoked salmon or Brie here. Indoors, this
pizzeria resembles a '50s takeout joint, but the
patio is always crowded late into the night in
summer.

Barrier-free, washrooms in basement. Unlicensed.
Patio. $

Other locations:
504 Queen West (see page 14)
2459 Yonge (see page 226)

23 PITA BREAK
565 Yonge, 968-1032

A falafel's a falafel, right? A coupla chickpea hockey pucks surrounded by iceberg lettuce and encased in a plain pita wrapper, with some hot sauce to make things interesting if you're lucky. Not here. For starters, they bake the flatbread themselves, and it's twice as thick as usual and comes in flavours like pesto, black olive, jalapeño pepper, organic spelt, and pumpernickel — there's even a breakfast raisin-and-cinnamon pita. They're stuffed with superb chickpea patties and topped with an almost-coleslaw of red cabbage. After finishing one of these fabulous falafels, you'll never feel awful about them again. Closed Sunday.

Barrier-free, washrooms in basement. Unlicensed, smoke-free. $

3 THE PITA PIT
235 College, 586-0202

See listing page 42.

Barrier-free, washrooms in basement. Unlicensed. $

BARS

61 THE BRUNSWICK HOUSE
481 Bloor West, 964-2242

Animal House, more like it. This perennially popular beer hall is a university student valhalla. Every Thursday through Saturday evening, hundreds of drunken collegians sit in the rear space at long, parallel benches and tables and bellow along with — or jeer at — septuagenarian chanteuse Irene. This silver-haired cheerleader likes it rowdy — she's been taking — and leading — the abuse for over 20 years!

Three steps at door, washrooms in basement.

40 THE DUKE OF GLOUCESTER
649 Yonge, 961-9704

Dark and smoky, the Duke looks almost exactly like the Rover's Return pub from TV's *Coronation Street* — leaded glass, mahogany panelling, and red-velvet-lined booths. Although the decor screams ye olde pubbe, the Duke's CD jukebox features the latest top-of-the-chart Britpop singles from the likes of Oasis, Blur, and Pulp. Sports fans compete at several dartboards while armchair athletes cheer on UK soccer matches piped

in by satellite TV.

20 steps at door, washrooms downstairs.

5 EIN STEIN
229 College, 597-8346

To the soothing sounds of AC/DC on the CD jukebox, students shoot pool and play pinball and foosball while watching sports on the massive projector TV at this subterranean beer hall, which is furnished with kitchen tables and chairs. Customers spend their government loans on half-price all-day dinners or Wednesday-only $4.95 all-you-can-eat pasta pig-outs.

12 steps at door, washrooms on same floor. Patio.

59 THE MADISON
14 Madison, 927-1722

Taking up two three-storey Victorian homes in the south Annex, the Madison is party central for the nearby University of Toronto. A maze of interconnected rooms, the club has a Brit pub look — all red-velvet banquettes and brass draught pumps. In the basement, there's an intimate spot for quiet drinking; the first floor houses a piano bar for those who like to sing along, and the second floor holds six pool tables and two working fireplaces. The third floor is completely non-smoking. During summer, the Mad's west-facing double-decker patio is such a hot spot that lineups snake down the alleyway and out front to the street. And no Rollerblades!

Eight steps at door, washrooms on same floor. Patio.

ENTERTAINMENT 🎫 ADMIT ONE

LIVE MUSIC

26 VOX CENTRAL
580 Yonge, 367-1928

Vox Central is the Yonge Street satellite of downtown's rock 'n' roll restaurant Vox. Located in the home of the late Gasworks — the heavy-metal nightspot immortalized in Mike Myers' *Wayne's World* — Central features retro Brit-rock combos Thursdays to Saturdays. Complementing the beat groups, blow-ups of '60s English pop stars shot by famed photographer Barry Wentzell adorn the club's walls.

Barrier-free. Fully licensed. Patio. $$

CINEMAS — FIRST RUN

52 THE UPTOWN
764 Yonge, 922-6361

SHOPPING

ART SUPPLIES

12 CURRY'S
490 Yonge, 967-6666

Curry's is one of Toronto's oldest artists'-supply depots. Offering more than just paint, canvas, and easels, Curry's also carries inexpensive do-it-yourself framing kits, and a wide range of pens and papers. Airbrush aficionados will want to check out *Airbrush Action*, a magazine dedicated to custom car painting and advanced graffiti-writing. Closed Sunday.

Other location:
344 Queen West (see page 21)

BEER STORES

49 THE BEER STORE
709 Yonge, 323-9213

Monday to Wednesday 10 a.m. to 8 p.m.
Thursday and Friday 10 a.m. to 9 p.m.
Saturday 9:30 a.m. to 9 p.m.
Sunday 11 a.m. to 6 p.m.
Closed holidays.

Barrier-free.

62 THE BEER STORE
720 Spadina, 323-0566

Monday to Wednesday 10 a.m. to 8 p.m.
Thursday and Friday 10 a.m. to 9 p.m.
Saturday 9:30 a.m. to 9 p.m.
Sunday 11 a.m. to 6 p.m.
Closed holidays.

BOOKS AND MAGAZINES — NEW

22 BAKKA
598 Yonge, 963-9993

Now located on Yonge Street, this former Queen

2 SAL'S TATTOO & BARBER SHOP
429 Spadina, 593-4161

An anachronism on a street of misfits, Sal's is a retro-looking barber shop. There's a great old-fashioned barber's chair where haircuts are undertaken, and a small screened-off area at the back where tattoos are applied. On the walls hang sample tattoos drawn in the '50s by Sailor Jerry, Amsterdam's most famous tattoo artist — wonderfully ornate anchors, hearts with daggers, and skulls 'n' crossbones that the staff here can reproduce. Very cool.

West denizen sells new and used hardcover and paperback speculative fiction as well as magazines like *Locus, Heavy Metal*, and *Starburst*, the official Trekkie bible.

57 THEATREBOOKS
11 St. Thomas, 922-7175

Not just theatrical titles — scripts, criticism, technique manuals — but also books about film, television, and other media.

4 UNIVERSITY OF TORONTO BOOKSTORE
214 College, 978-7900

Textbooks, titles from the University of Toronto Press, trade books, and general press remainders. Regularly scheduled reading and lecture series.

COMICBOOKS AND 'ZINES

17 GREY REGION
550 Yonge, 975-1718

Comic-book collectors who have to have the latest American issue of their consuming passion the moment it's available know about Grey Region, a shop that sells US titles at US cover prices the first week they're released. As well, this crowded store with the giant gumball machine chained to the front door carries Pez dispensers, die-cast toy cars, and model airplanes. If you have any G.I. Joes or Transformers you want to unload, Grey Region will pay you cash for them.

15 1,000,000 COMIX
530 Yonge, 934-1615

We'll take their word for it — if there aren't a million, then there're sure a lot of 'em. As well as the latest comic titles and a wide range of used ones, this comprehensive shop carries *Star Wars* and *Star Trek* action figures, Beanie Babies, and a number of Japanese anime videos.

COMPUTERS

㉑ MEDIASCAPE
592 Yonge, 960-8585

With Toronto's largest selection of computer gaming software, Mediascape also offers a networked gaming facility at the back of its store. There, a dozen computers with Pentium II 333 MHz processors, 17-inch monitors and 3D video cards allow gamers to challenge each other to showdowns over Dune 2000, Quake 2, and Duke Nukem 3D. Speedy Internet connection, too.

CRAFTS

(55) BRIDGEHEAD TRADING
18 Roy's Square, 975-8788

Bridgehead — the trading arm of Oxfam — supports worldwide grassroots economic development by buying directly from co-operatives. Subsequent profits are returned to developing countries where they are used to promote social justice and self-sustaining industries. Think trade, not aid. Besides their famous organic coffee, Bridgehead sells wind-up wireless radios, Balinese xylophones, and Eco jackets made from recycled plastic pop bottles.

DRUGS

㊸ TORONTO HEMP COMPANY
667 Yonge, 923-3556

Although it's only one flight above the street, this company has a high profile. As well as your basic stoner paraphernalia — papers, bongs, blacklight posters — the store also carries do-it-yourself manuals like the *Marijuana Grower's Guide, Mushroom Cultivator* and back issues of *High Times* magazine. Check out the line of clothing made from hemp — jeans and baseball caps. In need of a belt? Try holding up your pants with some good old hemp hemp.

DISCOUNT STORES

⑬ HOLCO SALVAGE SALES
522 Yonge, 922-5842

THE MADISON: Four floors of darts, draught, and engineering students.

FASHION — NEW CLOTHING

35 ROCK WORLD
627 Yonge, 944-0714

In the '60s, Yonge Street was lined with stoner emporia where heads could score their essential black-light posters and chillums. They still can 30 years later at Rock Variety, a shop that carries hippie necessities. As well, they carry a wide range of official band T-shirts — from Metallica and the Misfits to fabulous Sex Pistols *Never Mind the Bollocks* Ts.

FASHION — VINTAGE CLOTHING

18 PLANET AID
554 Yonge, 921-6937

A non-profit organization founded to help people in need throughout the Third World, Planet Aid collects and sells used clothes from its Yonge Street store. A percentage of the money raised goes to service groups such as Hope Zambia, who help educate that country's population — 40% of whom are HIV-positive — about the spread of AIDS. Not only do customers help a good cause, but they can find some great stuff on the racks of donated clothing.

37 SOUTH PACIFIC
637 Yonge, 925-6464

8 TRIBAL RHYTHM
171B College, 595-5505
See listing page 29.

FASHION — SHOES

51 TWINKLE TOES
760 Yonge, 960-3693
See listing page 29.

HEALTH AND BEAUTY

42 LUSH
663 Yonge, 924-5874
See listing page 30.

HIKING AND BACKPACKING

41 CENTRAL SURPLUS
657 Yonge, 924-5200

33 MONSTER RECORDS
664 Yonge, 975-1829

Members of the KISS Army — this place is for you! Not only does this collector's record shop sell official KISS merchandise — Ace Frehley inaction figures, scary Gene Simmons face masks — it also has a KISS pinball machine. That works. Others will want to check out the shelves full of used rock tomes and back copies of *Rolling Stone*, *Details* and *Guitar Player*. Attention fogies — lots of 78s, too.

LIQUOR AND WINE STORES

19 LCBO
545 Yonge, 923-8498

Monday to Wednesday 9:30 a.m. to 6 p.m.
Thursday to Saturday 9:30 a.m. to 9 p.m.
Sunday 11 a.m. to 6 p.m.
Closed holidays.

56 LCBO
55 Bloor West, 925-5266

Monday to Friday 9:30 a.m. to 9:30 p.m.
Saturday 9:30 a.m. to 6 p.m.
Sunday 11 a.m. to 5 p.m.
Closed holidays.

MEMORABILIA

28 HOLLYWOOD RENAISSANCE
630 Yonge, 967-4598

Stacked with movie posters, lobby cards, and photo stills, Hollywood has Toronto's largest selection of movie memorabilia. If you're looking for original copies of TV- and film-shooting scripts, official *Absolutely Fabulous* T-shirts or a billboard-sized poster of your favourite chop-socky Hong Kong action flick, chances are this movie-lover's paradise has it.

33 MONSTER RECORDS
664 Yonge, 975-1829
See Hot Spot this page.

MUSIC— CDS, RECORDS & TAPES

50 CD REPLAY
762 Yonge, 513-1144
See listing page 172.

(29) DISC-COUNTS
599 Yonge, 925-9006

Alongside its very limited selection of current CDs, Disc-Counts sells mostly used CDs and cassettes, and a few rock mags.

(53) SUNRISE
721 Yonge, 498-6601

Houses a Ticketmaster outlet.
See listing page 123.

(16) URBAN SOUND EXCHANGE
542 Yonge, 967-3866

SKATEBOARDING

(20) SHRED CENTRAL
19 St. Nicholas, 923-9842

A rundown warehouse space packed with ramps and half-pipes, Shred Central is a skateboarder's paradise — no security guards to chase you away from the downtown skyscraper plazas, no annoying pedestrians, and no one over the age of 15. For a flat rate of $7, skaters, bladers, and BMXers get unlimited access to the graffiti-sprayed facility. And most importantly, you can come and go all day with no restrictions, dude.

TATTOOS AND PIERCINGS

(2) SAL'S TATTOO & BARBER SHOP
429 Spadina, 593-4161

See Hot Spot page 155.

(24) WAY COOL TATTOOS
604 Yonge, 929-2285

See listing page 68.

SLEEMAN
All Natural Ales & Lagers

Great food!
Vegetarian-
friendly!
Smoke-free
dining

Cream of Vegetable Soup
Mushroom, Zucchini & Sweet pepper Soup
Mussels Marinara
Californian Green Salad
Sweet Potato, cheddar, Spinach Pie
Grilled Duck on Multi Grain
Grilled chicken Breast
Create Your Own Pasta
Penne Or Fettucini
Tomato, Rose or Basil Pesto
Add, Veggie, chicken, or Salmon

ELIZABETH

By The

By The Way Café

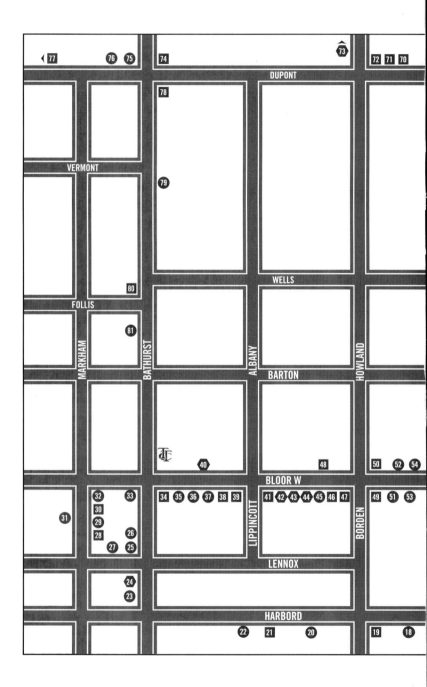

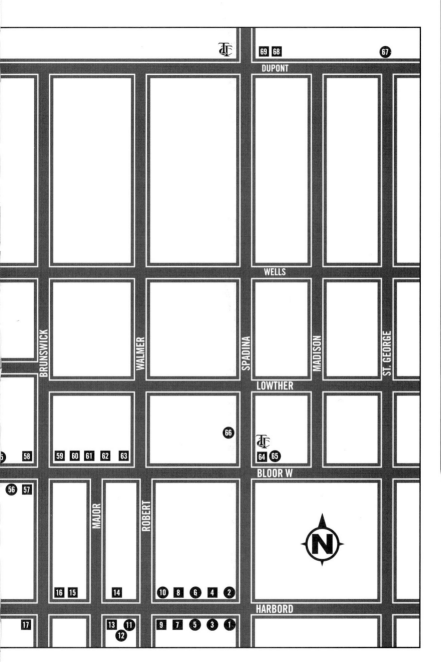

THE ANNEX

Formerly a bedroom community for students and teachers at the nearby University of Toronto, the Annex is now a mix of urban professionals and still-struggling students. From the bookstores of Harbord to the bustle of Bloor's pubs and clubs, this is a quarter that never quits.

FOOD & DINING

RESTAURANTS

78 **ANNAPURNA**
1085 Bathurst, 537-8513

Followers of Hindu meditation guru Sri Chinmoy wait on tables and cook in the kitchen of this plain-Jane vegetarian resto. Half the menu offers spice-lite dishes like noodle casserole or baked potato with mushroom gravy, but the south Indian items really kick. The Sri Lankan assortment dinner for two or more is a good introduction to Annapurna's capabilities. Closed Sunday.

One step at door, washrooms in basement. Unlicensed, smoke-free. $

70 **BISTRO TOURNESOL**
406 Dupont, 921-7766

Southern French. Closed Sunday and Monday.

One step at door, washrooms in basement. Fully licensed, smoke-free. $$

19 **BOULEVARD CAFE**
161 Harbord, 961-7676

In gastronomic centres like New York City and London, Peruvian cuisine is the latest rage. After all, the Incas were the South American civilization that introduced peppers, tomatoes, and potatoes to the rest of the world. Ahead of everyone else as usual, Toronto has been home to the Boulevard Café, a cantina that serves Peruvian fare, since

the early '80s. Lots of grilled seafood and searing hot sauces set the taste buds on fire. Sunday brunch features Eggs Boulevard — spicy scrambled eggs, sausage, and black turtle beans on three-grain toast.

One step at door, washrooms on same floor. Fully licensed. Patio. $$

60 **CEDAR'S LEBANESE CUISINE**
394 Bloor West, 923-3277

Behind its glass-block facade, Cedar's presents Middle Eastern mezes and mains in a semi-formal room that resembles a Greek taverna. Lebanese fries dusted in ground coriander, lamb-stuffed grape leaves, and falafel are just some of the more traditional dishes. Weekday lunches are all-you-can-eat affairs.

Barrier-free. Fully licensed. $$

63 **GOLDFISH**
372 Bloor West, 513-0077

See Hot Spot page 165.

72 **INDIAN RICE FACTORY**
414 Dupont, 961-3472

Consistently voted NOW readers' favourite Indian restaurant, the Factory's looks haven't changed since it opened in the late '70s — brown corduroy banquettes and macramé wall hangings. Ignore the decor and focus on plates piled high with fiery curries, puffy pakoras, and terrific tandoori chicken. There's much here for vegetarian palates, too. Cool down the spice-fire with Kingfisher beer.

One step at door, washrooms on same floor. Fully licensed. $$

14 **KENSINGTON KITCHEN**
124 Harbord, 961-3404

Mediterranean.

Two steps at door, washrooms in basement. Fully licensed. Patio. $$

7 **LATITUDE**
89 Harbord, 928-0926

One of the newest additions on a street famed for its bookstores, Latitude advertises itself as a wine bar — bottles of plonk are piled high behind the counter. The room has a fresh ambience that matches the menu's contemporary, clean flavours

HONEST ED'S: A little bit of Las Vegas lights up the corner of Bathurst and Bloor.

— Latin-with-attitude, hence Latitude. Green-and ripe-mango salad, avocados stuffed with vine-ripened tomatoes, grill-pressed Cubano sandwiches, and pumpkin-seed-encrusted free-range chicken breast are typical of their fusion-without-confusion fare.

Three steps at door, washrooms in basement. Fully licensed. Patio. $$

9 **MESSIS**
97 Harbord, 920-2186

Harbord is home to a wide range of eateries, from those dishing up cheap student eats to those offering haute cuisine in chi-chi surroundings. Messis is on the pricey end of the scale but delivers the gourmet goods. Begin with roasted Vidalia onion stuffed with chèvre and toasted walnuts, then tuck into parmesan-crusted rack of lamb over polenta with eggplant caponata. Think of Messis as a gastronomic breeding ground — some of the city's hottest new chefs got their start here.

One step at door, washrooms in basement. Fully licensed. Patio. $$$

59 **NATARAJ**
394 Bloor West, 928-2925

Perennially popular, this upscale Indian eatery

doesn't get carried away with the firepower. A large crowd of U of T students and elders in Birkenstocks means there's usually a wait for a table. But the whole head of yogurt-marinated cauliflower fired in a tandoor oven is worth the delay, as is just about everything else, including tandoori chicken, shrimp, and lamb. Vegetarian curries tend to be full of frozen vegetables — shame! — but the bhindi bhaji of fresh okra and tomato is the real thing. The lunchtime $7.95 all-you-can-eat buffet has limited offerings but still satisfies.

One step at door, washrooms on same floor. Fully licensed. $$

13 **OLIVE & LEMON**
119 Harbord, 923-3188

Chef Giancarlo Carnevale — the former owner of pricey Giancarlo Trattoria and the less formal College Street Bar — gets even more laid-back at this relaxed neighbourhood bistro. Carnevale keeps the menu Sicilian: grilled fish and veggies with — what else? — olive oil and lemon squeezes. A zoo since day one, this two-room wonder isn't for those in a hurry. Reservations recommended. Closed Monday.

One step at door, washrooms in basement. Fully licensed. $$

PIZZA GIGI: Old-school Neapolitan pies every day till 4 a.m.

62 **SERRA**
378 Bloor West, 922-6999

Sleekly chic with its dark mahogany tables and bar, this diminutive Italian café is a great place to meet for a light lunch or a sizable supper. The open kitchen turns out such dishes as wine-steamed mussels, warm-goat-cheese salad, and a smoked-salmon sandwich slathered in mascarpone. Designer pizzas from a wood-burning oven are topped with such gourmet fare as tiger shrimp, leeks, snow peas, and feta cheese.

Barrier-free, washrooms in basement. Fully licensed, smoke-free. $$

28 **SOUTHERN ACCENT**
595 Markham, 536-3211

Except for in the dreaded dead of winter, diners can eat outdoors on a covered, heated patio at this New Orleans–style eatery. Fanciful fare includes a salade niçoise à la Creole, vodka-splashed oysters on the half-shell, and blackened rack of lamb. Lagniappe is the in-house boutique that sells Southern Accent's own mugs, hot sauces, and official cookbook.

Three steps at door, washrooms in basement.

Fully licensed. Patio. $$$

4 **SPLENDIDO**
88 Harbord, 929-7788

In the '80s, the upwardly mobile flaunted their newfound riches through conspicuous consumption. The big-buck restaurants like Centro and North 44 still attract the power elite, as does the splendiferous Splendido. Theatrically dressed tables draw the air-kiss set to a menu that features such Cal-Ital appetizers as foie gras terrine that approaches $17, and mains like roasted leg of venison that tops the menu at $32. You want fries with that, hon? Five bucks extra. Closed Sunday.

Barrier-free. Fully licensed. $$$

30 **TRUE GRITS**
603 Markham, 536-8383

A multi-level soul-food restaurant from the folks responsible for Southern Accent, this funky N'Awlins-bordello-esque eatery is more down-home and less pricey than its soul sister down the street. Cajun cookin' is the theme here: meaty pork ribs basted with bourbon, southern-fried chicken, jambalaya. Side dishes include grits (surprise!), candied yams, and garlic mashed potatoes. For dessert, pecan pie or boozy bread pudding. Tapas — hush puppies, black-eyed-pea fritters — are served till 2 a.m. closing. Closed Sunday and Monday.

Four steps at door, washrooms on second floor. Fully licensed. Patio. $$

48 ZIZI TRATTORIA
456 Bloor West, 533-5117

Except for the plastic grapes, everything here sings traditional trattoria. No fusion food, no wood-fired ovens — just straight-ahead Italian fare cooked with flair and finesse. Start with grilled-radicchio salad, then follow with vodka penne or champagne risotto. There's cognac-nipped shrimp, grilled rack of lamb, and Atlantic salmon, too.

One step at door, washrooms upstairs. Fully licensed. $$

CAFES AND COFFEE HOUSES

58 BY THE WAY
400 Bloor West, 967-4295

Its wonky mural and its summer patio at a prime people-watching intersection make this sunny café a popular spot. Featuring a mix of Mediterranean-style starters and veggie-friendly Thai mains, By the Way is more of a neighbourhood haunt than a chic chow place and is often filled mid-afternoon by parents with strollers in tow. Weekend brunch fare includes Eggs Dilemma — poached with dill — as well as veggie Tex-Mex selections.

Barrier-free, washrooms in basement. Fully licensed, smoke-free. Patio. $$

47 DOONEY'S
511 Bloor West, 536-3293

One step at door, washrooms in basement. Beer and wine. Patio. $$

77 FAEMA
672 Dupont, 535-1555

This cavernous café with the ambiance of a used-car showroom crossed with the Sistine Chapel (there's a mini reproduction of Michaelangelo's famous painting hovering behind the bar) brews up Faema's own brand of beans on Faema's namesake espresso machines. Biscotti, sandwiches, gelato, and free newspapers to peruse, too.

Barrier-free. Unlicensed, smoke-free. $

63 GOLDFISH
372 Bloor West, 513-0077

Despite looking like the departure room of Stockholm International Airport, this cool contemporary cantina has surprisingly warm service and a menu that intrigues. Unusual culinary combos such as beet ravioli, cranberries, and curried cream sauce shouldn't work, but do. Duck appears in prosciutto-thin slices as an appetizer, and as shredded confit on a thin-crust pizza with goat cheese. This streamlined bistro brings downtown chic to the Annex, but unlike Queen West, Goldfish is an attitude-free zone. Reservations are essential, especially for weekend brunch.

Barrier-free, washrooms in basement. Fully licensed. $$

57 FUTURE BAKERY
483 Bloor West, 922-5875

Grab a plastic cafeteria tray and join the queue of budget-minded students and Annex residents for Eastern European–style soup and cabbage rolls. Once a family-run business, this franchise has begun to raise prices and institutionalize the food. Its prolonged popularity is due to the fact that you can order a coffee and a blintz, sit in the window, and people-watch for hours on end.

One step at door, washrooms in basement. Fully licensed. Patio. $

Other location:
793 Queen West (see page 59)
2199 Bloor West (see page 229)

80 GRAPEFRUIT MOON
968 Bathurst, 534-9056

Behind its rustic facade, this charming neighbourhood noshery offers a smoke-free hangout every day till 8 p.m. for locals grabbing a quick coffee before they pick up/drop off the kids. After 8, the dinner crowd materializes for veggie chili, do-it-yourself quesadillas, and daily specials. Saturday and Sunday brunch.

One step at door, washrooms in basement. Fully licensed, smoke-free. $

38 HEY GOOD COOKING
238 Dupont, 929-9140

There's not much to look at, aside from a mural depicting regular customers, but H.G.C. serves up economical not-strictly-vegetarian dinners and snacks. After scanning the chalkboard menu and placing your order at the counter, wait for the singing staff to bring it to your table. Soups are garden fresh, and a substantial wedge of spinach-and-squash pie comes with brown rice, steamed zucchini, and a basil-dressed salad of romaine, red cabbage, and brussels sprouts (!). Impressive. Takeout mini-rotis satisfy midnight munchies.

Barrier-free. Unlicensed, smoke-free, cash only. $

34 INSOMNIA
563 Bloor West, 588-3907

"The Internet is a strange place. Don't surf alone," cautions the illuminated marquee over the entrance to this cyber-café. A row of curtained booths conceal Net-connected computer terminals where you can browse cyberspace, paying by the hour. Or watch the large-screen TV on one of several comfy couches while munching state-of-the-art pizza and panini. Tarot readings are held at midnight and live jazz and blues sets are put on occasionally. Weekend brunch.

One step at door, washrooms in basement. Fully licensed. $$

15 MOMO'S
196 Robert, 966-6671

Middle Eastern.

Three steps at door, washrooms on same floor. Fully licensed, smoke-free. Patio. $$

64 SECOND CUP
324 Bloor West, 920-7601

See listing page 17.

Barrier-free, washrooms in basement. Unlicensed. Patio. $

41 SECOND CUP
537 Bloor West, 531-7185

See listing page 17.

Barrier-free. Unlicensed. Patio. $

8 TIK TALK
96 Harbord, 964-6414

Four steps at door, washrooms in basement. Unlicensed, smoke-free. Patio. $$

DELIS AND DINERS

50 MONTREAL'S DELICATESSEN
440 Bloor West, 966-8881

This deluxe delicatessen dishes up substantial sandwiches made with Montreal smoked meat — *quel surprise!* — smoked turkey, or corned beef. Eggy chopped liver, chunky coleslaw, and crunchy dill pickles keep customers happy round the clock — Montreal's never closes.

One step at door, washrooms on same floor. Fully licensed. Patio. $$

Other location:
160 Adelaide West (see page 109)

74 VESTA LUNCH
474 Dupont, 537-4318

Narrow, washrooms in basement. Unlicensed, cash only. $

JUICE BARS

46 JUICE FOR LIFE
521 Bloor West, 531-2635

Voted best vegetarian-friendly resto by NOW readers three years in a row, this totally vegan juice bar reaches beyond dairy-free smoothies and rejuvenating elixirs. Healthy green salads, slammin' sandwiches, and noodle noshes are served to regulars who lounge at tables and take in the Bloor blur. In summer, the front opens to the street.

Barrier-free, washrooms in basement. Unlicensed. $$

Other location:
336 Queen West (see page 17)

68 JUICE IT UP
258 Dupont, 926-1200 ext. 28

One step at door, washrooms in basement. Unlicensed, smoke-free. $

TAKEOUT

17 HARBORD FISH AND CHIPS
147 Harbord, 925-2225

In a whitewashed concrete bunker on Harbord close by Central Tech high school, this vat o' fat churns out ultra-crisp halibut and haddock with sides of gargantuan fresh fries and prefab coleslaw. Oh, and packets of tartar sauce. We defy four adults to finish the prodigiously proportioned newspaper-wrapped supper described as "dinner for two." Lineups form around six, and you can always escape the intense heat from the fryers at one of their sidewalk picnic tables.

One step at door, no washrooms. Unlicensed, smoke-free, cash only. Patio. $

21 **PIZZA GIGI**
189 Harbord, 535-4444

Open till 4 a.m. every night, Gigi throws a helluva pie. Forget the pine nuts and the smoked salmon — Gigi dresses its 'za with old-school toppings like pepperoni, green pepper, and pineapple chunks. They will make a thinner contemporary crust if you insist. Pick up or home delivery.

Four steps at door, washrooms in basement. Unlicensed. $

BARS

61 **JAMES JOYCE IRISH PUB**
386 Bloor West, 324-9400

Irish pub.

Barrier-free, washrooms in basement.

49 **KILGOUR'S**
507 Bloor West, 923-7680

Sports bar.

Seven steps at door, washrooms on same floor. Patio.

39 **PAUPER'S**
539 Bloor West, 530-1331

A two-storey neighbourhood hang with a rooftop patio, there's always a party happening at Pauper's. Check out the half-price Happy Hour food menu — burgers, Buffalo chicken wings, fish and chips — as well as the regularly priced build-it-yerself pizza and fajitas. And if you like to sing along, the piano bar welcomes would-be Sinatras Wednesday through Saturday evenings.

Two steps at door, washrooms in basement. Patio.

16 **ROWERS**
150 Harbord, 961-6277

Sports bar.

Seven steps at door, washrooms on same floor.

43 **LEE'S PALACE**
529 Bloor West, 532-1598

Lee's Palace has the best sightlines of any live music venue in town. The large stage towers over a sunken mosh pit at the front, and tables ring the room on several levels. Of course, if the headliner is some starting-out superstar such as the Tragically Hip, Nirvana, Red Hot Chili Peppers, Oasis, Alanis Morrisette, or Blur, all of whom have all played here, you might not see anything except the person in front of you.
Barrier-free. Fully licensed.

ENTERTAINMENT

LIVE MUSIC

44 **525 WEST**
525 Bloor West, 537-3044

Velvet sofas and really ugly lamps make up the decor at this blooze-bar-slash-restaurant. Various bands play rockin' tunes Thursday to Saturday nights, and the kitchen stays open till 2 a.m. Offering not much beyond pub grub — almost everything is deep-fried — the menu includes zucchini sticks, onion rings, burgers, and steaks.

Barrier-free, washrooms in basement. Fully licensed.

43 **LEE'S PALACE**
529 Bloor West, 532-1598

See Hot Spot listing this page.

DANCE CLUBS

42 **DANCE CAVE**
529 Bloor West, 532-1598

Upstairs from Lee's Palace, the Dance Cave features DJs spinning '70s glam rock, '80s indie and goth golden oldies, and current alt hits for clubbers more into posing than tripping the light fantastic. Tom Cruise alert: portions of the great actor's *Cocktail* flick were shot in this aircraft-hangar-like space.

16 steps at door, washrooms on same floor. Fully licensed.

THE ANNEX

CINEMAS — REVIVAL

40 THE BLOOR
506 Bloor West, 532-6677

The flagship of the Festival chain, the Bloor is the largest of their movie theatres. Like the others, it presents double bills of recent box-office hits and critically acclaimed films, as well as special programs of documentaries, cult flicks, and classics. Midnight screenings Friday and Saturday. A $6 one-year membership, although not compulsory, reduces the admission price of $6.50 to only $3.50.

Other Festival locations:
The Capitol (see page 227)
The Fox (see page 204)
The Kingsway (see page 230)
The Music Hall (see page 193)
The Revue (see page 216)
The Royal (see page 77)

THEATRE

24 BATHURST STREET THEATRE
736 Bathurst, 533-5561

Most Annex residents are aware of the independent theatre productions and music concerts put on at this former United church. But how many know that the building, besides accommodating two performance spaces, is also home to several political groups? The church takes the revenue generated by hall rentals and uses it to help underwrite the space it provides to such subversive organizations as the Coalition for Lesbian and Gay Rights Ontario, Women and the Environment, and the Toronto Vegetarian Association.

Barrier-free.

73 TARRAGON THEATRE
30 Bridgman, 531-1827

Since the early '70s, the Tarragon has been commissioning and then presenting new works by Canadian playwrights. Once a warehouse, the building is now divided between the Main Space, with 200 seats, and the Extra Space, a 100-seat venue for more intimate performances. The Tarragon stages seven productions during its season, from September to May, and independent companies mount plays there during the summer months.

Barrier-free.

TORONTO WOMEN'S BOOKSTORE: Polemics, theory, and sex-positive information.

SHOPPING

BEER STORES

76 **THE BEER STORE**
500 Dupont, 537-4882

Monday to Thursday 10 a.m. to 10 p.m.
Friday 10 a.m. to 11 p.m.
Saturday 9:30 a.m. to 11 p.m.
Sunday 11 a.m. to 6 p.m.
Closed holidays.

BICYCLES

52 **CURBSIDE**
412 Bloor West, 920-4933

Selling top-of-the-line carbon-fibre dream machines and refurbished clunkers, this busy bike
shop has a Zefal pump chained to a parking me-
ter out front for cyclists low on air. Free! Inside,
you'll find courier bags, skateboard equipment,
in-line skates, and ice skates. They do bike and
skate rentals and skate-sharpening, as well.

BOOKS AND MAGAZINES — NEW

26 **A DIFFERENT BOOKLIST**
746 Bathurst, 538-0889

This bookstore's titles reflect works concerning
gay and lesbian, First Nations, black, and Asian
issues aimed at children and adults. Coffee
drinking and browsing encouraged. Closed Sunday.

53 **BOOK CITY**
501 Bloor West, 961-4496

This literary institution sells local and international magazines and newspapers as well as current bestsellers, perennial favourites, and remainders. Don't forget your weekly copy of NOW
from the rack out front.

Other locations:
348 Danforth (see page 194)
1950 Queen East (see page 205)

31 **DAVID MIRVISH BOOKS ON ART**
596 Markham, 531-9975

Books on art, obviously.

22 **PARENTBOOKS**
201 Harbord, 537-8334

Books for kids as well as their moms and dads.

84 **SEEKERS**
509 Bloor West, 925-1982

For those on an inner quest, this below-street-
level shop specializes in guide books to self-
knowledge. Titles on Eastern and Western philoso-
phies, mysticism, Zen, Taoism, and Sufism, as
well as good old general-interest and self-help
books are featured in this laid-back book room.
CDs and hemp products, too, man.

82 **THIRD WORLD BOOKS AND CRAFTS**
942 Bathurst, 537-8039

1 **TORONTO WOMEN'S BOOKSTORE**
73 Harbord, 922-8744

For over 25 years this feminist bookstore has provided a forum for women writing about women.
Books on sex and sexuality, abuse and healing,
and AIDS, among other topics, line the shelves of
this completely accessible community centre. A
wide selection of fiction and magazines — *Off
Our Backs, Diva, Bitch* — is for sale as well.
Where else could a video titled *Suburban Dykes*
and a self-help manual called *Total Car Care for
the Clueless* rub shoulders on the same shelf?

BOOKS AND MAGAZINES — USED

5 **ABOUT BOOKS**
83 Harbord, 975-2668

Secondhand scholarly, out-of-print, and antiquarian volumes.

2 **ATTICUS BOOKS**
84 Harbord, 922-6045

Scholarly tomes on philosophy, medieval studies,
linguistics, and science.

10 **CAVERSHAM BOOKSELLER**
98 Harbord, 944-0962

Books on psychoanalysis, psychotherapy, psychia-
try, and psychology.

11 **THE CONSTANT READER**
111 Harbord, 972-0661

New and used books for children. Closed Monday.

THE ANNEX

COMIC BOOKS AND 'ZINES

29 THE BEGUILING
601 Markham, 533-9168

Part store and part art gallery, this bookshop displays original work by 'zine illustrators. Classic reprints of *American Splendor* and *Love and Rockets* can be found next to bins loaded with current titles and Marvel and D.C. collectibles. Superhero T-shirts, exhibition posters, and a wide selection of Japanese anime, too.

25 YESTERDAY'S HEROES
742 Bathurst, 533-9800

Sure, they've got comics, but there's a lot more here for the serious collector of pop-culture ephemera. They might be mere freebies to you, but for those in the know, *X-Files, X-Men, Star Wars,* and *Star Trek* bubblegum cards are highly sought-after. Besides a couple of in-store video games, you'll find Spiderman bandannas, Spice Girls action figures, and *South Park* cuddly toys.

COMPUTERS

75 CPUSED
488 Dupont, 533-2001

They do sell brand-new systems, but CPUsed — as its name suggests — specializes in used computers. Since computer geeks usually trade in last year's models to buy the latest state-of-the-art machines, lots of bargains can be found here. Can I interest you in a laptop that was only used by a little old lady to surf the Net on Sundays? Quick repairs, and a large stock of new and slightly less new Macs to boot, to boot. Closed Sunday.

DISCOUNT STORES

33 HONEST ED'S
581 Bloor West, 537-1574

As gaudy as a Las Vegas gambling den and lit by a gazillion light bulbs, this mazy barn of a bargain bin is a great place to shop for those things you just have to have — cheap kitchenware, socks and underwear, a gilt-sprayed ceramic bust of Elvis. There's always a lineup to get in when it opens at 11 a.m., and to pay you line up again for a longer time than you took shopping. Kitschy Ed's

is worth a visit just for its wacky in-store signs such as "Only our floors are crooked."

ECOLOGICAL

55 GRASSROOTS ENVIRO PRODUCTS
408 Bloor West, 944-1993

See listing for Earthlygoods page 194.

FASHION — NEW CLOTHING

66 NATIVE CANADIAN CENTRE
16 Spadina Road, 964-9087

Besides offering cultural programs, the Native Centre sports a gift shop that sells work crafted by aboriginal artisans. You won't find any tacky tourist souvenirs here; instead, discover such beautifully produced goods as one-of-a-kind ribbon shirts, intricate beaded jewellery, and ultracomfy fur-lined leather moccasins. The rewards are twofold — you get in touch with the glory of an ancient culture, and the profits your purchases generate are plowed back into the centre's services and activities.

FASHION — VINTAGE CLOTHING

37 RAG DOLL
555 Bloor West, 530-0003

Alongside the usual used jeans, leather jackets, and Hawaiian shirts, Rag Doll breaks the '80s fashion barrier by selling puffy silver ski jackets and striped velour pullovers. Racks of hockey sweaters hang next to brand new skate gear by Adrenalin and never-used '70s roller skates — with glitter laces! — to tempt true fashion plates. Hello Kitty pencil cases and purses, too. Closed Monday.

36 VINTAGE BRIDE
555 Bloor West, 530-0025

Beautifully preserved antique wedding gowns, hats, veils, gloves, and beaded bags are displayed next to chiffon cocktail dresses and fake fun furs. Nice day for a white wedding? Closed Monday.

FOOD

12 HARBORD BAKERY
115 Harbord, 922-5767

Sure, you'll find the expected bagels, breads, and

RING MUSIC: Why yes, I do know the chords to "House of the Rising Sun."

blintzes at this bakeshop in the heart of the Harbord Street village, but there's much more for the adventurous foodie. Salvadorean empanadas, Greek spanakopita, and Pita Break's amazingly thick, flavoured flatbread. Head here for customized birthday cakes, homemade preserves, and their own bulk peanut butter as well.

65 **NOAH'S NATURAL FOODS**
322 Bloor West, 968-7930

The largest health-food supermarket in the neighbourhood, Noah's stocks the usual assortment of supplements, herbs, and homeopathic aids. The busy shop also has a wide variety of organic produce and grains. Down the back and over to the side, their in-house café — Sunni's — sells sugar- and dairy-free casseroles and salads by the pound.

HOME FURNISHINGS — NEW

27 **ASHANTI ROOM**
28 Lennox, 588-3934

This former church rectory was once the headquarters of *Contrast*, Toronto's first black-activist newspaper. Its political idealism is carried on by this grassroots group dedicated to promoting the

micro-businesses that produce or import the items on sale here. A wide selection of African-inspired textiles are on offer, as well as wall hangings and pillows from Zimbabwe, boldly patterned dinnerware, and children's books, toys, and games. Cool alert: local designer B.I.T.H.'s Rastafarian tea cosies! Closed Monday.

18 **THINGS JAPANESE**
159 Harbord, 967-9797

A spare space as stylish as its stock, the shop features, well, Japanese things. Kimonos — to be worn or displayed as fashionable wall hangings — paper fans, and doorway curtains join cast-iron teapots, tea ceremony sets, and packages of green tea on the boutique's minimally stacked shelves. CDs, Japan guidebooks and cookbooks, too. Closed Monday.

LIQUOR AND WINE STORES

67 **LCBO**
198 Dupont, 922-7066

Monday to Friday 9:30 a.m. to 10 p.m.
Saturday 9:30 a.m. to 9 p.m.
Sunday 11 a.m. to 6 p.m.
Closed holidays.

20 GOOD FOR HER
181 Harbord, 588-0900

A sex-positive shop offering merchandise that appeals to women and their admirers — silk-screened pillows, greeting cards, strap-ons, and harnesses. Good For Her also rents such videos as *Viva La Vulva* and sells books like *Devil Babe's Big Book of Fun*. Seminars — Tie Me Up and Pleasure Me, Bottoms Up — are held regularly. Women-only hours are observed on Thursdays from 11 a.m. to 2 p.m. and Sundays starting at noon. Closed Monday.

MUSIC — CDS, RECORDS & TAPES

45 CD REPLAY
523 Bloor West, 516-0606

Lined with Frost fencing, this mainstream record store buys and sells used CDs and videos. New copies of current top-40 hits; posters and T-shirts, too.

Other location:
762 Yonge (see page 157).

35 PRIMAL SCREAM
561 Bloor West, 588-9292

You wouldn't expect a store with such a manic name to be so soothing, but the Scream is one of the most relaxing spaces in town. An aquarium full of tropical fish burbles away and welcoming couches at the rear of the shop make a great place to chill. CDs both new and used are sold, as well as videos, books, and 'zines.

MUSICAL INSTRUMENTS

6 RING MUSIC
90 Harbord, 924-3571

The autographed promo shots on the wall attest to Ring's stature among local musicians. Here, you'll find a platinum disc by Blue Rodeo dedicated to Ring's own guitar slingers, plus glossies from such other Canadian legends as Gordon Lightfoot and Martha and the Muffins. Lots of vintage and not-so-vintage guitars, amps, and stomp boxes as well as expert repairs make Ring an essential stop for musos. Closed Sunday.

NEW AGE

56 ETERNAL MOMENT
497 Bloor West, 924-3780

A sign outside this spiritual superstore prophetically states, "Conversations with God now available." Besides a talk with the Big Dude Upstairs, you'll find candles, chimes, crystals, and fortune-telling crystal balls. You can also have your baby-to-be's natal chart done and your tea leaves read.

3 WONDER WORKS
79A Harbord, 323-3131

PET SUPPLIES

23 ANNEX PET SUPPLY
718 Bathurst, 588-1925

Next door to the Annex Animal Hospital, this pet shop offers the usual leashes and bulk foods alongside such treats as ostrich jerky, peanut-butter-flavoured dog biscuits, and cat grass. Especially cool are salt-proof Muttluks for dogs and Beastie Band punk-style cat collars in happy-face, fish-bone, or skull 'n' crossbones motifs.

SEX

20 GOOD FOR HER
181 Harbord, 588-0900

See Hot Spot listing this page.

VIDEO

79 AFTER DARK
1043 Bathurst, 533-7500

Cult classics and killer B-movies are what you'll find at After Dark, a video shop stocked with esoteric tapes. Their business card describes the kind of things you'll find here as, "Weird, wonderful, wild and worse." Underground and offbeat gems by anti-auteurs John Waters, Andy Warhol, and Russ Meyer — not to mention many impossible-to-find flicks — are all available for rent at this outlet that stays open every night except Sunday till 4 a.m.

32 SUSPECT VIDEO
605 Markham, 588-6674

See listing page 34.

YORKVILLE

Yorkville Park

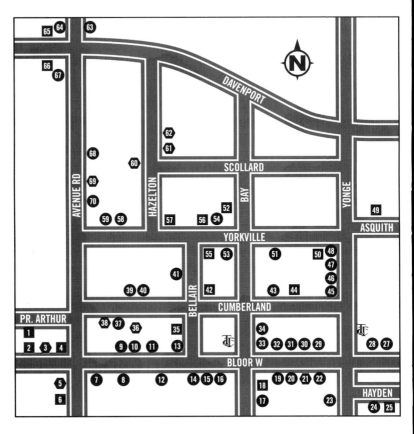

YORKVILLE

Once a hippie enclave — folkies Joni Mitchell and Neil Young played the Village's coffee-house circuit here in the '60s — Yorkville is now Toronto's chicest address. But it's not all designer labels and limousines — look deeply and you'll find the last vestiges of Toronto's most far-out spaces.

FOOD & DINING

RESTAURANTS

49 **INDOCHINE**
4 Collier, 922-5840

Indochine has one of Yorkville's best meal deals. For $7.95, diners can choose from such dishes as pad thai with green-mango salad, Vietnamese curried chicken, or Thai purple-basil beef. With them comes jasmine rice, a spring roll, and a bowl of hot 'n' sour soup. Despite its low prices, there's nothing cost-cutting about Indochine's pleasant yellow room dotted with brown-paper-over-linen tables and decorated with a colourful street-scene mural. Closed Sunday.

One step at door, washrooms in basement. Fully licensed. $

6 **JK ROM**
100 Queen's Park Circle, 586-5577

Acclaimed chef Jamie Kennedy — the JK to the Royal Ontario Museum's ROM — makes the best french fries in town. Of course, at this exceptionally swank restaurant they're called frites and they come with a marvellous lemon mayonnaise instead of ketchup. Open only for midday meals, this restaurant on the museum's roof is a favourite with the ladies who lunch. And their escorts.

Barrier-free. Fully licensed. Patio. $$$

52 **MORI**
1280 Bay, 961-1094

A casual Japanese noodle house and sushi bar on the fringe of Yorkville, Mori is a great spot for inexpensive eat-in or takeout meals — especially during the Film Festival. Choose from an assortment of bargain-basement-priced all-veggie futomaki or all-in-one udon-noodle dinners. Konichiwa.

10 steps at door, washrooms on same floor. Fully licensed. Patio. $

25 **SUSHI EI**
15 Hayden, 515-1957

On a narrow side street not far from the tumultuous corner of Yonge and Bloor, this minuscule Tokyo-authentic sushi bar serves up super-fresh seafood-and-rice rolls. Sit at the small sushi bar and point at whatever strikes your fancy, or order from the à la carte menu — bento-box meals of tempura, green salad, and miso soup, or soy-soaked salmon-teriyaki dinners. Closed Sunday.

Barrier-free. Fully licensed, smoke-free. $$

CAFES AND COFFEE HOUSES

57 **BOUFFE**
102 Yorkville, 924-8869

A hard-to-come-by patio seat overlooking the passing Yorkville parade of made-for-TV-movie stars, wannabe supermodels, and the hoi polloi can cause hefty damage to the pocketbook. But cheap and chic Bouffe — the low-rent but high-

HOT SPOT

55 **CAFE NERVOSA**
75 Yorkville, 961-4642

Named for the coffee shop on TV's *Frasier* — Kelsey Grammer is said to have once walked by, smirked, and kept walking — the French doors to this leopard-skin-and-wrought-iron-bedecked space open onto the corner of Yorkville Avenue and Balliol, one of the nabe's busiest intersections. Inexpensive-for-the-area panini and salad platters are as immense as the diet pizzas are wafer-thin. Upstairs, things get a little darker in the cigar lounge (cough). Spotted: Sporty Spice Girl Melanie Chisholm.

Six steps at door, washrooms on second floor. Fully licensed. Patio. $$

quality offshoot of the pricey Parisian boîte Zola — offers this, a view, and more. Classic bistro fare such as mussels moulinière, frogs' legs, and braised rabbit is matched by attentive service. Inside, burgundy banquettes beckon, while Edith Piaf serenades the unromantic and romantic alike. Closed Monday.

Six steps at door, washrooms on same floor. Fully licensed. Patio. $$

JK ROM: Lunch among the ruins.

2 **GREG'S ICE CREAM**
200 Bloor West, 961-4734

All-natural ingredients have helped keep Greg Mahon's fabulous homemade ice-cream concoctions in demand for 18 years. Current fave flavours include Japanese green tea and flame-roasted marshmallow, in cones or banana splits, and calorie-watcher sorbets. Take-home treats by the litre, too.

Seven steps at door, washrooms on same floor. Unlicensed, smoke-free, cash only. $

55 **CAFE NERVOSA**
75 Yorkville, 961-4642

See Hot Spot page 175.

2 **GREG'S ICE CREAM**
200 Bloor West, 961-4734

See Hot Spot this page.

65 **HAVANA**
233 Davenport, 968-1097

A tiny two-table coffee house, Havana is permeated by the aroma of roasted beans and the sounds of light jazz wafting from a 'blaster. You can sip a latte while standing at the window-view counter and flipping through the pages of the latest issue of a fashion magazine. Closed Sunday.

One step at door, no washrooms. Unlicensed, smoke-free. $

42 **LETTIERI**
94 Cumberland, 515-8764

See listing page 16.
Barrier-free. Fully licensed. Patio. $

56 **SECOND CUP**
70 Yorkville, 964-0876

See listing page 17.
Barrier-free. Unlicensed. Patio. $

50 **WANDA'S PIE IN THE SKY**
7A Yorkville, 925-7437

Wanda bakes spectacular pies — chocolate-pecan, lemon meringue, and thick double-crusted marvels she calls "very berry." As well, she creates gorgeous cakes such as calorie-intense strawberry cheesecake — available, like the pies, whole or by the slice. This tiny café offers vegetarian sandwiches and soups to enjoy before the afters in very relaxed surroundings. In summer, the front garage-door-style window opens to the street.

One step at door, washrooms on same floor. Unlicensed, smoke-free. Patio. $

DELIS AND DINERS

65 **AVENUE COFFEE SHOPPE**
222 Davenport, 924-5191

A quintessential diner, the Avenue so looks the part that it's constantly being used as a location for film and television-commercial shoots. Once the movie lights are off, the diner reverts to an old-fashioned lunch counter featuring milkshakes, pancake breakfasts, and banquet burgers. It's a favourite with the showbiz set, so check out the autographed photos of past Avenue customers Liza Minnelli, Whoopi Goldberg, and Robert De Niro, or purchase a Roots-designed Avenue Diner leather jacket.

One step at door, washrooms in basement. Unlicensed, smoke-free. $

35 **FLO'S**
10 Bellair, 961-4333

Flo's is a postcard-perfect replica of the kind of diner that never really existed in the '50s. With its wraparound booths, Coca-Cola memorabilia, and chrome lunch counter, Flo's brings back Happy Days with its retro menu of burgers, fries, and deluxe grilled cheese sandwiches. Sure, there's thin-crust pizza and salade niçoise for foodies, but for those wanting to relive the era correctly, go straight for the open-faced hot turkey sandwich with a side order of fries. And gravy.

Four steps at door, washrooms in basement. Fully licensed. Patio. $$

BARS

1 **THE DUKE OF YORK**
39 Prince Arthur, 964-2441

See listing page 154.
Nine steps at door, washrooms in basement.

18 **PANORAMA**
55 Bloor West, 967-0000

If you suffer from claustrophobia or acrophobia — or both — Panorama, the penthouse bar on the 51st floor of the Manulife Centre, won't be your idea of a place to party. After a two-minute ride in a cramped elevator, you step out into an elegant nightclub in the clouds. Two outdoor terraces — one facing north towards tree-shrouded Rosedale, the other south to the downtown core and islands beyond — are lined with patio furniture and a sure-grip rubber carpet. No one's been blown away — yet.

Barrier-free. Patio.

44 **THE PILOT**
22 Cumberland, 923-5716

See Hot Spot this page.

4 **THE ROOF**
4 Avenue Rd., 924-5471

The rooftop bar at the Park Plaza — or whatever they're calling the hotel these days — has been a literary landmark for more than 50 years. And bartender Harold Rochberg has been there since day one. Such writers as Mordecai Richler, Graeme Gibson, and Margaret Atwood (whose novel *Cat's Eye* has a scene that takes place in the bar) and publisher Jack McClelland used to come here to knock back a few, exchange witty banter, and engage each other in cerebral arm-wrestling contests. What *Gourmet* magazine calls one of North America's ten best saloons was once Toronto's only licensed patio. Although the terrace still overlooks the downtown skyline, it's been reduced to only seven tables.

Barrier-free. Patio.

ENTERTAINMENT

COMEDY CLUBS

3 **COMEDYWOOD DOWNTOWN**
194 Bloor West, 966-9663

See listing page 230. Closed Sunday, Monday, and Tuesday.

22 steps at door, washrooms on same floor. Fully licensed.

GALLERIES AND MUSEUMS

61 **ARTCORE**
33 Hazelton, 920-3820

A small but influential gallery, Artcore showcases

44 **THE PILOT**
22 Cumberland, 923-5716

One of Toronto's oldest bars — and at one time the longest stand-up in town — the Pilot has been around since the early '40s. So have some of its regulars. A popular watering hole associated with the literary crowd, this very dark room features live jazz performances every Saturday afternoon. Check out the rooftop patio and another out front for Yorkville's least snooty scene. Closed Sunday.

Two steps at door, washrooms in basement. Patio.

the work of emerging artists as well as the well-established. They represent not only Canadian artists — Dougal Graham and Sawan Yawnghwe among them — but also such prominent American and European talent as Sandro Chia, Dennis Oppenheim, and Mimmo Paladino, too. Closed Sunday and Monday.

60 **MIRA GODARD GALLERY**
22 Hazelton, 964-8197

One of Toronto's oldest art galleries, the Mira Godard has been representing and showing Canadian and international artists since the early '60s. With two airy floors of exhibition space, the gallery regularly shows work by Alex Colville, Mary Pratt, Robert Motherwell, David Milne, and Lucian Freud.

5 **ROYAL ONTARIO MUSEUM**
100 Queen's Park, 586-5549

Canada's largest museum, the ROM is home to an internationally acclaimed collection of Chinese artifacts dating back to the sixth century A.D. As well, don't miss the 13 re-assembled prehistoric skeletons in the Dinosaur Gallery, and the Bat Cave Gallery, a recreation of a Jamaican lair complete with over 4,000 faux flying beasties. Fake snakes, too. You pay to get in during regular hours, but admission is free every day from 5 to 6 p.m. (except Tuesdays when it's free 7 to 8 p.m.).

61 **SABLE-CASTELLI GALLERY**
33 Hazelton, 961-0011

The Sable-Castelli Gallery specializes in Canadian contemporary artists such as Betty Goodwin, Joanne Tod, and David Craven. It's affiliated with New York

YORKVILLE

City's famed Castelli Gallery, and owner Jared Sable is one of the country's leading art dealers.

CINEMAS — FIRST RUN

38 **THE CUMBERLAND FOUR**
159 Cumberland, 964-5971

21 **THE VARSITY**
55 Bloor West, 961-6303

ATTRACTIONS

69 **HAZELTON LANES**
55 Avenue Rd, 968-8600

Hazelton Lanes is a decidedly upscale two-level shopping mall with over 90 shops. Although such top-drawer boutiques as Gianfranco Ferre and Chez Catherine can be found here, other not-quite-so-pricey outlets like home-accessory depot Design Directives, tasty 'n' tasteful takeout café Hazelton Gourmet, and the Classical Record Store offer affordable stuff for the hoi polloi.

36 **VILLAGE OF YORKVILLE PARK**
Cumberland and Balliol, 392-1111

Part sculpture and part urban oasis, this once-controversial park has bloomed into one of Toronto's most relaxing spaces. Designed by American landscape artist Martha Schwartz, the public space made headlines when it was revealed that the city had paid a quarter of a million dollars for the piece of the Canadian Shield — that's the big rock — that stands in the centre of the square. It's a very big rock, mind. Now that the furor has faded and the plantings have grown, the Village of Yorkville Park is a great place to chill.

SHOPPING

BICYCLES

64 **PEDLAR CYCLES**
152 Avenue Road, 968-7100

BOOKS AND MAGAZINES — NEW

9 **CHAPTERS**
110 Bloor West, 920-9299

Chapters' flagship store has four floors for biblio-

philes. On the main floor you'll find a selection of new releases and current bestsellers — some autographed — as well as an extensive array of magazines and an in-house café complete with working fireplace. Down a circular staircase, the basement houses a CD department, a small stage area for musical performances, and another café. The second floor is devoted to business books and multimedia CD-ROMs, and the third to general fiction, non-fiction reference books, and travel guides, as well as an area where author's readings are held next to a fireplace. Children's books, too.

Other location:
Richmond West at John (see page 52)

48 **THE COOKBOOK STORE**
850 Yonge, 920-2665

With Toronto's most thorough selection of cookbooks and food-related titles, this store is a foodie's Shangri-La. Many celebrated food writers have put in a personal appearance here, among them Julia Child, Emeril Lagasse, Martha Stewart, and diet-guru Richard Simmons — unfortunately not together (the mind boggles!). As well, they sell culinary magazines like *Saveur, Vegetarian Times*, and *Chile Pepper*.

17 **INDIGO**
55 Bloor West, 925-3536

Indigo belies its mega-bookstore tag — with its sub-divided departments, Indigo is more like a cluster of small specialist shops than an anonymous superstore. As well as current bestsellers — some discounted — it has a large local and international magazine section, an adult-oriented CD collection, and a café decked out with wicker armchairs and marble-topped tables.

Other location:
2300 Yonge (see page 227).

46 **LICHTMAN'S**
842 Yonge, 924-4186

See listing page 113.

59 **MAISON DE LA PRESSE INTERNATIONALE**
124 Yorkville, 928-2328

More than a French-language newspaper and magazine stand, Maison carries titles from around the world. Obviously, the emphasis here is on Francophone books and journals from Quebec, France, and Africa, but the bustling shop also offers such diverse publications as the *International Herald Tribune*, the *Prague Post*, and UK cycling bible *On Your Bike*. Michelin maps and guidebooks en français, aussi.

51 **OMEGA CENTRE**
29 Yorkville, 975-9086

Omega Centre specializes in New Age titles. This free-form space has a well-stocked magazine rack with such publications as *Sedona: The Journal of Emergence*, *Alternative Press Review*, and *Light of Consciousness*, and it also carries books on fortune telling, alternative medicine, and personal growth. As well, you can stock up on crystals, essential oils, and "magickal" amulets, or just relax on couches to soothing CDs, surrounded by dream-catchers and wind chimes.

FASHION — ACCESSORIES

34 **JOSEPHSON'S**
60 Bloor West, 964-7070

Owned by the affable Dr. Josh — he also owns the Cookbook Store — Josephson's is Toronto's premier optician. As well as providing eye exams, the modish shop carries eyewear by such designers

as — deep breath — LA Eyeworks, Cartier, Jean Paul Gaultier, Yohji Yamamoto, Thierry Mugler, Martine Sitbon, Claude Montana, Sonia Rykiel, Phillipe Starck, Jil Sander, and Paul Smith. No Ray-Bans, though.

Other location:
2300 Yonge (see page 227)

14 **TIFFANY AND COMPANY**
85 Bloor West, 921-3900

Don't bother coming for breakfast unless you've brought your gold card. An outlet of the famous New York jeweller, this heavily guarded store features gold and diamond *bijoux* by designers Elsa Peretti and Paloma Picasso.

FASHION — NEW CLOTHING

28 **THE BAY**
2 Bloor East, 972-3333

See listing page 114.

11 **BENETTON**
102 Bloor West, 968-1611

One of several Benetton franchises in town, this outlet focuses on the Italian design company's

PRADA: The chicest name in minimal millennial fashion.

unisex sportswear and groovy kids' line. Don't miss its free mini-catalogues.

⑦ CLUB MONACO
157 Bloor West, 591-8837

See listing page 24.

㉛ EDDIE BAUER
50 Bloor West, 961-2525

Once an outdoorsy outfitter, Eddie Bauer has evolved into a J. Crew–style men's and women's haberdasher. Though canoes and snowshoes still hang from the walls, they're there strictly for display purposes.

Other location:
Eaton Centre (see page 121)

㉙ EMPORIO ARMANI
50 Bloor West, 960-2978

A beautifully minimalist space that takes up two floors linked by a dramatic marble staircase, this street-front offshoot of Holt Renfrew (see listing below) has its own separate Bloor Street entrance. As well as Armani's pricey togs, the designer's boutique carries a small selection of housewares — $30 coffee mugs (worth $2, tops, minus the

Armani logo), $35 ashtrays, and $95 sets of plastic salad tongs.

③ ENDS
140 Avenue Road, 968-7272

Ends-of-the-line, seconds, and remainders — they all end up at Ends, a bargain-hunter's paradise. There's always a colourful assortment of socks and sweaters on the carts out front, and when everything's half price or less, it's hard not to find something you'll need eventually. And sometimes you can come across recognizable name brands and famous designer labels, too.

Other locations:
1930 Queen East (see page 205)

㉝ THE GAP
60 Bloor West, 921-2225

See listing page 25.

㊴ HOAX COUTURE
114 Cumberland, 929-4629

See listing page 25.

㉜ HOLT RENFREW
50 Bloor West, 922-2333

Holt Renfrew is a one-stop high-fashion outlet

THE COOKBOOK STORE: Where Martha Stewart and Emeril Lagasse hang when in town.

featuring men's and women's designer clothing. Over three floors the store houses boutiques with menswear by Dolce & Gabanna, Donna Karan, Gucci, Helmut Lang, Jil Sander, and John Bartlett and womenswear by Christian Lacroix, Givenchy, Richard Tyler, Ungaro, and Valentino. Accessory lines include those by Gucci, Kate Spade, and Fendi. Pooped from shopping? Relax in the downstairs food court while nibbling on sushi or thincrust pizza.

23 LE CHÂTEAU
772 Yonge, 964-7755

See listing page 24.

8 PRADA
131 Bloor West, 513-0400

Painted the palest of pale greens, Prada is probably Yorkville's coolest couture outlet. The Bloor Street location is the latest for the Italian designer who also operates shops in Milan, New York, and Tokyo. Wall units display Prada's famous clunky '70s-revival handbags, and a few strategically positioned racks hold minimalist black-on-black men's and women's clothing. To complete the retro look, add a pair of the designer's Japanese-inspired square-toed shoes or sandals.

63 ROOTS
195 Avenue Road, 927-8585

See listing page 121.

12 ROOTS
95A Bloor West, 323-3289

See listing page 121.

45 STRICTLY HARDCORE
4 Cumberland, 922-1533

Possibly Yorkville's tiniest — and funkiest — retail outlet, this b-boy boutique carries such essential streetwear-designer names as Fubu, Helly Hansen, Kangol, and Ecko Unlimited, as well as Phat Farm jeans and Toronto's own Too Black Guys T-shirts. Along with crocheted fishermen's caps by local hatter Yaadi, Strictly sells DJ compilation tapes and hardcore hip-hop mags like *The Source Sports*, *Blaze*, and *Stress*.

20 SUNDE
55 Bloor West, 944-8406

Body-conscious and sophisticated, German-born

15 VERSACE
83 Bloor West, 920-8300

Behind a double iron gate and beyond the massive urns at the entrance lies Yorkville's most opulent designer boutique. Positively palazzo-like, Versace is a stunning space that showcases the late Italian designer's clothes and home accessories to dazzling effect. As well as highlights from the couture collection, the shop also stocks its mid-range Istante line. Mid-range? Try $5,700 for a leather biker's jacket almost identical to ones for sale on Queen West for $150 — but then, those don't come with a Versace label.

Roland Heizinger and Hong Kong native Jennifer Chiu's designs for Canadian company Sunde emphasize detailed workmanship. The team specializes in structured jackets, pants, skirts, dresses, and shirts that are both streamlined and sensual. Formerly of Boy London, Chiu also oversees Sunde's knitwear division.

Other location:
508 Danforth (see page 195)

41 UNCLE OTIS
26 Bellair, 920-2281

See listing page 28.

15 VERSACE
83 Bloor West, 920-8300

See Hot Spot this page.

16 VERSUS
77 Bloor West, 929-5966

A tall, airy space adjacent to its pricier couture cousin, Versus features Versace's slightly more economical — $295 jeans and $225 T-shirts — casual-wear collection.

FASHION — VINTAGE CLOTHING

22 DIVINE DECADENCE
55 Bloor West, 324-9759

Toronto's longest-lasting vintage-clothing shop, Divine Decadence has been in business for over 25 years. You won't find plaid lumberjack shirts and used Levi's here — Divine specializes in glamorous gowns from the Edwardian era through the flapper-tastic '20s, and designer evening

WANDA'S PIE IN THE SKY: Seconds?

wear from the '40s and '50s. This elegant emporium has a wall of vintage wedding gowns and sells fabulous frocks found in the closets of aristocratic South Americans. Actress Lauren Hutton is a regular customer.

FASHION — SHOES

10 NIKE
110 Bloor West, 921-6453

More of a multi-media experience than a shoe store, Nike is certainly impressive. You enter a pipe-gridded pavilion lit by huge TV projectors screening furiously edited sports highlights — all extreme-sport athletes flashing the Nike logo, of course. Over two floors, a mind-boggling array of sport shoes is displayed in pavilions decorated with inspirational slogans and dedicated to different types of sports activities — basketball, tennis, and women's workouts.

FOOD

43 DINAH'S CUPBOARD
50 Cumberland, 921-8112

Think of Dinah's Cupboard as a pantry for the rich and powerful. If it's the cook's night off, you can pick up prefab gourmet dishes like chicken-apricot couscous, vegetarian samosas, and smoked glazed ham. The truly clueless can't fail with pre-steamed mixed veggies and stir-fried noodles. Owned by kitchen whiz Dinah Koo — who also operates the chic Tiger Lily's eatery on Queen West (see listing page 16) — the Cupboard also carries imported teas and coffee beans as well as her own line of haute salad dressings. Closed Sunday.

24 UPTOWN NUTHOUSE
11 Hayden, 922-1517

Fancy an alternative to pricey movie-house popcorn saturated in fake butter? Across the street from the Uptown theatre, this peanut emporium offers snacks for those bored with jujubes. Roasted, salted cashews, meaty macadamias, and undyed pistachios make blockbuster movie munchies. Closed Sunday.

HAIR — SALONS

70 VIDAL SASSOON
37 Avenue Rd., 920-1333

Once the official hairdresser of swinging Carnaby Street, Sassoon's legacy is an international chain of salons. This one still gives some of the best cuts in town. Closed Sunday.

HEALTH AND BEAUTY

13 THE BODY SHOP
86 Bloor West, 928-1180

See listing page 30.

40 LUSH
116 Cumberland, 960-5874

See listing page 30.

HOME FURNISHINGS — NEW

37 ICE
163 Cumberland, 964-6751

Situated directly across the street from the Four Seasons Hotel — the swanky hostelry popular with visiting movie stars — ICE is chock full of oddball gifts. Celebrities — and not-so-swells — shop for things like *I Love Lucy* flannel pyjamas, *Star Wars* jean jackets, Jackie Onassis paper dolls, and silver-vinyl dog collars that promise to make your pet "look like Elvis in Las Vegas." Tintin devotees will want to check out the merchandise sporting the cartoon character's likeness — watches, T-shirts, and shoulder bags.

LIQUOR AND WINE STORES

19 **LCBO**
55 Bloor West, 925-5266

Monday to Friday 9:30 a.m. to 9:30 p.m.
Saturday 9:30 a.m. to 6 p.m.
Sunday 11 a.m. to 5 p.m.
Closed holidays.

68 **LCBO**
87 Avenue Rd, 924-9463

Monday to Friday 9:30 a.m. to 9 p.m.
Saturday 9 a.m. to 6 p.m.
Sunday noon to 5 p.m.
Closed holidays.

MUSIC— CDS, RECORDS & TAPES

30 **HMV**
50 Bloor West, 324-9979

See listing page 122.

54 **L'ATELIER GRIGORIAN**
70 Yorkville, 922-6477

A musical workshop, L'Atelier is a specialty record store offering one of Toronto's most complete classical sections. You'll find expensive, imported multi-disc CD box sets that no one else in town carries, as well as opera and classical performance DVD videos. Don't miss its extensive jazz and world-music departments, either.

27 **SUNRISE**
Bay-Bloor Centre, 498-6601

Houses a Ticketmaster outlet.
See listing page 123.

NATURAL REMEDIES

47 **THOMPSON'S HOMEOPATHIC**
844 Yonge, 922-2300

With some of the most beautiful wooden display cabinets in town, Thompson's is one of Toronto's oldest herbalists.

SEX

53 **LOVECRAFT**
63 Yorkville, 923-7331

From gag gifts to gags, Lovecraft sells sexually

LOVECRAFT: A sex shop for the whole family.

oriented devices that promote laughter and/or pleasure. Canada's oldest sex shop, Lovecraft is downright wholesome. Sure, there are the prerequisite naughty lingerie, vibrators, and how-to videos, but the brightly lit store also stocks such tame items as T-shirts with suggestive slogans and — for the truly past-it — walking canes complete with horn and rearview mirror.

58 **SENSORIA**
128 Yorkville, 966-4226

The more straitlaced sister store to Queen West's Condom Shack (see listing page 33), Sensoria is an emporium specializing in erotic aids. As well as romantic CDs and books with titles like *101 Great Quickies*, Sensoria celebrates the sensual with its line of love lotions, massage oils, and herbal relaxation masks. No raunchy sex toys here — well, hidden in a back corner you can find paint-on condoms and a Love Mask for "keeping your lover in the dark." Some may require more than a blindfold to do that.

Lolita's Lust

THE DANFORTH

Once known mainly for its many Greek restaurants, the Danforth is now a cosmopolitan boulevard of eateries, designer knick-knack shops, and pricey clothing boutiques. Sure, the souvlaki joints remain, but the avenue is also home to Cuban, Indian, and Caribbean eateries, most staying open late into the night.

FOOD & DINING

RESTAURANTS

10 ALLEN'S
143 Danforth, 463-3086

Looking like a saloon straight out of New York City, complete with a Wurlitzer jukebox programmed with golden oldies, Allen's features an amazing cross-section of microbrews and single-malt scotches. Early in the evening, the few booths up front and the many linen-topped tables are filled by serious beverage samplers who also partake of the booze-soaked menu — chicken-liver pâté sozzled with whisky, steak stew braised in beer, and fish and chips battered in ale.

Barrier-free, washrooms in basement. Fully licensed. Patio. $$

48 ASTORIA
390 Danforth, 463-2838

Greek.

Barrier-free. Fully licensed. $$

49 AVLI
401 Danforth, 461-9577

Beneath stucco archways, and sporting red and green accents atypical for the Danforth, this noisy, narrow room offers a menu that may be Greek but certainly isn't Greece-y. Unlike the heavy-handed stodge served by neighbouring restaurants, Avli's fare is as light as phyllo. Start with a correct lettuce-free Greek salad and follow with deftly grilled lamb chops. Veggie dips and meat pies make proper accompaniment to shots of ouzo. Suave service keeps on top of the ruckus.

One step at door, washrooms in basement. Fully licensed. Patio. $$

2 CAFE BRUSSEL
786 Broadview, 465-7363

Incredibly busy for Sunday brunch, when they serve such fare as Brie omelets, this dimly lit bistro is Toronto's sole Belgian eatery. Not that different from French, the dinner menu touches on all the bistro standards — onion soup, frites with mayonnaise, and slow-cooked stews. A large and varied choice of European lagers and ales is on tap, and a deep wine selection is on offer. Closed Monday.

One step at door, washrooms in basement. Fully licensed. Patio. $$$

.73 CHINCHILLA LOUNGE
513 Danforth, 465-9630

Describing the fare as "steaks and cocktails"

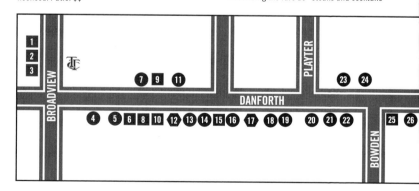

LA CARRETA: Going Cuban on the Danforth — an avenue known for its Greek grub.

doesn't do justice to this swanky saloon upstairs from swelegant Lolita's Lust, one of the Danforth's top dining destinations. Yes, there are cowboy rib-eyes to chow down and Broken-Down Lawnmowers to swill. But there are also whole butter-sauced lobsters, tandoori-spiced grouper, and portobello mushrooms stuffed with bacon, onion, and sage. And french fries. Closed Sunday and Monday.

16 steps at door, washrooms on same floor. Fully licensed. $$$

76 CHRISTINA'S
535 Danforth, 463-4418

The most noteworthy feature of this cavernous restaurant is its Web site — www.greektown.com — which lists Christina's familiar Greek-Ital hybrid menu and announces the awards the eatery has won (including Best Greek Restaurant, NOW magazine Readers' Poll 1996). But it's the snapshots of celebrities who've dined here that set it apart from the other eateries on the strip. Look for the photo of *Friends'* hunk Matt LeBlanc on a date

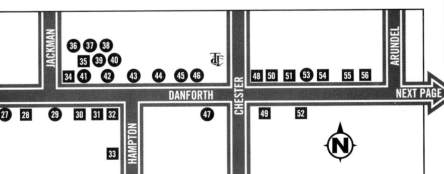

NEXT PAGE

67 FANCY SHOES
507 Danforth, 463-4166

Just like the nearby Lolita's Lust, whose owners have recently launched this place, the front window here is also painted over, leaving only a narrow slit through which to peer inside. It's named for imaginary gangster Carmen "Fancy Shoes" Travolta, but there's nothing fictitious about this casual Italian eatery's deliciously traditional antipasto, pasta, and grilled-meat menu. Warning: when you order an entree, that's exactly what you get. Side dishes cost extra. Closed Sunday.

Barrier-free, washrooms in basement. Fully licensed. $$$

in the early '90s with big-haired disco diva Alanis — she wasn't Morissette yet. The mind boggles!

Barrier-free. Fully licensed. Patio. $$

67 FANCY SHOES
507 Danforth, 463-4166

See Hot Spot this page. Closed Sunday.

Barrier-free, washrooms in basement. Fully licensed. $$$

79 THE FRIENDLY GREEK
551 Danforth, 469-8422

Many of the tavernas that line the Danforth serve interchangeable but filling Greek grub. It's as if there's one massive subterranean kitchen that supplies them all with grilled souvlaki on a stick, rosemary-and-lemon-flecked roast potatoes, oily rice, and Greek salad. They all look the same, too — a mid-'80s mix of high-tech halogen and over-

wrought iron. Well, the food's the same here as everywhere else, but the decor makes the Friendly Greek unique: whitewashed stucco walls, blue Hellenic trim, and murals depicting Aegean scenes. It's corny, but it's authentic.

Barrier-free, washrooms in basement. Fully licensed. $$

86 GREEK OLIVES
752 Danforth, 466-1414

Greek.

Barrier-free. Fully licensed. $$

83 IL FORNELLO
576 Danforth, 466-2931

See listing page 39.

Barrier-free. Fully licensed. Patio. $$

55 KALYVIA
420 Danforth, 463-3333

Greek.

Barrier-free, washrooms in basement. Fully licensed. Patio. $$

61 LA CARRETA
469 Danforth, 461-7718

The Danforth is the last place you'd expect to find a Cuban restaurant. But handsome host Jose Garcia, a former co-owner of chi-chi Ba-Ba-Lu'U in Yorkville, goes against type with this charming cantina. You can make a meal from the tapas menu alone — cornmeal tamal wrapped in corn husks and doused with fire-alarm hot sauce, crisp deep-fried-plantain baskets of shrimp, and placid yucca dressed with oil and garlic. Not only do they serve a fabulous Latin brunch on weekends, but

THE DANFORTH

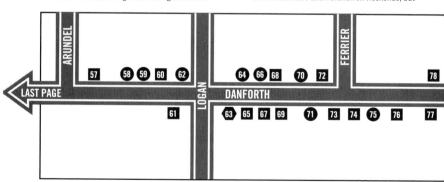

they also serve it after midnight Thursday through Saturday. Free salsa lessons every Sunday.

Barrier-free, washrooms in basement. Fully licensed. Patio. $$

3 **LILY SUSHI BAR**
784 Broadview, 778-8543

Darker than most Japanese restaurants — all navy accents among the usual hanging lanterns and travel posters — the sushi bar here slithers down one side of the room while more formal tables crowd the other. As Christmas lights twinkle overhead, regulars nosh on straightforward sushi and sashimi and typical teriyaki and tempura dinners.

One step at door, washrooms in basement. Fully licensed. $$

74 **LOLITA'S LUST**
513 Danforth, 465-1751

Through a peek-a-boo slit in the olive-green facade, you can just make out Lolita's clandestine interior. What you see is a souped-up '50s diner — reupholstered dinette suites, bare light bulbs, and soda-fountain stools lining a lunch counter — that's been turned into a winner. To call the menu Mediterranean doesn't give it its due. Greek and Italian flavours mingle with those of North Africa to create a truly contemporary experience.

Barrier-free, washrooms in basement. Fully licensed. $$$

35 **MARIKO**
348 Danforth, 463-8231

Located in the Carrot Common, a New Age shopping plaza, this cheery and charming eatery offers generous portions and reasonable prices for eat-in or takeout. Teriyaki, tempura, and sukiyaki may now be commonplace, but Mariko's sushi has something the others lack — a choice of brown rice instead of white. All dinners, such as fresh sashimi or vegetarian yosenabe casserole, come with miso soup, brown rice, and spicy sunomono pickles.

Barrier-free. Fully licensed. $$

51 **MEGAS**
402 Danforth, 466-7771

Greek.

Barrier-free. Fully licensed. Patio. $$

60 **MEZES**
456 Danforth, 778-5150

One of the snazzier spaces on the strip, Mezes features — guess what? — mezes, the Greek version of tapas — just right for snacking, or combine them for a major pig-out. Wriggly wrought iron and vines wrap themselves around a tiered room that's family-friendly and sophisticate-cool. Best: grilled shrimp, octopus and calamari doused in olive oil and lemon, home-cooked eggplant purée, zippy tzatziki, and nut-studded, honey-drenched baklava.

Barrier-free. Fully licensed. $$

82 **MR. GREEK**
568 Danforth, 461-5470

Greek.

One step at door, washrooms on same floor. Fully licensed. $$

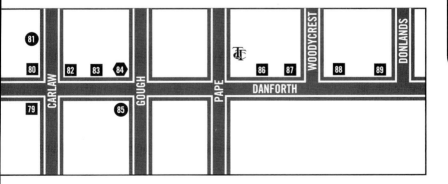

52 **MYTH**
417 Danforth, 461-8383

Open till 4 a.m. on Friday and Saturday night, this mammoth eatery-cum-pool hall housed in a former movie-house opens out front to embrace the Danforth's raucous street life. Things get crazy indoors, too. Reservations are a good idea, but even without them, the turnover's so quick in this very '90s brown-on-brown room that a table's bound to be available any minute. The food? Greek, Italian, Californian, with side trips to Cuba and France.

Barrier-free. Fully licensed. Patio. $$

54 **OCTAVIA**
414 Danforth, 461-3562

With its swanky College Street look, this spanking-new beanery may seem out of place on a street that speaks mostly Greek. Velour club chairs and banquettes occupy one raised area, while in summer less private tables spread onto the sidewalk through open French doors. Cosmopolitan Mediterranean mains — grilled octopus, black-ink linguini — mix with California salads, Ital veal and Thai satays.

Barrier-free, washrooms in basement. Fully licensed. Patio. $$

56 **OMONIA**
426 Danforth, 465-2129

Greek.

Barrier-free. Fully licensed. $$

68 **OUZERI**
500A Danforth, 778-0500

Once past the prismatic glassed-in foyer, you enter a free-flowing cantina rimmed with TV sets tuned to the sports channel. Terrazzo tables and wicker chairs are scattered over two levels, and the wine rack climbs to the ceiling. Mediterranean mains lean toward grilled salmon and lamb pies. Large garage doors open onto the avenue during the swelter of summer.

Barrier-free, washrooms in basement. Fully licensed. Patio. $$

72 **PAN**
516 Danforth, 466-8158

One of the most popular spots on the Danforth, Pan is beginning to show its age. The chartreuse-over-purple walls could use a new coat of paint.

Still, the mostly upmarket Greek menu continues to impress. Meze starters, such satisfying salads as roasted beets and green beans with lemony toasted walnuts, and the grilled sea-bass entree cause lineups after 8 p.m. A painting over the bar states cryptically, "You've done it already."

One step at door, washrooms on same floor. Fully licensed. Patio. $$$

57 **PAPPAS GRILL**
440 Danforth, 469-9595

Greek.

Barrier-free. Fully licensed. Patio. $$

31 **SHER-E-PUNJAB**
351 Danforth, 465-2125

One of the oldest Indian spots in the city, Sher-E-Punjab features the Bengali fare of the subcontinent's north. Despite its age, this is a surprisingly modern space — a split-level room festooned with mirrored wall-hangings that reflect light from halogen fixtures. Traditional dishes include chicken tikka masala, pork vindaloo, veal korma, and curries of chicken, goat, or shrimp. And from the tandoor oven, rich red chicken and puffed 'n' stuffed naan.

Two steps at door, washrooms in basement. Fully licensed. $$

28 **SILK ROAD**
341 Danforth, 463-8660

A simple space equipped with stacking chairs, purple tables and travel photos, this small eatery offers MSG-free dishes from Thailand, China, and Japan. Map your route to satiation with such dishes as hot-and-sour soup, Mongolian beef skewers, curried seafood-fried rice, and Grandma Wong's spicy tofu. Vegetarians will want to try Buddha's Delight, a healthy mix of mushrooms — wood ears, tiger-lily buds, tree moss — and vermicelli. Closed Monday.

Barrier-free, washrooms in basement. Fully licensed. $$

15 **THE WILLOW**
193 Danforth, 469-5315

Tex-Mex.

Two steps at door, washrooms in basement. Fully licensed. $$

CUTTY'S HIDEAWAY: In a dancehall stylee — cutting the rug to reggae riddims.

CAFES AND COFFEE HOUSES

25 DARK CITY
307 Danforth, 461-1606

The dimly lit Dark City is appropriately decorated in sumptuous coffee tones — lots of mahogany to offset the gold tin ceiling and deep-purple walls. Naturally, there's plenty of coffee on offer, as well as fruit juice, cider, and tea. Regulars snack on pita pizzas, pumpkin pie, and prepared salads while lounging on couches and reading the free magazines, or leaning on the elbow-high wraparound counter. Anti-Starbucks motto: "No shareholders, just coffee."

One step at door, washrooms in basement. Fully licensed. Patio. $

50 DEMETRE CAFFE
400 Danforth, 778-6654

One step at door, washrooms in basement. Unlicensed. Patio. $

80 ILLIADA
550 Danforth, 462-0334

This Greek coffee house caters mostly to twentysomethings who stare sullenly at each other while smoking, downing espressos, and sampling honey-sweet snacks.

Two steps at door, washrooms on same floor. Unlicensed. $

78 LETTIERI
544 Danforth, 465-6474

See listing page 16.

Two steps at door, washrooms on same floor. Fully licensed. $$

65 MOCHA MOCHA
489 Danforth, 778-7896

So nice they named it twice, this cafeteria-style café-slash-lunchroom dishes up mainly vegetarian vittles. Spicy veggie ragout, chickpea and guacamole pita sandwiches, and mega-muffins make Mocha busy from early in the morning till well past the time the street lights come on.

Barrier-free, washrooms in basement. Beer and wine, smoke-free. $

89 THE ONLY CAFE
972 Danforth, 463-7843

A crowded, smoky neighbourhood diner just beyond the borders of trendy Greektown, the Only is an oasis on a decidedly down-at-the-heels stretch of the Danforth. Guinness on tap and massive egg breakfasts guarantee that every seat at the lunch counter is taken on weekends.

Barrier-free, washrooms in basement. Fully licensed. Patio. $

77 **P.A.M.'S**
541 Danforth, 406-2856

Barrier-free, washrooms in basement. Unlicensed, smoke-free. $

32 **SECOND CUP**
355 Danforth, 466-6295

See listing page 17.

Barrier-free. Unlicensed. Patio. $

33 **TIMOTHY'S**
348 Danforth, 461-2668

Barrier-free. Fully licensed. Patio. $

JUICE BARS

33 **GIMME A SQUEEZE**
176A Hampton, 461-8168

Not the quietest spot on the Danforth — the juicer roars away like a buzz saw as it turns veggies into special tonics — but it's certainly the healthiest. Nourishing elixirs include those good for the gallbladder (apple, pear, lime, and ginger) and the liver (apple and beet). For an extra boost, add a shot of wheat grass, ginseng, or echinacea.

Barrier-free. Fully licensed, smoke-free. $

TAKEOUT

88 **BONA PIZZA PASTA**
818 Danforth, 406-5000

For traditionalists, Bona will whip up old-school doughy pepperoni pizzas, but foodies flock to her for wafer-thin gourmet pies topped with a choice of pine nuts, prosciutto, capers, Brie, smoked salmon, roasted garlic, artichokes, and more. Large pasta entrees — pink-sauced ravioli, vegetarian lasagna — coupled with creditable Caesar salad create alternative takeouts.

Barrier-free, washrooms in basement. Unlicensed. $

87 **CARIBBEAN QUEEN**
780 Danforth, 406-1446

Not much more than a donut shop littered with nearly dead houseplants, what the Queen lacks in decor it makes up for in the fiery fare of Trinidad.

Spicier than Jamaican jerk, the chicken here is nutty with allspice and aflame with Scotch bonnet peppers. Vegetarian rotis — squash, chickpea channa, potato — oxtail dinners and spectacularly spiced homemade mango pickle are not to be missed. Closed Sunday.

Barrier-free, washrooms in basement. Beer and wine. $

1 **MAGIC OVEN**
788 Broadview, 466-0111

Everybody makes gourmet pizza nowadays — they start with an ultra-thin crust and then toss on the oddest toppings they can think of. This neighbourhood pizzeria goes even further. Veterans of Gerrard East's India Town, the owners take the classic pie and give it a Thai or Bengali twist. To wit: Thai Magic, with lemon-grass chicken, mushrooms, basil, anise, and coriander, or Tandoori Magic, with red-spiced chicken, potato, ginger, coriander, and green chilies.

One step at door, washrooms in basement. Unlicensed, smoke-free. $

BARS

30 **THE AULD SPOT**
347 Danforth, 406-4688

On a street known for its Greek joints, the Auld Spot pub is as Irish as they come. The Cranberries croon on the CD player as Guinness flows from the taps and regulars fill the small room with animated banter. Despite the pub's decor, the grub's surprisingly pan-global — carrot-and-artichoke soup, Louisiana bouillabaisse, and salads with an Asian twist.

Barrier-free, washrooms in basement.

8 **DORA KEOGH**
141 Danforth, 778-1804

Next door to Allen's is its less formal cousin the Dora, a no-frills Irish pub with a Celtic vibe. Sit in the semi-private snug or reserve the kitchen for a private dinner party featuring feasts of simple Irish stew and soda bread. First-timers are made to feel like long-lost relatives.

Barrier-free.

6 **THE OLD NICK**
123 Danforth, 461-5546

An inviting neighbourhood pub with plaid carpets

and whitewashed walls, the Nick is particularly popular with partyers on Friday and Saturday nights. The menu ventures slightly beyond typical bar food to offer quesadillas, veggie wraps, and quiches du jour. Brunch on weekends.

One step at door, washrooms in basement.

ENTERTAINMENT

LIVE MUSIC

9 **BLACK SWAN**
154 Danforth, 469-0537

A very smoky bloozecan, the Swan features live music most nights in their second-floor show-room, ranging from Chicago blues to roots and alt-rock. Downstairs at the back, there're a coupla pool tables and assorted video-trivia terminals. Despite the boy's-club atmosphere, women have actually been sighted here.

Barrier-free, washrooms in basement. Fully licensed. Patio.

84 **CUTTY'S HIDEAWAY**
538 Danforth, 463-5380

Once past the gigantic metal detector, you climb a staircase that leads to this spacious second-storey Jamaican dance hall. Occasionally, you can catch a live concert here, but mostly it's recorded Island grooves. Fancy yourself the next Bob Marley or Shabba Ranks? Then try your luck on Thursday's Karaoke Night. DJs and sound crews spin wicked tracks Friday and Saturday till the early hours, then start again on Sunday at four in the afternoon.

16 steps at door, washrooms on same floor. Fully licensed.

POOL HALLS

63 **BILLIARDS ACADEMY**
485 Danforth, 466-9696

Up a long flight of stairs, this overhauled pool hall is probably not what you expect. All dark purples and maroons — and carpeting! — the multi-windowed space holds 10 tables, each of them lined with a different colour of felt. A row of TVs picks up sports from a satellite dish and a small bar serves drinks and pub grub: chicken wings, burgers, and fries.

12 **THE MUSIC HALL**
147 Danforth, 778-8163

Part of the Festival chain that screens double bills of recent independent and Hollywood hits, this 1,000-seat cinema is also the location of many film shoots. Hard to believe, but this 75-year-old theatre doubled for Studio 54 in the recent Mike Myers flick. The Music Hall is often used as a concert venue, too, for performers as diverse as the electric James Brown and the soporific Cowboy Junkies — not on the same bill, of course!

20 steps at door, washrooms on same floor. Fully licensed.

CINEMAS — REVIVAL

12 **THE MUSIC HALL**
147 Danforth, 778-8163

See Hot Spot listing this page.

SHOPPING

BICYCLES

5 **CYCLEMANIA**
113 Danforth, 466-0330

A distinct lack of snobbery — my bike's better than your bike — sets this friendly cycling shop apart from the competition. A line of used clunkers sits out front, and a wall of top-of-the-line frames hangs inside. Bike rentals, winter storage, and free air, too.

Other location:
945 Bloor West (see page 219).

BOOKS AND MAGAZINES — NEW

11 **ANOTHER STORY**
164 Danforth, 462-1104

Not just another bookshop, Another Story focuses on gender, race, and class issues as well as alternative lifestyles. It's not all academic, though. There's quite a large children's literature section, and lots of international fiction, poetry, and self-published tracts. Book launches and readings are held regularly, too.

CARROT COMMON: A vegetarian's valhalla — organic grocery, homeopathic dispensary, and more.

42 BOOK CITY
348 Danforth, 469-9997

See listing page 169.

COMPUTERS

29 CD-ROM STORE
345 Danforth, 778-4048

Computer geeks will find much to keep them amused at this CD-ROM central. Reference texts, gardening manuals, and home-improvement how-to's are all available on disc. Both PC- and Mac-friendly, the outlet offers a wide selection of sports, games, and entertainment packages as well as MIDI keyboards, graphic-production software, and add-ons such as external speakers and joysticks.

CRAFTS

22 THE CLAY ROOM
279 Danforth, 466-8474

Ever fancied getting into ceramics, but can't be bothered with all that pottery stuff? This storefront gallery gets rid of the hard part. Start by choosing your about-to-be masterpiece from among such *objets* as precast teapots, dinner plates, or vases, and paint it yourself at one of the space's large tables. Your instant heirloom is then clear-glazed and fired in the store's own kiln. And if you'd like to paint with a bunch of friends, you can book the place for a private party. Closed Monday.

21 EL PIPIL
267 Danforth, 465-9625

For an eclectic mix of crafts and clothes from all around the world, El Pipil is the place to shop. Colourful robes, practical knapsacks, and ornate jewellery hang from the ceiling, spill off shelves, and flow onto the sidewalk. Named for an indigenous Salvadorean tribe — El Pipil means the people — this populist boutique buys directly from artists rather than corporate suppliers.

ECOLOGICAL

46 EARTHLYGOODS
372 Danforth, 466-2841

To get the slightest buzz, you'd have to smoke an entire field of the low-THC hemp that's grown to make this environmentally friendly merchandise. But here, you can buy all kinds of stuff made from the fibre-yielding plant: cargo pants, loafers, jeans, massage oils, lip balm and, er, twine. Recycled inner tubes get transformed into fashionable shoulder bags and rubber rucksacks, and old tires get a new life as doormats. Too cool or what?

FASHION — ACCESSORIES

53 **NIK NAK**
412 Danforth, 465-7703
See listing page 23.

FASHION — NEW CLOTHING

66 **MS. EMMA DESIGNS**
496 Danforth, 465-5069
See listing page 26.

71 **REPLAY**
511 Danforth, 778-4647
See listing page 27.

36 **ROBIN KAY**
348 Danforth, 466-1211
See listing page 27.

70 **SUNDE**
508 Danforth, 463-4112
See listing page 181.

FOOD

62 **ACROPOLE BAKERY**
458 Danforth, 465-1232
Greek breads and pastries.

69 **ATHENS PASTRIES**
509 Danforth, 463-5144
The specialties at this modern Greek café are marvellous phyllo-wrapped pies stuffed with spinach, ground meat, or mild cheese. Linger over cups of industrial-strength coffee accompanied by honey-drenched baklava, or rush home with your bounty and serve it as bite-size cocktail hors d'oeuvres.

35 **THE BIG CARROT**
348 Danforth, 466-2129
Founded in 1983, the co-op–run Carrot health-food store is unlike any other. What started as a

hole-in-the-wall retail shop has expanded into a mini-mall of several stores called Carrot Common. At its heart is the Big Carrot, an organic groceteria serving the Riverdale community. Baked goods, hydroponic produce, and macrobiotic prepared soups, stews, and salads are just some of the items on sale. In-store demonstrations, vegetarian cooking classes, and a newsletter with recipes are also available.

58 **SUCKERS**
450 Danforth, 405-8946
With a sales counter that appears to be built from oversized yellow lozenges, Suckers supplies the essentials for anyone who's a sucker for sweets. Tie-dyed bubble gum, parking meters full of lollipops, candy for days, T-shirts and lava lamps.
Other location:
1566 Yonge (see page 228)

45 **SUGAR MOUNTAIN**
364 Danforth, no phone
See listing page 52.

85 **SUN VALLEY**
583 Danforth, 469-5227
This store's large fruit and vegetable selection and aisles of gourmet goodies— more like a mall, really — offers as close to the variety and quality of Kensington and St. Lawrence Markets as you'll find in Greektown. The sizable clientele guarantees that everything here has a short shelf-life.

GIFTS

47 **BLUE MOON**
375 Danforth, 778-6991
Certain that gifts can make a difference, this boutique supports craftspeople in the Third World by trading with them directly. Blue Moon's criteria are that the producers receive a fair price for their work, provide healthy working conditions, and are aware of the environmental impact of their products. Many of the beautifully made and reasonably priced *objets d'art* wouldn't be out of place at a much fancier design store. And with each purchase — even of a fashionable batik bathrobe — you make a personal and political statement.

43 **PULP**
348 Danforth, 462-2812
This picayune cubbyhole sells off-the-wall greet-

ing cards, postcards, and Curious George calendars, as well as such toiletries as soaps, perfumes, and lotions. Ribbons, gift wrap, and glittery stickers bundle everything up.

HAIR — BARBERS

81 HAIR CARE JIM'S
792 Carlaw, 465-7656

OK, it's listed in the phone book as Jim's Barber Shop, but the sign painted on the window of this garish yellow clip joint clearly says "Hair Care Jim's." And so it — and he — is known. There's none of that unisex stuff here — although he will perform "ladies' short cuts." (Don't ask.) The room is spartan, just two old-fashioned barber's chairs, a rotating barber's pole, and a display of men's essential grooming aids — Bay Rum booster, Quo Vadis aftershave and cans of Gillette Foamy shaving cream. Closed Sunday.

HEALTH AND BEAUTY

37 KNOW YOUR BODY BEST
348 Danforth, 466-1515

Stressed? Back out of whack? Know Your Body Best has all for what ails ya. Registered massage therapists every one, the staff offer a wide variety of massage tools that resemble S & M toys. Spiky balls, pain erasers, and, best of all, bongers — a hard rubber ball on a flexible rod that works wonders on shoulder tension and comes with its own newsletter — share space with more common-looking facial massagers, wrist supports, and water-filled pillows.

Other location:
1908 Queen East (see page 207)

26 PLANET EARTH
309 Danforth, 463-1773

Preservative-free and hand-crafted from scratch, Planet Earth's cosmetics are made in their "kitchen" daily. A Canadian company, Planet Earth produces a line of home-spa products that includes Jacuzzi seltzers, gourmet hair food, and musk skin cream, all made from natural ingredients. Every item's contents are listed, along with its expiry date.

Other location:
473 Church (see page 144).

HOME FURNISHINGS — NEW

75 ALTERIORS
527 Danforth, 466-3622

The height of quiet, understated good taste, this upscale shop features household items — sofas, pillows, screens, chenille throws — that remain discreet despite their expensive price tags.

14 DESIGN ZONE
175A Danforth, 462-1875

It's difficult to single out any one item at this houseware and kitchenware shop, since it's piled floor-to-ceiling with well-designed gadgets and gear. Here are a few things we especially liked: wrought-iron table lamps with zebra-print shades, oversized martini glasses and matching swizzle sticks, scented candles with brass snuffers, and wicker picnic hampers. And for a modest donation to AIDS hospice Casey House, your purchase will be gloriously gift-wrapped.

16 ELAN
199 Danforth, 406-3629

Don't even think of riding off with the '50s Firestone Super Cruiser bicycle parked out front of this savvy shop — it's bolted in place to the sidewalk. Past the bike, you'll find a line of brand new retro-looking overstuffed sofas and vintage knick-knacks that give a contemporary look of old and new. Stock is constantly changing, so if you like it, you'd better buy it now — it won't be there when you come back.

38 GARDEN'S PATH
320 Danforth, 466-0116

When you walk into this florist's, you're greeted by a whistling parrot. It's not some animatronic doorbell, but an actual bird. The shop is full of flowers both fresh and dried, and houseplants and floral arrangements climb around wrought-iron topiary supports. Water splashes into a small fountain that doubles as Polly's bath.

20 LILY LEE
261 Danforth, 461-1017

Devoted to clean-lined and natural-fibre accessories, Lee's stylish shop features retro-inspired lighting fixtures, comfy multi-coloured cushions and most of the Canadian-owned Umbra line of affordable housewares. Works by local artisans

Jane Hill, Jan Koven, and Terry Craig illustrate the shop's design philosophy of simplicity.

27 **MARTHA STURDY DESIGN**
315 Danforth, 465-2464

See Hot Spot listing this page.

HOME FURNISHINGS — KITCHEN

64 **COOK'S PLACE**
488 Danforth, 461-5211

Apple corers, bottle openers, corkscrews, egg beaters, food mills, graters, and grinders . . . everything a chef could want — beginners and old hands alike. For the truly obsessed foodie, a TV monitor at the back of the shop is tuned to the Food Network. Watch as TV chef Emeril Lagasse finishes off his latest gourmet creation by shouting, "Bam!"

LIQUOR AND WINE STORES

18 **LCBO**
213 Danforth, 469-4724

Monday to Saturday 9:30 a.m. to 10 p.m.
Sunday 11 a.m. to 6 p.m.
Closed holidays.

MUSIC — CDS, RECORDS & TAPES

19 **THE MUSIC CHAMBER**
217 Danforth, 406-1641

A record store the size of your bedroom, the Chamber specializes in mainstream classical and jazz standards. The Three Tenors, Frank Sinatra, and Ella Fitzgerald are all represented with CD greatest-hits collections.

4 **SAM THE RECORD MAN**
105 Danforth, no phone

See listing page 123.

13 **URBAN SOUND EXCHANGE**
161 Danforth, 406-0630

44 **WILD EAST COMPACT SOUND**
360 Danforth, 469-8371

At the top of the turquoise stairs that lead to the second floor, you'll find a minimally decorated, austere room where the focus is on the best in

27 **MARTHA STURDY DESIGN**
315 Danforth, 465-2464

Vancouver sculptor-turned-jewellery-designer Sturdy embraces minimalism. Moving beyond her work in metals and stones, the artist now produces limited-edition cast-resin tables, benches, and pedestals. Reminiscent of '70s-era Gucci, her colourful crafts have been featured on the cover of Vogue magazine and sold in boutiques throughout Europe and the Far East. And now on the Danforth!

CDs and vinyl. The shop stocks a comprehensive cross-section of electronica categorized as techno, ambient, synthbeats, minimalist, and good ol' German blip-rock. The jazz and classical sections are equally well catalogued.

NATURAL REMEDIES

39 **THE BIG CARROT WHOLISTIC DISPENSARY**
348 Danforth, 466-8432

Connected to the main store, though it also has its own separate entrance, the homeopathic branch of the Carrot provides a full-service healing centre. Experienced and savvy staff supply info on naturopathic supplements, herbal remedies, and vibrational essences, as well as books, pamphlets, and videos.

24 **OTTWAY HERBALIST**
300 Danforth, 463-5125

Founded in 1930, this holistic-remedy clinic offers free consultations with a staff of European-trained doctors and pharmacists. Over 3,500 herbs and herbal cocktails are for sale. They also print a free newsletter that announces in-house blood tests and information on new products.

Other location:
453 Church (see page 144)

23 **THUNA HERBALIST**
298 Danforth, 465-3366

Out front, a 75-year-old Toledo weight scale offers to tell your weight for free. Don't fret — it's always too high. Inside the herbal apothecary, therapists offer various treatments — naturopathy, chiropractic, acupuncture, reflexology, and Ojibway, western, or Chinese herbalism. They also sell cooking spices and bran cookies encouragingly dubbed Bowel Buddies.

NEW AGE

40 **GIFTS FROM THE EARTH**
320 Danforth, 465-4579

These gifts come from way down inside Mother Earth — most of them are mined in quarries. Pore over crystals, onyx pyramids, and healing stones while New Age muzak soothes you into another consciousnezzz. . . . Sorry, I dozed off there. You'll find spirit catchers, beeswax candles, extremely essential oils and incense here, too.

PET SUPPLIES

7 **SMALL WONDERS**
140 Danforth, 462-3773

More than a pet store, this animal-friendly community centre offers pet grooming on the premises — or you can rent the space and do it yourself — as well as advice on breed selection, and fashions for both you and your pooch or Persian. The custom-made studded collars would look just as cool on you. Once you've met the owner's Doberman and Rottweiler — don't be afraid, they're sucks, really — your new friends will gladly accept a Yuppy Puppy dog treat. This animal-friendly haven also carries a line of vegetarian pet food.

VIDEO

59 **GREEK CITY VIDEO**
452 Danforth, 461-6244

17 **REVUE VIDEO**
207 Danforth, 778-5776

From cult classics to Hollywood blockbusters and indie documentaries, the Revue stocks an impressive range of titles for rent or sale. They post a top-40 chart of current faves, and sort older films by country of origin and director. Besides the works of such cinematic greats as Fellini, Scorsese, and the Bergmans — Ingmar and Ingrid — you'll find the complete works of French comic genius Jacques Tati.

Boardwalk

THE BEACH

Whatever you do, don't call it the Beaches. There's only one beach and locals insist the name of their neighbourhood is singular. Rollerblade, bike, or stroll along the lakeside boardwalk. Take in the annual jazz festival in Kew Gardens, or browse Queen Street East's many quirky boutiques.

FOOD & DINING

RESTAURANTS

40 **AKANE-YA**
2214A Queen East, 699-0377

This small, austere eatery — grey walls, black lacquered furnishings, translucent shoji screens — dishes out upmarket Japanese dinners. Sushi combos, veggie or shrimp tempura, teriyaki platters, and super soba-noodle soups may be pricier than elsewhere, but the price guarantees the first-rate quality of the fish. Because space is limited, weekend reservations are a must. Closed Monday.

Barrier-free, washrooms in basement. Fully licensed, smoke-free. Patio. $$$

48 **ANTOINETE**
2455-1/2 Queen East, 698-1300

This petite eatery's size makes reservations mandatory — that, and the homemade pasta that draws customers to the Beach from all over our Ital-mad city. Eschewing nouvelle cuisine, chef-owner Antoinette Sacco's menu features old-school minestrone and ravioli. Her only concession to fusion cooking is a Caesar salad that sits on a crisp cumin-speckled pappadum. Tricoloured gnocchi plump with smoked chicken, peppers, and basil are sauced with vine-ripe tomatoes. And what could be more traditional for dessert than tiramisú? Closed Sunday and holidays.

Barrier-free. Fully licensed. $$

47 **EL PERRO**
2282 Queen East, 690-9030

The team behind the Santa Fe–style Tejas beanery (see page 202) turns to the cuisine of Spain for this cantina's menu. Light snacks are nibbled at the tapas bar, and substantial suppers are served on the raised rear level. Unusual for this style of cooking, most dishes are low in fat. *¡Ay caramba!* Closed Monday.

Barrier-free, washrooms in basement. Fully licensed, smoke-free. Patio. $$

18 **IL FORNELLO**
1968 Queen East, 691-8377

See listing page 39.

Barrier-free. Fully licensed. $$

11 **JAMAICA SUNRISE**
1959 Queen East, 691-2999

This comfortable bistro brings a little bit of the Islands to the Beach. While retro reggae gently rocks, regulars dig into jerk chicken, oxtail, or curried-goat dinners, all sided with rice 'n' peas,

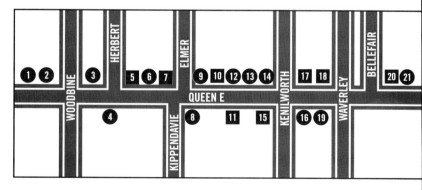

fried dumplings, and tossed greens. Tricoloured Rasta pasta and veggie rotis will satisfy non-carnivores. Wash it all down with homemade ginger beer, carrot juice, or the soda called Ting.

One step at door, washrooms in basement. Fully licensed. $$

38 PEPPINO'S ON THE BEACH
2343 Queen East, 699-3552

The prettiest — and priciest — spot in the Beach, this beautifully decked out Italian trattoria in a Victorian house overlooks two gardens. The front-yard patio is the perfect place for moonlit summer dinners, and the inside dining room is ablaze in light and white linen year round. Ital fare runs from traditional prosciutto-and-melon antipasti to black-ink cuttlefish risotto. Closed Monday.

11 steps at door, washrooms on same floor. Fully licensed, smoke-free. $$$

24 RICHARD'S
2066 Queen East, 698-2066

Open for dinner seven nights a week, this homey bistro features a market-fresh menu. The eclectic fare ranges from Brie with snails to warm goat-cheese-and-mango salad and Bismarck herring starters. Mains tend toward such classics as chicken Kiev and apple-stuffed pork tenderloin. Casual and never stuffy, Richard's has been a Beach favourite for more than 20 years.

Four steps at door, washrooms in basement. Fully licensed. $$

54 ROSETTA
924 Kingston Rd, 690-6081

Kingston Road, a desolate strip that runs from the

MERSINI: College cool goes to the Beach.

lake to Scarborough, is an unlikely locale for such an upscale eatery. Once a greasy spoon — the lunch counter still stands, but now they serve martinis instead of banana splits — Rosetta's has retro lime-green booths that are the perfect setting for romantic dinners. Toned-down fusion fare whose ingredients sing rather than shock, and smooth but never obsequious service make this tiny gem shine. Closed Sunday and Monday.

Barrier-free, washrooms in basement. Fully licensed. $$$

52 TEJAS
2485 Queen East, 694-2643

Right where the Queen streetcar turns to make its journey westward, this extremely cool cantina is nestled among the Beach's tall trees. Featuring Santa Fe fare with little fat, the menu goes beyond the usual burrito-and-refried-bean combo plates served at most Toronto tacoterias. Mesquite-smoked chicken makes several appearances. For dessert, there's retro Key lime pie. And don't miss the frozen slushy margaritas!

One step at door, washrooms in basement. Fully licensed, smoke-free. $$

50 SATAY ON THE ROAD
2306 Queen East, 698-8618

Diners sit under bamboo awnings at this mainstream Thai eatery. Slim pickings for vegetarians; except for a few curries, the menu here is mostly meat. Skewered satays — chicken, beef, pork, lamb, squid, or scallop — come with a nippy dip, and the pad thai rice noodles are tart with tamarind and covered in crushed peanuts. Free iced tea with everything. Closed Monday.

Barrier-free. Fully licensed, smoke-free. $$

Other locations:
1570 Bayview (see page 225)
2003 Avenue Road (see page 225)

51 SPIAGGIA
2318 Queen East, 699-4656

The tables in this bright and breezy room are set far apart — perfect for private dining. The chalk-board outlines a modern Mediterranean menu featuring such familiar fare as steamed mussels, grilled calamari, and veal Marsala. Even more romantic, the rear room is dimly lit for dining *à deux*. More sociable diners can take in the Beach's street scene from Spiaggia's curbside patio.

Three steps at door, washrooms on same floor. Fully licensed. Patio. $$$

52 TEJAS
2485 Queen East, 694-2643

See Hot Spot this page.

15 WHITLOCK'S
1961 Queen East, 691-8784

In an all-wood store built in 1891 that's been declared a historic site by the city, this casual bistro boasts an antique shop's worth of attractive clutter. However, the restaurant's menu is fairly *au courant*. Escargots exotiques, vegetable spring rolls, Cajun snapper, and baby back ribs are typical dinner and brunch items. Many veggie mains.

One step at door, washrooms in basement. Fully licensed. $$

5 WICKERHEAD
1910 Queen East, 693-5980

Only open for weekend brunch, this cosy restaurant has its housefront painted to resemble an oversized woven basket. Wickerhead boasts a chef formerly of Centro — one of the priciest meal tickets in town — but the menu here rings in at half the price of his former employer's. Start with organic mixed greens, or try scones with apricot-and-almond preserves and apples sautéed in maple syrup, all topped with crème fraîche. Ex-

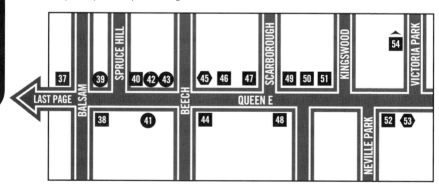

actly what "Eggs Flexibility" is isn't explained. Closed Monday to Friday.

Six steps at door, washrooms on same floor. Fully licensed. Patio. $$

29 **YUMEI SUSHI**
2216F Queen East, 698-7705

An unpretentious and pretty sushi bar, Yumei isn't in the same class as the more expensive Akane-Ya, but serves satisfying rice-and-seafood combos. Semi-private booths line one side of the room and more public tables take up the rest. A few Korean dishes appear, notably bulgoki (marinated sliced sirloin), and kalbi (beef ribs). Weekday all-inclusive lunch specials and takeout are available, too.

Barrier-free, washrooms in basement. Fully licensed. $$

CAFES AND COFFEE HOUSES

31 **MERSINI**
2120 Queen East, 699-9444

Under twinkly ceiling pin lights or outdoors on the curbside patio under the stars, this Mediterranean eatery is as close as the Beach gets to College cool. A mishmash of mesh and marble, the restaurant's decor corresponds to its fusion of Mediterranean fare. Greek mezes such as stuffed vine leaves and pickled octopus share the menu with Italian grilled cheese sandwiches with prosciutto and roasted peppers. Or go Belgian with waffles.

Barrier-free. Fully licensed. $$

37 **MIXED DELIGHTS**
2180 Queen East, 690-7649

A mixed bag of goodies— bulk coffee beans, blackballs and jujubes — are for sale in this very dark, intimate room spotlit by halogen lamps. Sip a cuppa out front on the rickety park bench or indoors at one of a few window seats. Make sure to check out the wall of signed celebrity photos: black-hatted Garth Brooks; Mr. Hockey himself, Wayne Gretzky; and curmudgeonly Lou Reed. Someone swiped the autographed glossy of Céline Dion, though.

Two steps at door, washrooms in basement. Unlicensed. $

35 **P.A.M.'S**
2142 Queen East, 693-6090

Two steps at door, washrooms on same floor. Unlicensed. $

46 **THE REMARKABLE BEAN**
2242 Queen East, 690-2420

This java mecca for rollerbladers sells eat-in or takeout coffee and snacks. Lounge on the sidewalk and watch the passers-by or grab some goodies to take to a double bill at the Fox cinema next door.

Barrier-free, washrooms in basement. Unlicensed, smoke-free. $

22 **THE ROASTERY**
2018 Queen East, 698-5090

One step at door, washrooms in basement. Unlicensed. $

DELIS AND DINERS

26 **CALIFORNIA SANDWICHES**
2197 Queen East, 699-1662

See listing page 74. Closed Sunday.

Barrier-free, washrooms in basement. Fully licensed, cash only. $

44 **THE GOOF**
2379 Queen East, 694-9696

Properly named the Garden Gate, this greasy spoon got its nickname when the "d" in the neon sign over the front door announcing "Good Food" burned out. Or so legend has it. The Goof is also allegedly a Chinese restaurant, but no one has been seen eating chow mein here since it opened in 1952. It's the all-day breakfasts that keep the jukebox-equipped booths full. Expect a lineup on weekends.

One step at door, washrooms in basement. Unlicensed, smoke-free. $

20 **SUNSET GRILL**
2006 Queen East, 690-9985

A grill that never closes, the Sunset serves up massive round-the-clock breakfasts of pancakes, French toast, or steak and eggs. Order through the open front window or venture into the restaurant's long, thin room and eat among the plastic plants. The farther in you go, the nicer the diner

R.C. HARRIS FILTRATION PLANT: Art deco icon.

gets. By the time you've reached the very back, you'll find yourself in a raised area under a sky-light, far from the open kitchen's smoky grill.

One step at door, washrooms in basement. Beer and wine, cash only. $

17 LICK'S
1960 Queen East, 362-5425

Is there an echo in here? After selecting your burger — Homeburger with cheese, turkey Gob-bler, or veggie — the cashier shouts, "Ordering!" The rest of the staff join in with "Ordering! Order-ing!" By the time you've run the gauntlet of condi-ments — "Relish?" "Relish!" — your head will be spinning. The meaty foil-wrapped burgers and hand-cut fries almost make the song-and-dance routine from the help bearable.

Two steps at door, washrooms in basement. Unlicensed, smoke-free. $

27 NOVA FISH AND CHIPS
2209 Queen East, 699-1885

Nothing's changed here since Nova opened just after the Second World War. A blank black-and-white facade fronts an ugly narrow space

watched over by a stuffed marlin mounted on the wall. Line up at the counter and order basic news-paper-wrapped halibut and chips. Douse 'em in salt and cider vinegar and devour 'em at one of the few Arborite-topped tables, or take 'em home to demolish in front of the TV. Closed Sunday and Monday.

One step at door, washrooms in basement. Unlicensed, smoke-free, cash only. $

BARS

49 FITZGERALD'S
2298 Queen East, 698-8588

Downstairs, this is a typical dingy Canadian beer parlour, complete with silently blinking video games and a TV tuned to TSN. By noon, the stand-up bar is lined with regulars arguing over last night's (insert sport here) game. But after dark, the upstairs space is transformed into a cocktail lounge. As a fire blazes, sophisticated Beach resi-dents down such cocktails as the Paralyzer mar-tini and Killer Kool-Aid. Platters of nachos or pakoras and samosas satisfy the munchies.

Two steps at door, washrooms on same floor. Patio.

ENTERTAINMENT

CINEMAS — REVIVAL

45 THE FOX
2236 Queen East, 691-7330
See listing page 168.

ATTRACTIONS

53 R.C. HARRIS FILTRATION PLANT
2701 Queen East, 392-2932

Featured in Michael Ondaatje's novel *In the Skin of a Lion*, and one of Toronto's most striking art deco structures, this beautifully designed water-works is often used as a backdrop for video and movie shoots. Surrounded by multi-tiered ter-races, the colossally cool building overlooks Lake Ontario — sunsets and sunrises here are particu-larly spectacular. Free one-hour guided tours of the interior are scheduled every Saturday at 10 a.m., 11:30 a.m. and 1 p.m.

SHOPPING

AROMATHERAPY

39 **THE AROMA SHOPPE**
2206 Queen East, 698-5850

Founded by aromatherapist and cosmetologist Jan Benham, this warm, wood-trimmed shop sells hand-blended hair and body products based on essential oils from the plant kingdom, all with a Celtic motif. Special one-day courses cover herbal soap-making, concocting your own makeup, and Reflexology 101. Full-time courses in aromatherapy are also offered.

AUDIO EQUIPMENT

1 **RING AUDIO**
1860 Queen East, 691-2336

Audiophiles flock to this shop specializing in non-transistorized stereos. TEAC and Revox reel-to-reel tape decks, studio-quality JBL speaker cabinets the size of refrigerators, and all-tube McIntosh and Fisher amps attract hi-fi fiends from all over. Amidst clear Plexiglas speakers festooned with pink and blue neon lighting, a poster collection depicts '50s Hollywood femme fatale Rita Hayworth. Closed Sunday and Monday.

BICYCLES

2 **BEACHES CYCLERY**
1882 Queen East, 699-1461

A bare-bones bike sales and repair shop, the Cyclery stocks the Giant and Norco lines. Closed Sunday.

43 **RE-CYCLE**
2230 Queen East, 698-3756

Here's a bike shop with a split personality. During warm months, it's a basic bicycle sales and service centre. But when winter weather comes, it morphs into a gift store. What gives? Seems the two owners see their business differently — so in the summer they stock inner tubes and sell moun-

tain bikes and in-line skates, but come November, they roll out the Umbra picture frames and wastepaper baskets. Go figure.

BOOKS AND MAGAZINES — NEW

13 **BOOK CITY**
1950 Queen East, 698-1444

See listing page 169.

8 **MEDIA ENCORE**
1939 Queen East, 699-5511

Not only does Media Encore sell used and remaindered books — and CDs — at half their sticker price, but they buy them as well. Their mission statement is "Easy to buy from, easy to sell to." One of the larger book emporia in the Beach, it also holds regular readings and discussion groups.

CRAFTS

12 **SIBONGILE**
1944 Queen East, 698-0021

Up a very long flight of stairs, this African gift shop nestles under the rafters of a Beach storefront. While world music lilts, check out the handmade wrapping paper, the beaded mats, and the wrought-iron hat stands. Drums and tambourines will appeal to anyone with a sense of rhythm.

FASHION — ACCESSORIES

3 **HATS GALORE**
1883 Queen East, 693-1076

Every item sold here except the umbrellas and the cowboy *chapeaux* is fashioned on the premises by the mad hatter. Choose from plush jesters' hats, straw boaters, 10-gallon Stetsons, panama hats, Australian bush hats, and tweed Sherlock Holmes deerstalkers — they even have sombreros. Most are available in women's, men's, and children's sizes.

FASHION — NEW CLOTHING

9 **ENDS**
1930 Queen East, 699-2271

See listing page 180.

HOT SPOT

33 **OVERKILL**
2130 Queen East, 691-4165

If you're ever stuck for gift ideas for teenagers — or for Peter Pan boomers who never made it past 20 — this cool boutique has just what you're looking for. Belts made from Chevrolet seat belts, expensive state-of-the-art sunglasses, and Overkill's own logo-embossed oversized sweatshirts make just about anybody look cool. To prove it, the shop displays an autographed copy of NOW magazine featuring cover boys and regular customers the Barenaked Ladies. Told ya — just about anybody!

33 **OVERKILL**
2130 Queen East, 691-4165

See Hot Spot this page.

32 **WILD WILD WEST**
2130 Queen East, 693-2668

Howdy, pardner! Urban cowboys and cowgirls will find all they require for bronco busting and/or line dancing at this Old West boot boutique. Bolo ties, silver belt buckles and Santa Fe–style ponchos help recreate the look of the American Southwest. Would-be Crocodile Dundees can fashion themselves in Australian outback outfits and dingo hats. Did we mention cowboy boots?

FASHION — SHOES

19 **NATURE'S FOOTWEAR**
1971A Queen East, 691-6706

A sensible shoe store for sensitive soles. Sandals and lace-ups from Birkenstock, Ganter, and Rieker as well as anti-stress Rolde walking shoes are on offer. Massage your tired toes with a Relax-A-Roller or pamper them in multi-hued wool-and-sheepskin Padraig slippers. Hand-knit woolly sweaters, too. Closed Wednesday, Sunday and holidays.

FOOD

30 **DOUGH HEAD'S**
2118 Queen East, 693-9770

Bread's the thing here — not the stuff you spend, but the dough that gets baked into loaves with honey and figs, spinach and feta, or green and black niçoise olives. In the back, bins brim with buns, baguettes, and bagels. For dessert, check out the panoply of flans, tortes, and tarts. If you're not in a hurry, sit at one of the few tables scattered about while savouring a gourmet sandwich. Cash only.

23 **THE NUTTY CHOCOLATIER**
2179 Queen East, 698-5548

There's plenty here to satisfy chocoholics of any age. Imported Belgian truffles — amaretto-, cognac- and champagne-spiked — British chocolate bars, and sponge taffy are just some of what's on offer. And if you can't think of a gift for a certain someone, how about a solid-chocolate fish named Larry, a herd of marzipan pigs, or a detective kit that includes a chocolate walkie-talkie, a chocolate badge, and kinky chocolate handcuffs?

7 **PASTA FRESCA**
1924 Queen East, 691-5999

Just inside the door, a pasta machine churns out the store's fresh noodles. Two types of tortellini — spinach or veal — and five types of agnolotti (including sweet potato) can either be topped with one of several homemade sauces and eaten on the premises, or taken home to be reheated. A blackboard menu announces the day's specials, and a freezer case holds more noodles and Italian ices.

10 **POP IT POPCORN**
1932 Queen East, 693-2999

A shop completely devoted to popcorn, Pop It pops a rainbow of colours and flavours — nacho, ketchup, and dill pickle being just a few. Raw kernels and seasonings for do-it-yourself popcorn pig-outs are sold here, too.

6 **SUGAR MOUNTAIN**
1920 Queen East, 690-7998

See listing page 52.

41 **SUNSET FOODS**
2359 Queen East, 690-4460

Those who like their food hot will find this terra-cotta-coloured gourmet shop a fire-eaters' heaven. Sauces with descriptive names like Endorphin Rush, Rasta Fire, and Sudden Death — which comes with a way-cool skull key chain

LUSH: Handmade and eco-conscious cosmetics sold by the kilo — and used by the tubful.

— are sure to set taste buds ablaze. Dried chili peppers and other Tex-Mex staples are available, as are jalapeño-decorated boxer shorts and red-pepper patio-light sets. Closed Monday.

HAIR — BARBERS

42 **NEIL'S HAIRCUTTING**
2218 Queen East, 691-8369

For more than 25 years, Neil has been cutting hair in his old-fashioned shop. The front window holds a jungle of overgrown plants and a turn-of-the-century barber's pole. Inside, Neil's customers sit on an antique chair surrounded by rec-room wood-panelled walls covered with autographed glossies of Maple Leafs hockey players and Blue Jays baseball greats.

HEALTH AND BEAUTY

14 **THE BODY SHOP**
1952 Queen East, 694-9936

See listing page 30.

3 **KNOW YOUR BODY BEST**
1908 Queen East, 690-7082

See listing page 196.

21 **LUSH**
2014 Queen East, 691-8822

See listing page 30.

HOME FURNISHINGS — NEW

16 **HANSON HOUSE**
1967 Queen East, 699-5125

No, this is not a boutique dedicated to the teenage trio from Oklahoma. There's nothing here that Hanson fans would want — unless they're into exquisitely tasteful objects. Velour pillows embroidered "Prince" on one side and "Frog" on the other, chrome crocodile nutcrackers, and sheet-metal refuse canisters labelled "Rubbish" are typical of the whimsy on offer.

LIQUOR AND WINE STORES

25 **LCBO**
2185 Queen East, 690-9876

Monday to Friday 9:30 a.m. to 9 p.m.
Saturday 9 a.m. to 9 p.m.
Sunday 11 a.m. to 6 p.m.
Closed holidays.

28 **WICCASHOPPE**
2211 Queen East, 693-9422

It's Halloween every day at this one-stop shop for witches and warlocks — good ones, of course. Stock up on homemade incense, detoxifying healing stones, mojo bags, and tarot cards. Fans of Norwegian death metal will find a horde of gargoyle statuettes, phallic gender candles, and glow-in-the-dark human skulls. The store sells bath salts, too. Closed Monday.

NEW AGE

28 **WICCASHOPPE**
2211 Queen East, 693-9422

See Hot Spot this page.

34 **WUNJO'S**
2134 Queen East, 699-3601

Think of Wunjo's as a supermarket of the supernatural. Offering classes in such New Age interests as yoga, belly dancing, and hands-on healing, this karmic community centre includes an art gallery, a gift shop with Native crafts, and a café serving samosas, empanadas, and organic cherry pie.

ROLLERBLADING

36 **PLANET SKATE**
2144 Queen East, 690-7588

The Beach is an ideal place to rollerblade — especially the lakeside boardwalk — and this streamlined boutique has everything a rad skater needs. Impressive high-tech wheels by Roces, Rossignol, Bauer, and K2 line the walls, and shelves hold Indian Motorcycle sweats and tees as well as Airwalk runners. For winter 'bladers, there are carbon-fibre hockey sticks and Bruzer fleece outerwear. And in the summer, the store offers in-line skating lessons and a kids' skate camp.

Dutch Dreams Ice Cream

AND BEYOND

Downtowners may find it hard to believe, but there is nightlife north of Bloor Street. Sure, the pickings get slimmer the farther you travel from Queen West, but all over Toronto there are neighbourhoods with treasures that only the local residents know and sometimes share.

HARBOUR & ISLANDS

FOOD & DINING

RESTAURANTS

THE RECTORY
Ward's Island, 203-6011

Other than a few hot-dog stands and fast-food restaurants, the Rectory is the only dining spot on the islands. Located just off the southernmost boardwalk, the Rectory is situated in an idyllic grove of shade trees far from the tourists and day-trippers. Chef Audrey Demers operates the contemporary-menu eatery from late May to Labour Day and only on weekends (reservations — especially for Sunday brunch — are essential). Closed Monday to Thursday.
Barrier-free. Unlicensed. Patio. $$

DELIS AND DINERS

CANARY GRILL
409 Front East, 364-9943

The Canary is hard to miss — it sits surrounded by bulldozed fields of industrial debris in a deserted area of the waterfront. A favourite of film crews — check out the autographed pics of Jane Seymour, Peta "Nikita" Wilson, and, er, '80s heavy metallurgists Killer Dwarves — this greasy spoon has lots of atmosphere and passable diner grub. Since there's a machine shop directly below, be sure to visit the Canary's washrooms — they vibrate!

Three steps at door, washrooms on same floor. Fully licensed. $

BARS

THE IRISH ROVER'S PUB
2 Villiers, 778-5352

Owned by the professional Irishmen famous for their '70s hit "The Unicorn" — surely, you remember the chorus: "There were green alligators and long-necked geese, some humpy-backed camels, and some chimpanzees"? — the Rover's is a waterfront Irish pub on the grand scale. Such traditional pub grub as bangers 'n' mash, Irish stew, and beer-braised beef in Rover's Pie is served alongside contemporary fare like French onion soup or chicken fingers in a basket. Mondays, Celtic bands perform, and Wednesdays through Sundays '60s-style combos rock the house.
Other location:
The Unicorn (see page 226)
Barrier-free. Patio.

ENTERTAINMENT

LIVE MUSIC

AIR CANADA CENTRE
40 Bay, 815-5500

Toronto's latest enormodrome, the Air Canada Centre is home to two of Toronto's professional sports teams — the NBA's Raptors and the NHL's Maple Leafs. A state-of-the-art facility with four Sony Jumbotrons and over 650 TV monitors — you can watch the game from the washrooms if you like — the facility is also used for concert performances by acts like the Rolling Stones and the Tragically Hip.

MOLSON AMPHITHEATRE
955 Lakeshore Boulevard West, 260-5600

Although it doesn't move, the high-tech Molson Amphitheatre has replaced the revolving-stage concert bowl at Ontario Place (a great place to spend half the show watching the headliners' backs). With a capacity of 16,000 — 9,000 seated and 7,000 general admission tickets on the lawn behind them — the venue has hosted performances by Elton John and the Spice Girls, and was the site of the Lilith Fair festival.

THE WAREHOUSE
132 Queen's Quay East, 869-0045

Part of the Guvernment entertainment complex, the Warehouse is a 2,000-capacity concert space in a, well, warehouse. Though some attempt has been made to glitz it up, it still remains a grim, cavernous room with appalling sound. That hasn't stopped the likes of the Rolling Stones, David Bowie, Prince, and the Backstreet Boys from appearing here.

DANCE CLUBS

THE DOCKS
11 Polson, 461-DOCK

The Docks isn't a nightclub — it's a theme park with dance music and a liquor license. Big? Try this: over 40,000 square feet of patio, a 4,700-square-foot outdoor swimming pool, an 18-hole miniature golf course, a 40-foot-tall rock-climbing wall, a 300-yard driving range, 35 bars, a 120-foot-drop Giant Swing Ride, special Foam Nights, live music concerts, and 16 outdoor pool tables — including one in the pool. Closed November to April.

THE GUVERNMENT
132 Queen's Quay West, 869-9261

You enter through a curvy fluorescent-cerise painted vestibule that leads to a monstrous 2,500-club-kid-capacity black-and-silver dance hall decked out in chain mail. Upstairs, the VIP lounge — the Drink — is a quieter room furnished with fuzzy purple sofas and fun-fur drapes. A third room, Tang — which, as its name suggests, painted screaming orange — hosts gay House Nights every Friday. Closed Sunday to Thursday.

Some areas barrier-free. Fully licensed. Patio.

GALLERIES AND MUSEUMS

POWER PLANT
213 Queen's Quay West, 973-4949

Can't find the Power Plant? Just look for the giant smokestack. In the same former ice house that is home to the du Maurier Theatre Centre, the Power Plant is an eclectic art gallery that focuses on multidisciplinary works by emerging and established artists. Past shows have included period photos by Warhol-documentor Billy Name and a multimedia history of the Queen West art scene of the '80s.

THEATRE

DU MAURIER THEATRE CENTRE
231 Queen's Quay West, 954-5199

A 425-seat theatre in a converted ice house at

UNIVERSAL GRILL: A former greasy spoon, the Grill has morphed into a deluxe diner with moxie.

Harbourfront , the Centre presents new music works, drama, performances by touring dance companies, and a series of children's concerts. Some areas barrier-free.

DANCE THEATRE

PREMIERE DANCE THEATRE
207 Queen's Quay West, 973-4921

Located on the third floor of the Queen's Terminal building, the Premier Dance Theatre is an intimate venue used by many local and touring performance companies. Both the Toronto Dance Theatre and Danny Grossman Dance Company present their fall and winter seasons here.

ATTRACTIONS

HARBOURFRONT
235 Queen's Quay West, 973-3000

Once an abandoned industrial wasteland along the waterfront, Harbourfront is now a revitalized culture and recreation centre that reflects the diversity of Toronto's multi-ethnic population. A series of converted warehouses and dock buildings, Harbourfront comprises theatres, art galleries, concert bowls, lakeside restaurants, cafés, and watering holes (see listings for du Maurier Theatre Centre and Power Plant). Perhaps its biggest attraction is the Harbourfront Reading Series, a weekly series of appearances by top Canadian and international authors that culminates in the annual International Festival of Authors (see listing page 237).

QUEEN'S QUAY TERMINAL
207 Queen's Quay West, 203-0510

Once a shipping terminal, this art deco building has been converted into a shopping concourse topped by luxury condominiums. Jutting out into Lake Ontario, the complex houses the Premier Dance Theatre (see above) as well as shops like the Japanese Paper Place (see listing page 65), Movado, and Tilley Endurables.

SKYDOME
1 Blue Jays Way, 341-3663

Located at the foot of the C.N. Tower — or the Space Needle, as the 'Merkins call it — the Sky-dome is home to former World Series champs the

Toronto Blue Jays. The roof retracts and the world's largest Sony Jumbotron lives here. Uh, that's about it.

WARD'S ISLAND

Before the islands were turned into parklands, people actually lived there. They still do on Ward's Island, an enclave of a few hundred winterized cottages on the far eastern end of the archipelago. Since cars aren't allowed on the island, a series of wooden boardwalks wind among the houses and along the waterfront, making a great bike ride.

SHOPPING

BEER STORES

THE BEER STORE
350 Queen's Quay West, 581-1677

Monday to Wednesday 10 a.m. to 8 p.m.
Thursday and Friday 10 a.m. to 9 p.m.
Saturday 9:30 a.m. to 9 p.m.
Sunday 11 a.m. to 6 p.m.
Closed holidays.

LIQUOR AND WINE STORES

LCBO
2 Cooper, 864-6777

Monday to Saturday 9 a.m. to 10 p.m.
Sunday 11 a.m. to 6 p.m.
Closed holidays.

SEX

NUDE BEACH
Hanlan's Point

On the far western end of the Toronto islands you'll find Hanlan's Point, Toronto's only nude beach. Well, beach is a bit of an exaggeration — it's more like a strip of crushed gravel next to an unswimmable, polluted lake. But there are a few dunes and some scrub pines to frolic amongst. And since it is now legal for women — and men! — to tan topless in public in Ontario, Hanlan's Point is rather, well, pointless.

QUEEN EAST

FOOD & DINING

RESTAURANTS

BONJOUR BRIOCHE
812 Queen East, 406-1250

Master baker Henri Faissen — formerly of chic Ellipsis on College Street — makes the best brioche in town. These airy rolls, rich with eggs and butter, are served with Bonjour's all-day breakfast and brunch menu. Lightly scrambled eggs topped with a smoked-salmon rosette are served with a kick-start of horseradish-chive sour cream and a dab of bright-red salmon roe. Saturdays and Sundays, the casual coffee-coloured room is a madhouse — expect a long wait for a table. Closed Monday.

One step at door, washrooms in basement. Beer and wine, smoke-free, cash only. $

HELLO TOAST
993 Queen East, 778-7299

Humourist Fran Liebowitz once wondered why there are restaurants in New York City called Bonjour Croissant but none in Paris called Hello Toast. Well, there is in Toronto. With a collection of antique toasters, and decked out with '40s dining-room furniture and a chandelier constructed from '50s fiberglass lamps, this kitschy kitchen serves first-rate lunches and pasta 'n' pizza dinners. But it's Toast's weekend brunch that's put the beanery on the map — deluxe eggs Benedict with smoked salmon on English muffins, or eggs Florentine with Mornay sauce. Don't miss the fabulous challah toast. Closed Monday dinner.

One step at door, washrooms on same floor. Fully licensed. $$

THE REAL JERK
709 Queen East, 463-6055

In a converted bank, Ed and Lily Pottinger operate an Island-idyll jerk shack that's one of Toronto's favourites — it usually tops NOW's Readers' Poll for best Caribbean restaurant. A table on the balcony's a great place to watch the rollicking action.

Old-school reggae rocks the sound system, Red Stripes are swilled, and jerk chicken with peas 'n' rice gets devoured. Instead of heading south for a winter getaway, grab the Queen car and head east!

One step at door, washrooms in basement. Fully licensed. $$

SEA BREEZE
1342 Queen East, 406-6060

An unassuming storefront, Sea Breeze serves up daily dim sum that's easily the equivalent of any of the bite-sized delicacies sold in downtown's Chinatown. Locals have kept this extremely modest dining room a secret for years — with only a few tables and a limited menu, the Sea Breeze has to be one of the cheapest meal deals in town. Some of the sum is downright weird — Oriental shrimp tacos? — but its crocodile-shaped dumplings are stuffed with delicious shrimp, crab, and crunchy bamboo shoots.

One step at door, washrooms in basement. Unlicensed, smoke-free. $

ENTERTAINMENT

LIVE MUSIC

THE OPERA HOUSE
735 Queen East, 466-0313

Once a movie theatre — and before that a vaudeville hall — the 650-seat Opera House has excellent sightlines. A number of local promoters regularly present concerts as well as fashion shows and fetish events.

Some areas barrier-free. Fully licensed.

SHOPPING

BEER STORES

THE BEER STORE
1285 Queen East, 465-2626

Monday to Friday 10 a.m. to 10 p.m.
Saturday 9:30 a.m. to 10 p.m.
Sunday 11 a.m. to 6 p.m.
Closed holidays.

FASHION — VINTAGE CLOTHING

GOODWILL
299 Coxwell, 465-8569
See listing page 114.

VALUE VILLAGE
924 Queen East, 778-4818
See listing page 219.

FOOD

KITCHEN WITCH EMPORIUM
1118 Queen East, 462-0020

Pie queen Skeeter Jones is quite a character. Regarded as a kitchen magician, Jones puts on a mock-bitchiness that regular customers ignore or love. But who gives a fig about attitude when her baked goods are so superb? Displayed on turn-of-the-19th-century stands, the sweet and savoury pies available here have earned Jones her culinary esteem — gorgeous double-crusted peach 'n' pecan tarts, and deep-dish meal-in-one combos such as rosemary-spiked lamb with potatoes, carrots, and buttery gravy. Seasonal soups, scones, turnovers, and sensational brownies like the frozen Oreo Treats have made the Witch a weekend must-stop in about-to-be-gentrifed Leslieville. Closed Monday.

HOME FURNISHINGS — USED

CLUTTERS
692 Queen East, 461-3776

ETHEL
1091 Queen East, 778-6608

MACHINE AGE MODERN
692 Queen East, 461-3588

PHIL'Z
770 Queen East, 461-9913
See listing page 78.

VAVOOM
1114 Queen East, 465-2770

ZIG ZAG
1107 Queen East, 778-6495

LIQUOR AND WINE STORES

LCBO
1656 Queen East, 691-9758

Monday to Thursday 9:30 a.m. to 10 p.m.
Friday and Saturday 9:30 a.m. to 11 p.m.
Sunday 11 a.m. to 6 p.m.
Closed holidays.

ROCK-CLIMBING

TORONTO CLIMBING ACADEMY
100A Broadview, 406-5900

In this 10,000-square-foot facility, the Academy offers state-of-the-art simulated rock-climbing for beginners and pros alike. Seventy multi-dimensional climbs — many with top-roping routes — have molded natural features like stalactites, overhangs, and crack climbs. As well, it provides special areas for bouldering, spelunking, and arch climbs. First-timers can take basic climbing-technique courses and the advanced can have training programs custom-designed to their level of skill. Shoes and harnesses can be rented, too.

SEX

THE TOOLBOX
508 Eastern, 466-8616

Toronto's oldest leather bar — and Toronto's only smoke-free gay bar — is located in a quiet working-class neighbourhood in the shadow of one of Ontario's leading motorcycle clubhouses, although the bikers inside the former Simcoe House are mostly the pretend kind. Lined with licence plates and *Drummer* magazine pin-ups, the Toolbox isn't really that different from Queen West's Black Bull — except the only female here is a Labrador Retriever. Rooms are available upstairs for overnight stays at Muther's Guesthouse, and every Sunday there's a potluck-style all-you-can-eat $10 brunch.

Smoke-free. Patio.

PARKDALE

FOOD & DINING

SHALA-MAR
391 Roncesvalles, 588-9877

One of Toronto's oldest Indian restaurants, Shala-Mar is a dark, romantic restaurant that serves mildly spiced and all-halal fare from northern India and Pakistan. Closed Monday.

One step at door, washrooms upstairs. Fully licensed. $$

CAFES AND COFFEE HOUSES

ALTERNATIVE GROUNDS
333 Roncesvalles, 534-6335

Barrier-free. Unlicensed, smoke-free. Patio. $

MITZI'S
100 Sorauren, 588-1234

That's right, there are no good restaurants in Parkdale. At least, that's what Mitzi's regulars might say to anyone wondering what this unassuming diner on a quiet street is like. Once a well-guarded secret, the word is out now about Mitzi's — fabulous weekend brunches with such selections as thick egg-bread French toast with strawberries and whipped cream, and lemon-poppy-seed pancakes studded with pecans. Weekdays, it's open from 7:30 a.m. to 7 p.m. for breakfast, sandwich lunches, and late-afternoon snacks. Really? In Parkdale? Closed Monday.

One step at door, two steps to washroom on same floor. Unlicensed, smoke-free, cash only. Patio. $$

SWALLOW
1544 Queen West, 535-1811

Don't let the ragtag tables and mismatched chairs put you off. There's some serious cooking going on here. While Patti Smith and Hank Williams Sr. croon on the CD player, tuck into a first-rate all-day breakfast. Two-fisted sandwiches — balsamic tuna salad, pressed roast-pork Cubano — flesh out a menu that also in-

Downtown skyline from the ferry.

cludes healthy salads, Tex-Mex veggie mains, and deluxe dinner entrees. The swingin' backyard patio doubles as an organic garden whose herbs find their way into Swallow's fabulous fare. Expect weekend lineups.

Barrier-free, washrooms in basement. Beer and wine. Patio. $

TAKEOUT

ALI'S ROTI SHOP
1446 Queen West, 532-7701

Trinidadian treats emanate from this Parkdale fast-food parlour. You can spice up three different styles of roti wrapper — dhalpoori, sada, and paratha — with roast duck, chewy conch, shrimp, or veggie fillings including pumpkin, eggplant, and chickpea channa. With its strictly donut-shop vibe, there's no reason to hang around. But Island specialties like salt-fish buljol with breadfruit and heat-relieving homemade soursop ice cream make return visits inevitable.

One step at door, washrooms in basement. Unlicensed, smoke-free, cash only. $

BACCHUS ROTI
1376 Queen West, 532-8191

In trendy California, foodies call them wraps —
here in multicultural Toronto they're better known
as rotis. What makes Bacchus unique is its
whole-wheat wrappers and Guyanese-flavoured
fillings — shrimp, spinach, squash, joined by
cheddar cheese, curried goat with X-rated hot
sauce, okra, cabbage, or chickpeas with tofu. Side
dishes such as crisply sweet plantain chips, Carib
double popovers, and peanut-butter cakes help
cause long lines at dinner hours. Closed Sunday
and holidays.

Barrier-free. Unlicensed, smoke-free. $

RICE & NOODLE
1533 Queen West, 535-6868

Warning: no one in their right mind would ever
want to eat in this exceptionally unattractive
restaurant. But foodie fans know the deal here is
the super Szechuan and Thai take-away — eggplant curries, basil chicken, and veggies with tofu
and peanut sauce. Home delivery, too.

One step at door, washrooms in basement. Unlicensed. $

ENTERTAINMENT

POOL HALLS

ACADEMY OF SPHERICAL ARTS
38 Hannah, 532-2782

To describe the Academy as just a pool hall
doesn't do it justice. This 5,000-square-foot
warehouse space — once the home of billiard
manufacturer Brunswick — has been converted
into an elegant Victorian-style club. With 15 antique pool tables predating the 1920s, the Academy also serves in its dining room first-class fare
like tandoori mahi mahi, soya-protein stir-frys,
and thin-crust mondo pizzas. Digging the scene:
actor Minnie Driver, six-steps-from Kevin Bacon,
and Rush rocker Geddy Lee. (Because they often
host corporate affairs, the club advises a call in
advance to ensure they're open to the public that
day.) Closed Sunday.

Six steps at door, washrooms on same floor. Fully
licensed. Patio.

CINEMAS — REVIVAL

THE REVUE
400 Roncesvalles, 531-9959

See listing page 168.

SHOPPING

BEER STORES

THE BEER STORE
1200 Dundas West, 536-3945

Monday to Wednesday 10 a.m. to 8 p.m.
Thursday and Friday 10 a.m. to 9 p.m.
Saturday 9:30 a.m. to 9 p.m.
Sunday 11 a.m. to 6 p.m.
Closed holidays.

THE BEER STORE
2135 Dundas West, 531-6512

Monday to Wednesday 10 a.m. to 8 p.m.
Thursday and Friday 10 a.m. to 9 p.m.
Saturday 9:30 a.m. to 9 p.m.
Sunday 11 a.m. to 6 p.m.
Closed holidays.

THE BEER STORE
65 Brock, 532-5702

Monday to Thursday 10 a.m. to 10 p.m.
Friday 10 a.m. to 11 p.m.
Saturday 9:30 a.m. to 11 p.m.
Sunday 11 a.m. to 6 p.m.
Closed holidays.

FASHION — VINTAGE CLOTHING

GOODWILL
28 Roncesvalles, 534-1686

See listing page 114.

SALVATION ARMY STORE
1447 Queen West, 536-3361

FOOD

GRANOWSKA'S
175 Roncesvalles, 533-7755

A Polish deli and bakery.

Barrier-free, washrooms in basement.
Unlicensed.

LCBO
11 Brock, 532-7283

Monday to Saturday 9:30 a.m. to 10 p.m.
Sunday 11 a.m. to 6 p.m.
Closed holidays.

LCBO
1230 Dundas West, 536-4634

Monday to Thursday 9:30 a.m. to 6 p.m.
Friday and Saturday 9:30 a.m. to 9 p.m.
Sunday 11 a.m. to 6 p.m.
Closed holidays.

ROCK-CLIMBING

JOE ROCKHEAD'S CLIMBING GYM
29 Fraser, 538-7670

Canada's first and largest indoor rock-climbing
facility, Rockhead's is owned by Bob Bergman, a
former Canadian sport-climbing champ. Whether
they are beginners or experts, patrons can do the
vertical on over 60 climbing routes, including a
35-foot mini-mountain and a 50-foot overhang.
Yearly and monthly memberships are available
— or you can pay your way as you hone your
skills. Equipment rentals, too.

CHINATOWN EAST

FOOD & DINING

RESTAURANTS

MIMI
688 Gerrard East, 778-5948

Spic-and-span spotless — not only are MiMi's tables covered in plastic, they're glass-topped as
well — this family-run restaurant serves Vietnamese fare that seems straightforward yet is
surprisingly complex. It's easy to assemble a major pig-out here for less than $10 per person from
dishes such as sugar-cane shrimp in rice-paper
roll-ups with leaf lettuce, raw bean sprouts,
shredded daikon and carrots, and crushed
peanuts. $3 Heineken, too.

Barrier-free, washrooms upstairs. Beer and wine. $

PEARL COURT
633 Gerrard East, 463-8778

Serving dim sum daily from nine in the morning
till four in the afternoon — and open every night

SWALLOW: Without question, Parkdale's finest food experience — low-key digs, upmarket fare.

till 4 a.m. — the Court is a family-size Cantonese restaurant specializing in seafood and a few Szechuan dishes.

Barrier-free, washrooms in basement. Fully licensed. $$

SHOPPING

BEER STORES

THE BEER STORE
800 Gerrard East, 463-1313
Monday to Wednesday 10 a.m. to 8 p.m.
Thursday and Friday 10 a.m. to 9 p.m.
Saturday 9:30 a.m. to 9 p.m.
Sunday 11 a.m. to 6 p.m.
Closed holidays.

LIQUOR AND WINE STORES

LCBO
932 Gerrard East, 466-1209
Monday to Thursday 9:30 a.m. to 6 p.m.
Friday 9:30 a.m. to 10 p.m.
Saturday 9:30 a.m. to 6 p.m.
Sunday 11 a.m. to 6 p.m.
Closed holidays.

BLOOR WEST

FOOD & DINING

RESTAURANTS

KOREA HOUSE
666 Bloor West, 536-8666
Korean-Japanese fare in a pagoda-like room.

One step at door, washrooms in basement. Fully licensed. $$

MUL RAE BANG-A
3 Christie, 534-6833
Smoky Korean restaurant with private booths.

One step at door, washrooms in basement. Fully licensed. $$

RIKISHI
833 Bloor West, 538-0760
Decorated with Japanese landscape paintings, geisha dolls, and bamboo wall-hangings, this tiny sushi bar offers a tasty alternative to red meat. While they do serve standard fare — sushi and sashimi combos, tempuras, and teriyakis — they also offer veggie versions on a separate menu that includes creations like daikon salad, udon noodle soup, and cucumber, avocado, and gourd rice wraps. Closed Monday.

Barrier-free, washrooms in basement. Fully licensed, smoke-free. $$

SEJONG
658 Bloor West, 535-5918
Like the other restaurants along Bloor, Sejong serves a mix of Japanese sushi and teriyaki dishes, and Korean barbecued meats. Ask for one of the semi-private shoji-screened rooms that line the wood-trimmed space. First, you're brought seven bowls of complimentary pickles — ranging from crunchy, mild seaweed strips to atomic cabbage kimchee — as well as miso soup and eggy custard. If you get too carried away on the starters, you may not have room for the mains — grilled salmon or vegetarian noodle casserole, say — by the time they arrive.

Barrier-free, washrooms upstairs. Fully licensed. $$

UNIVERSAL GRILL
1071 Shaw, 588-5928
Following a tried and true recipe for success — take a down-at-the-heels diner, refurbish its fittings to original quality, and update the menu — the Grill has been crowded from the get-go. Venetian blinds slice the light like in a '40s film noir, while the kitchen pumps out comfort food that's elevated to gourmet level. As Superfly Curtis Mayfield croons, diners soak up the retro atmosphere at booths built for four, but if you expect to get one, reserve in advance (especially for weekend brunch). The curbside patio's noisy during the day as trucks lumber by but grows quiet once the moon rises. Closed Monday.

Two steps at door, washrooms in basement. Fully licensed. Patio. $$

TROPICAL CORNER
612 Bloor West, 534-6675

For the same price as a burger at a fast-food chain, foodies with a taste for the out-of-the-ordinary can dine at this Salvadorean cantina. It ain't fine dining, but the pork-, cheese-, or veggie-stuffed pupusas — try 'em with a side of pickled slaw — and the beef and potato empanadas are filling and go down well with a mango, blackberry, or tamarind natural-juice shake.

Barrier-free, washrooms in basement. Unlicensed, smoke-free. Patio. $

ENTERTAINMENT

LIVE MUSIC

CLINTON'S
693 Bloor West, 535-9541

A classic tavern that looks like the interior of a log cabin, Clinton's upstairs room showcases some of Toronto's best up-and-coming performers, as well as established stars returning to where they first got started. Downstairs, a more progressive and intimate performance space — Shaman's Closet — spotlights esoteric electronica, free jazz, and other off-the-wall music.

One step at door, washrooms on same floor. Fully licensed.

SHOPPING

BEER STORES

THE BEER STORE
323 Symington, 536-4852

Monday to Wednesday 10 a.m. to 8 p.m.
Thursday and Friday 10 a.m. to 9 p.m.
Saturday 9:30 a.m. to 9 p.m.
Sunday 11 a.m. to 6 p.m.
Closed holidays.

THE BEER STORE
904 Dufferin, 536-8924

Monday to Wednesday 10 a.m. to 8 p.m.

Thursday and Friday 10 a.m. to 9 p.m.
Saturday 9:30 a.m. to 9 p.m.
Sunday 11 a.m. to 6 p.m.
Closed holidays.

BICYCLES

CYCLEMANIA
945 Bloor West, 533-0080

See listing page 193.

BOOKS AND MAGAZINES — NEW

DEC BOOKROOM
836 Bloor West, 516-2966

Established by the Development Education Centre, this bookstore provides information about struggles for social and political change around the world.

FASHION — VINTAGE CLOTHING

VALUE VILLAGE
1319 Bloor West, 539-0585

Overflowing with bargain-priced secondhand clothing and housewares, Value Village has many treasures you'll uncover if you dig deep enough. Other locations:
924 Queen East (see page 214)
2119 Danforth (see page 230)

FOOD

HO DO KWA JA
656 Bloor West, 538-1208

No visit to Korea Town is complete without a look in the window of this shop named for the Korean donut-like pastries they produce. A conveyor belt carries half-moulds that are filled with crushed walnuts, sweet bean paste, and, finally, batter. The halves are joined mechanically, then passed over gas jets to emerge as golf-ball-shaped baked goods.

KARMA CO-OP
739 Palmerston, 534-1470

Open since 1972 and only to members — but anyone is welcome to join — the store stocks organic foods and natural products, both unprocessed and prepared. The inventory includes fresh fruit and veg, free-range eggs, bulk grains, organic meats, and household and personal care goods. Once a member, you are able to vote on policy decisions and elect the board of directors.

LIQUOR AND WINE STORES

LCBO
879 Bloor West, 536-4340

Monday to Thursday 9:30 p.m. to 6 p.m.
Friday and Saturday 9:30 a.m. to 9 p.m.
Sunday 11 a.m. to 6 p.m.
Closed holidays.

MUSICAL INSTRUMENTS

LONG AND MCQUADE
925 Bloor West, 588-7886

An institution long known to Toronto musicians, L & M carries everything from keyboards to kazoos to kettle drums, and they rent equipment, too. Aisles of guitars — including some vintage models — PA systems, and brass instruments take up every square inch of this two-storey music supermarket. The place is home to neophyte fretwankers whose renditions of the masterworks of Metallica blast through very loud amplifiers. Closed Sunday.

SEX

METRO THEATRE
677 Bloor West, 533-9131

A 10-year-old poster advertising porn superstar Marilyn Chambers' *Insatiable* sets the tone at this seedy triplex movie-house. Now that every dirty old man has a VCR, the popularity of these ancient skin-flicks that run all day from 10 a.m. is mystifying. Maybe it's the social element? The marquee says that, as well as old movie posters, they sell car batteries, too! Perhaps if the film doesn't turn you on, the battery will.

WEST ST. CLAIR WEST

FOOD & DINING

RESTAURANTS

FERRO
769 St. Clair West, 654-9119

See Hot Spot page 221.

THE GEM
1159 Davenport, 654-1182

With its jukebox, eclectic bric-à-brac, and lunch counter complete with stools, the Gem is like a '50s diner. Sort of. No malt shoppe was ever decked out in red and black or featured such fare as rigatoni with feta, sun-dried tomatoes, and spinach in a tomato and garlic sauce. Casual, funky, and fun.

One step at door, washrooms in basement. Fully licensed. $$

LA BRUSCHETTA
1317 St. Clair West, 656-8622

Because of the number of American movies made in town, Toronto is often referred to as Hollywood North. So where do the tinseltown celebs hang out? Believe it or not, this off-the-beaten-track trattoria is one of their favourite spots. But you don't have to be a celebrity to be treated like family — all are welcomed equally by the Piantoni family. And when the grub — homemade Italian antipasto, fettuccine Giuliana with brandied cream, and textbook tiramisù — is as good as the greeting, everyone's a VIP. Closed Sunday.

Barrier-free, washrooms in basement. Fully licensed. $$$

MAÑANA MEXICANA
813 St. Clair West, 656-7099

There is no such thing as an authentic Mexican restaurant in Toronto. We have lard-heavy rice 'n' bean tacoterias and modern Santa Fe–style cantinas. But mole? No way! Mañana is the exception to that rule of tongue. It helps that the cook is an actually from Mexico and has a deft touch with seafood and chicken entrees — try calamari sizzling on a cast-iron plate and drenched with earthy chipotle, or chicken coated with ground pumpkin seeds. With a splash of hot sauce, the nacho-and-salsa combo skyrockets.

One step at door, washrooms in basement. Fully licensed. Patio. $$

MIRAFLORES
816 St. Clair West, 656-3402

Recently acclaimed by food writers as the cutting-edge food of the 21st century, the ancient cuisine of Peru is a mostly unknown fare — although, around the globe, people eat tomatoes, potatoes, and peppers every day. Miraflores is an informal room whose cuisine runs from cheap 'n' cheerful to haute — marinated beef heart, seafood ceviche, and beet, cassava, and Yukon Gold potato salad. Beware the atomic-strength hot sauce! Closed Wednesday.

Barrier-free, washrooms in basement. Fully licensed. $$

TAKEOUT

ALBERT'S REAL JAMAICAN FOOD
542 St. Clair West, 658-9445

Taxi drivers, club kids, and Forest Hill society matrons form a line that snakes out the front door for Albert's famous takeout jerk-chicken dinners. Delicately spiced, the fowl comes bone-in, Island-style, and is ladled over a mess of rice and pigeon peas. Decor is minimal — the obligatory Bob Marley poster, natch — and the drink of choice is the JA soda dubbed Ting.

One step at door, no washrooms. Unlicensed, smoke-free, cash only. $

CHURRASCO OF ST. CLAIR
679 St. Clair West, 658-0652

Toronto's tastiest chicken shack is a foodie destination of note — and not just for those who can't be bothered to cook. It doesn't make any difference what time you show up, there's always a throng waiting for their spice-rubbed charcoal-grilled birds doused with honeyed hot sauce. Side 'em with roasted potato puffs, serviceable salads, and loaves of Portuguese cornbread, and you've got yourself an instant feast. Don't worry — the queue moves quickly. Closed Monday.

Barrier-free. Unlicensed, smoke-free. $

HOT SPOT

FERRO
769 St. Clair West, 654-9119

At Ferro, a little bit of swanky College Street comes to St. Clair West, a neighbourhood that combines a downtown mindset with old-world manners — and parking, too! With a stainless-steel washroom and wrought-iron details that bounce sound, Ferro can be very noisy. It's incredibly busy, especially on Friday and Saturday nights, so come early if you want to join in the raucous atmosphere. Huge portions of pasta and pizza mean everyone goes home with a doggy bag.

Barrier-free. Fully licensed. Patio. $$

DUTCH DREAMS
78 Vaughan, 656-6959

On a street of Italian trattorias and jerk-chicken take-aways, Dutch Dreams offers a taste of Holland. Elaborately decked out in a Dutch motif — blue-and-white Delft-style wallpaper, clogs on shelves, windmill bric-à-brac — this incongruous ice cream parlour sells over 50 flavours of ice cream and frozen yogurt and serves them up in cones decorated with sprinkles, chocolate chips, and silver bullets. It also prepares Baked Alaska, Dutch waffles, and Peach Melba. On sweltering summer evenings, expect very long lineups.

Two steps at door, washrooms in basement. Unlicensed, smoke-free. $

LA PALOMA GELATERIA
1357 St. Clair West, 656-2340

An old-world-style ice-cream parlour that specializes in Italian ices.

Barrier-free, washrooms in basement. Unlicensed. Patio. $

SHOPPING

BEER STORES

THE BEER STORE
1083 St. Clair West, 654-7100

Monday to Wednesday 10 a.m. to 8 p.m.
Thursday and Friday 10 a.m. to 9 p.m.
Saturday 9:30 a.m. to 9 p.m.

Sunday 11 a.m. to 6 p.m.
Closed holidays.

FASHION — VINTAGE CLOTHING

SALVATION ARMY STORE
920 St. Clair West, 651-2825

Closed Sunday.

FOOD

CENTRO TRATTORIA AND FORMAGGIO
1224 St. Clair West, 656-8111

One of the city's top gourmet shops, Centro specializes in Italian cheese, pasta, and olive oil.

TRE MARI BAKERY
1311 St. Clair West, 654-8960

An Italian bakery, Tre Mari supplies bread and pastries to some of Toronto's top restaurants.

LIQUOR AND WINE STORES

LCBO
908 St. Clair West, 654-4240

Monday to Saturday 9:30 a.m. to 10 p.m.
Sunday 11 a.m. to 6 p.m.
Closed holidays.

DELIS AND DINERS

COMMISSO BROTHERS AND RACCO
8 Kincort, 651-7671

Almost a bargain-priced Italian bulk-food emporium — where else can you find gallon-sized tins of anchovies? — Commisso's never closes. Which is good news for anyone who gets a craving for a sloppy tomato-sauced pounded-veal and green-pepper sandwich on a Calabrese bun at five in the morning.

One step at door, no washrooms. Unlicensed, smoke-free. $

WEST EGLINTON WEST

FOOD & DINING

TAKEOUT

SHANTY'S
1806 Eglinton West, 785-1205

If a film crew ever wanted to shoot in a picture-perfect JA jerk shack, they'd be hard-pressed to find a more authentic place than this Oakwood Village takeout joint. With seating for six, Shanty's is a tiny place that takes its highly spiced Island fare seriously. They're on "Island time," too, as the Jamaican saying goes — dishes like fried red-snapper escovitch and salt cod with scrambled-eggs-esque ackee "soon come" eventually.

Barrier-free. Unlicensed, smoke-free, cash only. $

VIV'S ISLAND TAKE-OUT
2641 Eglinton West, 653-1234

The culinary cognoscenti have followed Vivienne Nelson from her humble beginnings at a lunch counter in Spadina's garment district and later digs in west-end Long Branch to the heart of Eglinton West's Caribbean community. This out-of-the-way Jamaican jerk shack cooks up aromatically spiced chicken and pork, and vinegar-marinated kingfish and tilapia. Open from 7:30 a.m. daily for those who like to begin the day with a spicy kick-start.

One step at door, washrooms in basement. Unlicensed, cash only. $

EGLINTON WEST

FOOD & DINING

RESTAURANTS

AUTOGRILL
495 Eglinton West, 489-0961

Once a bank, this space has been redesigned to resemble the kind of upmarket diner found in style-conscious northern Italy. It's very bright and airy, almost a new-car showroom, with moulded plywood chairs, Formica-topped tables, terrazzo floors, and fluorescent tubes. The old vault's been converted into a wine cellar. In keeping with the theme, the menu offers mostly pizza, pasta and panini choices. Popular with families as well as late-night swingers, Autogrill is a rarity — great grub and a fabulous space. *La dolce vita!*

Barrier-free, washrooms in basement. Fully licensed. $$

HOUSE OF CHAN
876 Eglinton West, 781-5575

Looking like an archetypal Chinese restaurant straight out of the '60s, House of Chan is one of north Toronto's most popular steakhouses. Sure, there's chicken fried rice and sweet-and-sour spareribs, but regulars are here for the steak — massive fillets deftly grilled and thinly sliced, sided with spuds and dill pickles. A zoo on Sunday nights.

One step at door, washrooms in basement.

VANIPHA LANNA
471 Eglinton West, 484-0895

See listing page 82. Closed Sunday.

Some areas barrier-free. Fully licensed. $$

ENTERTAINMENT

THE EGLINTON
400 Eglinton West, 487-4721

Toronto's finest example of an art deco movie-house, the large-screen Eglinton offers an alternative to cramped cinema complexes.

FASHION — ACCESSORIES

NIK NAK
450 Eglinton West, 489-2853

See listing page 23.

UPTOWN

FOOD & DINING

RESTAURANTS

FIVE DOORS NORTH
2088 Yonge, 480-6234

North Toronto knows the Nose, owner Gio Rana's other restaurant on upper Yonge Street which is actually called Gio's. Even more confusing, Five Doors North is really seven doors north and hiding behind a sign that advertises Futon World. Lost? That's the idea. For Five Doors offers even better southern Italian fare than its more famous nosy compatriot. With funky decor — confession booths, the futon-store cocktail lounge — that says Queen Street more than Yonge and Eligible, this is a worthy addition to the neighbourhood's pantheon of pasta parlours. Closed Sunday and holidays.

Barrier-free. Fully licensed. $$

FORKCHOPS
1440 Yonge, 944-8501

See listing page 150.

One step at door, washrooms in basement. Fully licensed, smoke-free. $$

FORKCHOPS
2311 Yonge, 480-9622

See listing page 150.

Barrier-free, washrooms upstairs. Fully licensed, smoke-free. $$

GIO'S
2070 Yonge, 932-2306

Known by many as the Nose because of the large proboscis that's suspended over the restaurant's front door, this bowling-alley-shaped space resembles a suburban rec room, complete with laundry hanging from the ceiling. You'd better be in a good mood before you visit because the staff relentlessly cajole, pester, and mock their clientele when not singing along to the Dean Martin on the sound system. The food? Old-school pastas, grilled lamb, and homemade desserts. Closed Sunday and holidays.

Barrier-free, washrooms in basement. Fully licensed. $$

QUEEN'S QUAY TERMINAL: Designer boutiques and luxury condos on the lakeshore.

GOVINDA'S
243 Avenue Rd., 922-5415

Yes, this is the vegetarian restaurant located in the Hare Krishna temple. And no, incense is not burned in this spare space that looks like a church basement because it is a church basement. The only thing that anyone will try to push down your throat is some of Toronto's best northern Indian vegetarian cuisine. Not only do you not have to tip the staff — the restaurant's strictly self-serve — but the $7 all-you-can-eat tab is tax-deductible. All this and takeout, too. Closed Sunday.

10 steps at door, washrooms in basement. Unlicensed, smoke-free, cash only. $

IL FORNELLO
1560 Yonge, 920-7347

See listing page 39.

Barrier-free, washrooms upstairs. Fully licensed. $$

JOV
1701 Bayview, 322-0530

Taking its name from its three owners' first initials, JOV is one of uptown's hottest meal tickets. So much so that mandatory reservations are only taken exactly one week ahead — not one day be-fore, not one after. Deluxe service, a low-key but luxurious room, and sometimes first-rate dishes (grilled calamari with vine-ripened tomatoes; lobster salad with mizuna lettuce, mushrooms, and sweet-corn 'n' papaya mayonnaise; duck confit with roasted figs) make the difficulty in obtaining a table worth the bother.

Barrier-free, washrooms in basement. Fully licensed, smoke-free. $$$

MISTRAL
1392 Yonge, 968-0030

Named for a cold and violent wind that whips off the Mediterranean to blanket the south of France with all manner of weather-related nastiness, Mistral the restaurant mixes classical Provençal fare with up-to-the-minute technique. In a warm-yellow room, the media gang gather at lunch, but a mixed crowd of Rosedale old money and downtown trendies make dinner more laid-back. Bouillabaisse, mussels moulinière, and steak et frites remain authentic but are given a lighter, modern touch.

Barrier-free, washrooms in basement. Fully licensed. $$

NOTHING IN COMMON
8 Birch, 975-9150

Taking its name from the fact that none of its

menu items have anything to do with each other (Hostess chips with onion dip — or prawns over spaghettini?) N.I.C. is nonetheless a lot of fun. A pint-sized coach house, it's painted bright red and outfitted with garage-sale finds. You'll find it hard to remain stony-faced when surrounded by Barbie lunch boxes, Kenner Easy-Bake Ovens, Slinkys, and Mr. Potato Head. Pasta and seafood mains and a substantial weekend brunch aren't bad, either.

Seven steps at door, washrooms upstairs. Fully licensed. $$

ROSEDALE DINER
1164 Yonge, 923-3122

This ain't the Rosedale Library, but it sure is the Rosedale Diner. With period decor that has been left intact, this circa '40s lunch counter offers contemporary cuisine that belies its surroundings — non-retro fare such as whole heads of roasted garlic with Portuguese cornbread, and its namesake burger with Brie and roasted red peppers. There are two small rooms and a shaded rear patio, but the best seats in the house are the twin tables for two in each of the street-side windows.

One step at door, washrooms in basement. Fully licensed. Patio. $$

SATAY ON THE ROAD
1570 Bayview, 440-0679

See listing page 202.
Barrier-free, washrooms in basement. Fully licensed, smoke-free. Patio. $$

SATAY ON THE ROAD
2003 Avenue Rd, 488-5153

See listing page 202.
Barrier-free. Fully licensed, smoke-free. Patio. $$

ZUCCA
2150 Yonge, 488-5774

Chef and owner Andrew Milne-Allan is one of Toronto's eat elite. His intimate north Yonge bistro — all pale-rose walls and warm wood accents — is a major fave with neighbourhood foodies. As well as being a beautiful restaurant, it has a Mediterranean-nuanced contemporary-Italian menu that draws raves for dishes like thin slices of rare veal in a crushed-walnut crust and drizzled with white-truffle oil, oven-roasted sea bass with potato and fennel in a balsamic vinaigrette,

and Amaretto crème caramel. Mondays and Tuesdays are risotto nights.

Barrier-free, washrooms in basement. Fully licensed, smoke-free. Patio. $$$

CAFES AND COFFEE HOUSES

ACE BAKERY
1360 Yonge, 968-8880

Featuring the stellar breads of one of Toronto's best bakeries, this is the café outlet of famous Ace. Bread-head owners Linda Haynes and Martin Connell make NOW readers' favourite loaves — 10 percent of the before-tax profits generated by their baked goods goes to their philanthropic Calmeadow Foundation, which promotes economic self-reliance in the form of home-based businesses across Canada and throughout the emerging world. Social responsibility realized through the sale of killer Calabrese and focaccia.

Barrier-free. Beer and wine. Patio. $$

ELECTRIC BEAN CYBERCAFE
10 Eglinton East, 481-2100

Here's this computer cantina's mission statement: "We will change the world, and we will have fun doing it." With over 50 terminals — as well as a high-speed T1 connection — the Bean offers some of the fastest Internet access in the city. They also offer e-mail accounts, computer games — Sony PlayStation, Nintendo 64, and Sega Saturn — and introductory classes for neo-Netizens. Two virtual-reality systems, too — Virtual Voyager and Alpine Racer 2.

Barrier-free. Fully licensed. $$

RAHIER
1717 Bayview, 482-0917

It doesn't get any better than Rahier. Belgian chocolatiers François and Sonia Rahier are divine bakers, and their patisserie on Bayview is a mecca for those with a sweet tooth. Displayed like jewels in a case, their astonishing gâteaux and tortes are named for famous French philosophers and artists. Perhaps a Proust (vanilla mousse over praline sponge cake)? Luscious fruit flans and chocolate florentines full of honey-drenched almonds are equally spectacular. Closed Monday.

Barrier-free. Unlicensed, smoke-free. $

TAKEOUT

GROUCHO'S
1574 Bayview, 482-3456

Do fries go with that shake?

Barrier-free, washrooms in basement. Beer and wine, smoke-free. Patio. $

JOEL'S GOURMET PIZZA
1718 Avenue Rd., 961-5635

See listing page 128.

Barrier-free. Unlicensed, smoke-free. $$

MASSIMO
2459 Yonge, 487-4449

See listing page 153.

Four steps at door, washrooms in basement. Fully licensed. Patio. $$

MY FAVOURITE
3 Macpherson, no phone

A tiny hole in the wall that's open only between May and September, it's one of the few outlets that carries Greg's superlative ice cream.

Barrier-free. Unlicensed. Patio. $

BARS

THE DUKE OF KENT
2315 Yonge, 485-9507

See listing page 154.

TORONTO CLIMBING ACADEMY: Get vertical.

Barrier-free, washrooms in basement.

THE REBEL HOUSE
1068 Yonge, 927-0704

The Rebel House bucks the uptown trend of sophisticated sleekness. This old House is positively rough — worn plank flooring, craggy wooden counters, and coarse stucco walls. But there's nothing unsavoury about the customers who fill both the downstairs and upstairs rooms and the parachute-covered patio out back, knocking back pints from 16 different draught pumps. The small menu goes beyond bar snacks with such all-Canadian fare as lamb-and-ale stew with shiitake mushrooms, and roast duck with cider-braised wild rice and cranberry-leek compote. Saturday and Sunday brunch, too.

Two steps at door, washrooms in basement. Patio.

SHARK CITY
117 Eglinton East, 488-7899

A popular spot with Yonge and Eligible singles, Shark City is home to a casually swank contemporary restaurant featuring Eurasian chow. Sporting an oceanic decor and mosaic tiles, the downstairs nightclub features DJs spinning Latin, jazz, and r 'n' b platters Thursday through Saturday evenings. Four bars, pool tables, and a large dance floor, too. Closed Sunday and Monday.

Some areas barrier-free. Fully licensed. Patio.

THE UNICORN
175 Eglinton East, 482-0115

See listing page 210.

One step at door, washrooms in basement. Patio.

ENTERTAINMENT

COMEDY CLUBS

YUK YUK'S
2335 Yonge, 967-6425

From its modest beginnings in the basement of the 519 Centre (see listing page 140) in the mid-'70s, Yuk Yuk's has grown to become Canada's largest chain of comedy clubs. The weekly schedule: Mondays are new-talent nights, Tuesdays improv, Wednesdays through Saturdays two-hour stand-up performances, and Sundays are for special one-off events. As well as Toronto native Jim Carrey, who got his start here as a 15-year-old impressionist, comics who have appeared at Yuk Yuk's include George Carlin, Howie Mandel, Rick Moranis, Emo Phillips, Rodney Dangerfield, Sandra Bernhard, and Jerry Seinfeld (not all at the same time).

Barrier-free. Fully licensed.

DANCE CLUBS

BERLIN
2335 Yonge, 489-7777

One of Yonge and Eglinton's busiest meat markets, Berlin is a second-floor dance complex with a fancy contemporary dining room. But most of the action takes place on the dance floor, where singles connect during Tuesday night salsa lessons, and later mambo to DJs and live Latin bands. Wednesdays are Swing Nights, and Thursdays women are admitted *sans* cover charge to groove to r 'n' b and house DJs. Fridays and Saturdays see more house DJs and live dance-rock musicians. Closed Sunday and Monday.

Barrier-free. Fully licensed.

CINEMAS — FIRST RUN

THE REGENT
551 Mt. Pleasant, 480-9884

THE YORK
101 Eglinton East, 486-5600

CINEMAS — REVIVAL

THE CAPITOL
2492 Yonge, 487-8852

See listing page 168.

SHOPPING

BEER STORES

THE BEER STORE
10 Price, 925-0366

Monday to Thursday 10 a.m. to 10 p.m.
Friday 10 a.m. to 11 p.m.
Saturday 9:30 a.m. to 11 p.m.
Sunday 11 a.m. to 6 p.m.

Closed holidays.
Barrier-free.

BOOKS AND MAGAZINES — NEW

INDIGO
2300 Yonge, 544-0049

See listing page 178.

LICHTMAN'S
1430 Yonge, 922-7271

See listing page 113.

LICHTMAN'S
2299 Yonge, 482-2462

See listing page 113.

SLEUTH OF BAKER STREET
1600 Bayview, 483-3111

Not just for Sherlock Holmes fans — although they do carry a large selection of Conan Doyle first editions and memorabilia — this old-fashioned bookstore, complete with sliding ladders, specializes in new as well as used crime and mystery titles. Closed Sunday and Monday.

COMIC BOOKS AND 'ZINES

SILVER SNAIL
2374 Yonge, 481-4152

See listing page 22.

FASHION — ACCESSORIES

JOSEPHSON'S
2300 Yonge, 484-4070

See listing page 179.

FASHION — NEW CLOTHING

ROBIN KAY
2599 Yonge, 485-5097

See listing page 27.

ROBIN KAY
394 Spadina Rd., 932-2833

See listing page 27.

ROOTS
1485 Yonge, 967-4499

See listing page 121.

FASHION — SHOES

AUSTRALIAN BOOT COMPANY
2644 Yonge, 488-9488
See Hot Spot listing page 65.

TWINKLE TOES
2582 Yonge, 322-6291
See listing page 29.

FOOD

SUCKERS
1566 Yonge, 934-0251
See listing page 195.

HEALTH AND BEAUTY

02 SPA BAR
2044 Yonge, 322-7733
What's the first thing an emergency worker gives to an accident victim? Oxygen. So, what's good for knocked-down pedestrians, winded athletes, and Michael Jackson must be good for the rest of us, right? Although medical opinion is divided, the folks at 02 believe that a quick inhale of the good stuff will cure what ails you. Make sure you're not smoking a cigarette at the same time — pure oxygen is highly flammable.

HIKING AND BACKPACKING

SPORTING LIFE
2665 Yonge, 485-1611

LIQUOR AND WINE STORES

LCBO
1121 Yonge, 922-0403
Monday to Saturday 9 a.m. to 11 p.m.
Sunday 11 a.m. to 6 p.m.
Closed holidays.

LCBO
1493 Yonge, 921-3235
Monday to Wednesday 9:30 a.m. to 7 p.m.
Thursday to Saturday 9:30 a.m. to 9 p.m.
Sunday 11 a.m. to 6 p.m.
Closed holidays.

LCBO
2300 Yonge, 487-4858
Monday to Saturday 9:30 a.m. to 9 p.m.
Sunday 11 a.m. to 5 p.m.
Closed holidays.

MUSIC — CDS, RECORDS & TAPES

SAM THE RECORD MAN
1500 Yonge, 324-8624
See listing page 123.

SAM THE RECORD MAN
2440 Yonge, 486-7462
See listing page 123.

VORTEX
2309 Yonge, 483-7437
See listing page 33.

SKATEBOARDING

BOARDSPORTS
2010 Yonge, 485-9463
Snowboarding, sailboarding, surfboarding, and wakeboarding, too.

TATTOOS AND PIERCINGS

WAY COOL TATTOOS
5203 Yonge, 226-4142
See listing page 68.

24–7 RESTAURANTS

FRAN'S
21 St. Clair West, 925-6337
See listing page 153.
One step at door, washrooms on same floor. Fully licensed. $$

FRAN'S
45 Eglinton East, 481-1112
See listing page 153.
Barrier-free. Fully licensed. $$

BEYOND BEYOND

FOOD & DINING

![RESTAURANTS]

DRAGON DYNASTY
2301 Brimley, 321-9000

Located in a suburban Scarborough mall, Dragon Dynasty is an upwardly mobile Cantonese eatery — just check out all the Benzes and Range Rovers in the parking lot. Dim sum is served daily from 11 a.m. until mid-afternoon, when its pricey seafood-heavy Cantonese menu takes over.

Barrier-free. Fully licensed. $$$

GRAND YATT
9019 Bayview, 905/882-9388

The dim sum rule of thumb says that the farther you get away from downtown Chinatown, the better the grub gets. The recent influx of Hong Kong money has settled in Toronto's northern suburbs, and Grand Yatt's as deluxe as you can get. Join the queue at the door and, once seated, order à la carte or from the cart. Biscuit-size chive pancakes and deep-fried sticky rice stuffed with red-bean paste and pork are certain pleasers. But beware the Phoenix Claws — boiled chicken feet marinated in vinegar. Yikes!

Barrier-free. Fully licensed. $$

THE GREEN MANGO
3006 Bloor West, 233-5004

See listing page 150.

Barrier-free. Beer and wine. $

MCNIE'S LOVELY GRUB
315 Burnhamthorpe, 231-6916

Etobicoke's on the way to the airport, but downtowners with a thing for fish and chips will want to make a beeline for this strip-mall chippie. Resembling a Victorian tea-room — doilies everywhere and a septuagenarian staff — the charming eatery features fare that goes beyond seafood and spuds. Specialties include such UK-centric grub as deep-fried haggis, blood pudding, mushy peas, and pickled beetroot. Closed Sunday and Monday.

Barrier-free, washrooms in basement. Unlicensed. $

KITCHEN WITCH: Antiques 'n' pie for a song.

RUBY
1571 Sandhurst Circle, 298-1638

Tucked away in a suburban mall in Scarborough, this upscale banquet hall serves up some of the best dim sum around. While trolleys trawl the aisles between linen-topped tables, you can savour steamers of shiu mye and har gow dumplings stuffed with seafood and veggies. Eventually, everything goes past — deep-fried tofu, oversized-wonton soup, pork pot-stickers — but sometimes dessert shows up in the middle of the proceedings. Friendly, helpful servers assist the uninitiated.

Barrier-free. Fully licensed. $$

![CAFES AND COFFEE HOUSES]

FUTURE BAKERY
2199 Bloor West, 769-5020

See listing page 165.

![BOWLING ALLEYS]

BOWLERAMA
2788 Bathurst at Glencairn, 782-1841

Five-pin and ten-pin bowling. Computerized scoring.

Fully licensed.

BOWLERAMA
5837 Yonge at Cummer, 222-4657

Five-pin and ten-pin. Computerized scoring. Fully licensed.

PLANET BOWL
5555 Eglinton West, 695-2695

48 ten-pin lanes. Computerized scoring. Fully licensed.

WILSON PRO BOWL
877 Wilson, 638-1753

30 lanes with five-pin and ten-pin bowling. Computerized scoring.

Fully licensed.

ENTERTAINMENT

COMEDY CLUBS

COMEDYWOOD
800 Steeles West, 905/761-0543

A subterranean and suburban comedy club on the fringe of Toronto, Comedywood is a 400-seat venue that presents such local and international stand-up acts as Mitch Hedberg and Bobcat Goldthwait. Closed Sunday, Monday, and Tuesday.

THE GUVERNMENT: I cover the waterfront.

20 steps at door, washrooms downstairs. Fully licensed.

CINEMAS — REVIVAL

THE KINGSWAY
3030 Bloor West, 236-1411

See listing page 168.

SHOPPING

BEER STORES

THE BEER STORE
380 Donlands, 429-7388

Monday to Wednesday 10 a.m. to 8 p.m.
Thursday and Friday 10 a.m. to 9 p.m.
Saturday 9:30 a.m. to 9 p.m.
Sunday 11 a.m. to 6 p.m.
Closed holidays.

FASHION — VINTAGE CLOTHING

VALUE VILLAGE
2119 Danforth, 698-0621

See listing page 219.

SKATEBOARDING

HOGTOWN
3246 Danforth, 698-2500

See listing page 54. Closed Sunday.

VIDEO

PLAYDIUM
99 Rathburn West, 905/273-9000

See listing page 54.

Almost everything else you need to know

SURVIVAL

AIDS INFORMATION

AFRICANS IN PARTNERSHIP AGAINST AIDS
924-5256

AIDS & SEXUAL HEALTH INFOLINE
392-2437

AIDS ACTION NOW
517 College, 928-2206

AIDS COMMITTEE OF TORONTO
399 Church, 340-2437

ASIAN COMMUNITY AIDS SERVICES
33 Isabella, 963-4300

CASEY HOUSE HOSPICE
9 Huntley, 962-7600

LESBIAN GAY BISEXUAL YOUTH HOTLINE
962-9688

PWA FOUNDATION
399 Church, 506-1400

STREET HEALTH
249 Sherbourne, 964-2459

TWO-SPIRITED PEOPLE OF THE FIRST NATIONS
45 Charles East, 944-9300

AIRLINES

AIR CANADA
130 Bloor West, 925-2311

AIR FRANCE
151 Bloor West, 922-3344

AIR ONTARIO
925-2311

ALITALIA
800/361-8336

AMERICAN AIRLINES
800/433-7300

BRITISH AIRWAYS
250-0880

JAPAN AIRLINES
130 Adelaide West, 364-7229

LUFTHANSA
360-3600

QANTAS
800/227-4500

UNITED
100 Front West, 800/241-6522

AIRPORTS

PEARSON INTERNATIONAL AIRPORT
247-7678

Situated in suburban Mississauga, Pearson International is Canada's busiest and largest airport, with three terminals that handle domestic and international flights. Easily accessed by expressway — about 45 minutes from downtown during non-rush hours — the airport is also serviced by limousines, express buses, and TTC public transit.

TORONTO CITY CENTRE AIRPORT
203-6942

After a brief $4 ferry ride from the foot of Bathurst Street, travellers can catch short inter-city turbo-prop flights from the small airport located at the western end of Toronto's islands.

TTC CONNECTIONS TO AIRPORT
363-4636

See listing page 244.

BANKS — OPEN SATURDAY

BANK OF CHINA
396 Dundas West, 971-8806

BANK OF MONTREAL
291 Spadina, 867-4759

CANADA TRUST
574 Bloor West, 534-9211

CITIBANK
463 Dundas West, 977-7272

HONGKONG BANK OF CANADA
222 Spadina, 348-8888

HONGKONG BANK OF CANADA
421 Dundas West, 598-3982

NATIONAL BANK OF CANADA
468 Dundas West, 977-6812

ROYAL TRUST
1554 Bayview, 974-1850

SCOTIA BANK
292 Spadina, 866-4612

SCOTIA BANK
363 Broadview, 465-3531

TORONTO DOMINION BANK
501 Dundas West, 982-2111

BOOZE DELIVERY

DIAL-A-BOTTLE
751-4222

Can't get to the beer store? For a fee of $6.45 — plus the cost of yer booze — these folks will deliver two cases of suds or three bottles of liquor directly to your front door. Don't forget to tip, you lazy sod. Closed holidays.

BUS LINES

AIRPORT EXPRESS
905/564-6333

Airport Express offers four connections to and from all three terminals at Pearson International Airport. Three subway stations have Airport Express service — Islington on the Bloor line, Yorkdale on the Spadina line, and York Mills on the Yonge line. Buses leave every 20 minutes from approximately 5 a.m. to midnight (cost: $6.75 to $8.30 one way).

In the downtown core the Airport Express bus operates during the same hours ($12.50 one way). As well as the Bus Terminal (610 Bay), the bus picks passengers up at the following hotels: the Colony Hotel (89 Chestnut), Delta Chelsea Inn (33 Gerrard East), the Sheraton Centre (123 Queen West), the Royal York Hotel (100 Front West), and the Westin Harbour Castle (1 Queen's Quay West).

To take the bus downtown from the airport, look for the Airport Express depot at Terminals One, Two, and Three. The buses then head to the subway connections or to the downtown hotels and bus terminal.

BUS TERMINAL
See listing page 120.

GREYHOUND
610 Bay, 367-8747

PMCL PENETANG-MIDLAND COACH LINES
695-1867

TRENTWAY-WAGAR
961-9666

CAR RENTAL

A PLUS CAR AND TRUCK RENTAL
1951 Yonge, 488-3684

A PLUS CAR AND TRUCK RENTAL
548A Church, 413-1222

AVIS
800/879-2847

HERTZ
620-9620

THRIFTY
134 Jarvis, 868-0350

TILDEN
Spadina at Queen West, 364-4195

WRECKS 4 RENT
77 Nassau, 585-7782

CONSULATES

CONSULATE GENERAL OF AUSTRALIA
175 Bloor East, 323-1155

CONSULATE GENERAL OF BRAZIL
77 Bloor West, 922-2503

CONSULATE GENERAL OF BRITAIN
777 Bay, 593-1267

CONSULATE GENERAL OF CUBA
5353 Dundas West, 234-8181

CONSULATE GENERAL OF DENMARK
151 Bloor West, 962-5669

CONSULATE GENERAL OF FINLAND
1200 Bay, 964-0066

CONSULATE GENERAL OF GERMANY
77 Admiral, 925-2813

CONSULATE GENERAL OF GREECE
365 Bloor East, 515-0133

CONSULATE GENERAL OF ICELAND
250 Yonge, 979-6740

CONSULATE GENERAL OF ISRAEL
180 Bloor West, 961-1126

CONSULATE GENERAL OF ITALY
136 Beverley, 977-1566

SURVIVAL

CONSULATE GENERAL OF JAMAICA
214 King West, 598-3008

CONSULATE GENERAL OF JAPAN
Toronto Dominion Centre, 363-7038

CONSULATE GENERAL OF PORTUGAL
121 Richmond West, 360-8260

CONSULATE GENERAL OF SPAIN
200 Front West, 977-1661

CONSULATE GENERAL OF SWEDEN
2 Bloor West, 963-8768

**CONSULATE GENERAL OF THE PEOPLE'S
REPUBLIC OF CHINA**
240 St. George, 964-7260

**CONSULATE GENERAL OF THE UNITED STATES
OF AMERICA**
360 University, 595-1700

EMERGENCY!

ADDICTION RESEARCH FOUNDATION
33 Russell, 595-6000

Drug and alcohol information line: 595-6111
Substance dependence: 595-6021
Addiction/Medicine Clinic: 595-6019
Opiate Clinic: 595-6019
Smoking Treatment Centre: 595-6019
Community programs: 595-6028
HIV program: 595-6079

AMBULANCE
911

ASSAULTED WOMEN'S HELPLINE
863-0511

**COVENANT HOUSE (EMERGENCY SHELTER
FOR YOUTH)**
20 Gerrard East, 598-4898

DISTRESS CENTRES
598-1121

FIRE DEPARTMENT
911

GERRARD MOBILE VET SERVICES
284-4610

KIDS HELP PHONE
800/668-6868

POISON INFORMATION CENTRE
813-5900

POLICE DEPARTMENT
911

S.O.S. FEMMES (FRENCH CRISIS LINE)
759-0138

THE TORONTO HUMANE SOCIETY
11 River, 392-2273

TORONTO RAPE CRISIS CENTRE
597-8808

VETERINARY EMERGENCY CLINIC
1180 Danforth, 465-3501

EMPLOYMENT CENTRES

As well as offering career counselling and posting job openings, many government-run job centres also provide free Internet access for the unemployed.

A.C.C.E.S. EMPLOYMENT RESOURCE CENTRE
425 Adelaide West, Suite 401, 921-1800

Free. One terminal.
Monday to Friday 9 a.m. to 5 p.m.
Closed Saturday and Sunday.
Barrier-free.

COMMUNITY INFO CENTRE
2696 Eglinton West, 652-2273

One terminal.
Monday to Friday 9 a.m. to 5 p.m.
Closed Saturday and Sunday.
Barrier-free.

DIXON HALL HUMAN RESOURCE CENTRE
58 Sumach, 863-0499

30 terminals.
Monday to Friday noon to 4 p.m.
Closed Saturday and Sunday.
Barrier-free.

**DUFFERIN MALL EMPLOYMENT RESOURCE
CENTRE**
900 Dufferin, 583-4700

20 terminals.
Monday to Friday 9 a.m. to 4 p.m.
Closed Saturday and Sunday.
Barrier-free.

**GOODWILL TORONTO EMPLOYMENT RESOURCE
CENTRE**
108 George, 362-4711

11 terminals.
Monday to Friday 8:30 a.m. to 4:30 p.m.

Closed Saturday and Sunday.
Barrier-free.

MIZIWE BIIK ABORIGINAL EMPLOYMENT CENTRE
415 Yonge, 591-2126

Three terminals.
Monday to Friday 9 a.m. to 5 p.m.
Closed Saturday and Sunday.
Barrier-free.

NEIGHBOURHOOD LINK CAREER CENTRE
2625 Danforth, 698-1332

20 terminals.
Monday noon to 7:30 p.m.
Tuesday and Wednesday 9:30 a.m. to 4:30 p.m.
Thursday noon to 7 p.m.
Friday 9:30 a.m. to 1 p.m.
Saturday 10 a.m. to noon.
Closed Sunday.
Barrier-free.

PARACHUTE COMMUNITY EMPLOYMENT CENTRE
468 Queen East, 363-1689

11 terminals.
Monday to Friday 8:30 a.m. to 4:30 p.m.
Closed Saturday and Sunday.
Barrier-free.

ST. CLAIR WEST EMPLOYMENT RESOURCE CENTRE
1345 St. Clair West

20 terminals.
Monday to Friday 9 a.m. to 4 p.m.
Closed Saturday and Sunday.
Barrier-free.

ST. STEPHEN'S YOUTH EMPLOYMENT RESOURCE CENTRE
1415 Bathurst, 537-5477

16 terminals.
Monday 9:15 a.m. to 7:30 p.m.
Tuesday 9:15 a.m. to 4:30 p.m.
Wednesday 9:15 a.m. to 1:00 p.m.
Thursday 9:15 a.m. to 1:30 p.m.
Friday and Saturday 9:15 a.m. to 1 p.m.
Closed Sunday.
Barrier-free.

TORONTO CENTRE FOR CAREER ACTION
777 Bloor West

One terminal.
Monday to Friday 8:30 a.m. to 5 p.m.
Closed Saturday and Sunday.
Barrier-free.

TORONTO SOUTH EMPLOYMENT RESOURCE CENTRE
70 University

16 terminals.
Monday to Friday 9 a.m. to 4 p.m.
Closed Saturday and Sunday.
Barrier-free.

WOODGREEN EMPLOYMENT RESOURCE CENTRE
1080 Queen East

22 terminals.
Monday to Thursday 9 a.m. to 4:30 p.m.
Friday and Saturday 9 a.m. to 12:30 p.m.
Closed Sunday.
Barrier-free.

WOODGREEN YOUTH JOB CENTRE
989 Danforth

16 terminals.
Monday to Friday 9 a.m. to 5 p.m.
Closed Saturday and Sunday.
Barrier-free.

YOUTH EMPLOYMENT SERVICES
543 Richmond West, 504-5516

16 terminals.
Monday to Thursday 9 a.m. to 5 p.m.
Friday 9:30 a.m. to 4:30 p.m.
Closed Saturday and Sunday.

FERRIES

TORONTO ISLAND FERRIES
392-8193

Ferries to the Toronto Islands leave from the docks at the foot of Bay Street next to the Harbour Castle Hilton Hotel. Year-round service is provided to the eastern-most island, Ward's Island, from 6:35 in the morning. The last ferry back from Ward's Island leaves at 11:45 p.m.

Service to Centre Island and Hanlan's Point runs from early April till mid-October and is discontinued during the winter. Ferries leave the Bay docks at least every 30 minutes from 9 a.m. (8 a.m. on weekends and holidays); the last ferry back from the islands leaves at 11:45 p.m. Though allowed year round on the Ward's Island ferry, bicycles are only permitted on the Centre Island ferry Monday to Friday.
Round trip tickets cost $4.

FESTIVALS & FAIRS

ARTSWEEK
977-2787

Held during the last week in September, ArtsWeek is

presented by Art Toronto. The nine-day celebration of creativity includes over 100 performances, screenings, readings, and exhibitions of work by more than 250 local artists. As well, the public is invited to behind-the-scenes tours of galleries, film studios, dance schools, architects' offices, and artists' studios.

THE BEACHES INTERNATIONAL JAZZ FESTIVAL
698-2152

It's not the Beaches — it's the Beach! Despite the misnomer, this completely free-admission fest is one of Toronto's most popular events. Held annually over four days in late July, it takes over Queen Street East between Woodbine and Beach avenues, turning the Beach into a zoo for the weekend. Traffic and public transit become a disaster. Gigs are held in storefronts, on street corners, in clubs, and in public parks. And it's not just restricted to jazz — the booking policy includes be-bop, swing, r 'n' b, reggae, and blues performers, from unknown local up-and-comers to international headliners like the Fabulous Thunderbirds.

CARIBANA
465-4884

Since it was first staged at Canada's 1967 centennial celebrations, Caribana has been Toronto's wildest street party. A cross between New Orleans' Mardi Gras and the Carnivals of the Caribbean, Caribana is North America's largest Afrocentric festival. The annual event draws tourists from around the world who come to watch and participate in Saturday's 12-hour (!) parade and Sunday's arts and music fair held on the Toronto Islands. Needless to say, chicken is jerked and rum is downed. Wicked!

DOWNTOWN JAZZ FESTIVAL
363-8717

Every June, Toronto jumps to the myriad sounds of jazz. With sounds ranging from Dixieland trad to funky acid, the 10-day festival takes over more than 40 downtown venues. Local musicians like Jane Bunnett and such international artists as Herbie Hancock, Sarah Vaughan, and Wynton Marsalis play to appreciative audiences in smoky clubs and special tents set up in downtown parks and parking lots.

GAY PRIDE DAY
927-7433

One of North America's largest parties, Gay Pride Day — weekend more like — attracts more than half a million revellers to the streets of Boystown. And you don't have to be that way to join in the fun — Sunday's Pride Parade down Yonge Street draws a bigger crowd than the Santa Claus Parade. After the parade, everybody descends on Church Street where big-name performers — Holly Cole, Scott Thompson, Carole Pope — take to stages set up on side streets. The festivities actually start about a week earlier with special arts events at Buddies in Bad Times Theatre (see listing page 141) and other neighbourhood spots. Late Saturday and Sunday nights, circuit parties take over the bigger dance clubs like the Guvernment (see listing page 211) and Industry (see page 62) while other shenanigans take place in the bars along Church, as well as those on Queen West and College Streets. Some restaurants even host Monday hangover brunches!

INTERNATIONAL FESTIVAL OF AUTHORS
973-4760

The star in the crown of Harbourfront's Reading Series, the annual International Authors Fest is a forum for contemporary authors of fiction, poetry, drama, and biography. Since its inception in 1990, the event has attracted world-renowned celebrity writers, Nobel laureates, Pulitzer, Booker, and Governor General's Award winners, as well as lesser-known authors anxious to have their work discovered by the reading public.

NORTH BY NORTHEAST (NXNE)
185 Danforth, 469-0986

In the short time since its inception in 1995, the North by Northeast (NXNE) Music Festival and Industry Conference has established itself as Canada's premier event for new music. Showcasing more than 400 acts from Canada, the U.S., and around the world at 26 downtown venues over three nights in mid-June, NXNE is recognized worldwide as both a musicians' festival and an essential music-industry gathering. During the day, over 2,000 music-lovers participate in panel discussions, song-writing sessions, and demo-listenings. At night, NXNE becomes a club-hopping marathon. Such multi-genre performers as Wild Strawberries, neo-folkie Hayden, and mondo-funksters Bran Van 3000 first made their big splash at NXNE.

TORONTO INTERNATIONAL FILM FESTIVAL
967-7371

Recognized as one of the top fests in the world, the Toronto International Film Festival is a 10-day event held every September that draws cinephiles from around the globe. Screenings are held in movie-houses in Yorkville and the downtown core, and every night of the festival, two different films are saluted with hot-ticket celebrity-studded galas. Highlights include Midnight Madness, Director's Spotlight retrospectives, tributes to contemporary world cinema, and a slew of glamorous parties.

WORD ON THE STREET
504-7241

Held in collaboration with ArtsWeek, Word on the Street occurs during the last weekend in September in Toronto, Halifax, Ottawa, Calgary, and Vancouver simultaneously. In Toronto, Queen Street West is closed to traffic for the day and tents and stages are erected to shelter booths manned by more than 250 publishers, booksellers, and literacy organizations. This popular events attracts more than 150,000 visitors annually.

FOREIGN EXCHANGE

AMERICAN EXPRESS
100 Front West, 363-3883

AMERICAN EXPRESS
50 Bloor West, 967-3411

BENDIX FOREIGN EXCHANGE
366 Bay, 366-9000

CURRENCIES INTERNATIONAL
2 Dundas East, 977-1690

FOREIGN EXCHANGE CENTRE
313 Yonge, 598-3769

FRIEDBERG & COMPANY
181 Bay, 350-2888

MONEY EXPRESS
240 Wellesley East, 925-6190

THOMAS COOK
55 Bloor West, 961-9822

WORLD CURRENCY EXCHANGE
245 Yonge, 214-4761

GAS STATIONS

ESSO
143 Avenue Rd., 921-8747
1110 Bathurst, 532-7332
998 College, 535-7565
333 Davenport, 964-1866
150 Dupont, 964-2250
553 Lakeshore Blvd. West, 203-0106
581 Parliament, 922-1884
307 Sherbourne, 925-8660

FRED'S GAS BAR
873 Queen West, 504-2673

OLCO
723 College, 533-4800

PETRO-CANADA
861 Avenue Rd at Chaplin, 489-0952
354 Harbord at Crawford, 532-4971
117 Jarvis at Richmond East, 216-6757
505 Jarvis at Wellesley East, 921-5059
536 Mt. Pleasant at Belsize, 486-1722
567 Shuter at River, 922-7890
55 Spadina at Clarence Square, 596-8835

ROYAL AUTO SERVICE
969 Queen West, 504-5089

TRI-SERVICE STATION
1056 Queen West, 536-4479

HOSPITALS

HOSPITAL FOR SICK CHILDREN
555 University, 813-1500

MOUNT SINAI
600 University, 596-4200

THE TORONTO HOSPITAL
200 Elizabeth, 340-4611

WOMEN'S COLLEGE HOSPITAL
76 Grenville, 966-7111

HOSTELS

GLOBAL VILLAGE BACKPACKER'S HOSTEL
460 King West, 703-8540

Once the historic Spadina Hotel — site of many arty hijinks in the '80s — the newly renovated hotel has been reborn as a hostel. Rooms are bright and clean — some even have their own baths — and occupancy is double. Check out the first-floor cocktail lounge straight out of the '40s — *The Last Detail* with Jack Nicholson was filmed here. Centrally located on the Spadina LRT line, this is the cheapest and safest spot to lodge downtown.

SIESTA NOUVEAU
15 Lower Sherbourne, 861-0947

Advertising itself as an "artist's compound in the heart of Toronto's action," this 45-bed bunkroom may be artistic, but it's a good half-hour walk or 15-minute streetcar ride away from Queen West. Offering double or triple occupancy, the newly converted space has escaped the grime of some of its competition. Although it's a relatively safe neighbourhood, you still wouldn't want to be roaming the streets around here late at night.

TORONTO INTERNATIONAL HOSTEL
76 Church, 971-4440

A member of the International Youth Hostel Federation, this downtown facility has 170 beds available in several configurations — singles, doubles, triples, quads, and dormitories for 10. Newly renovated, the hostel features kitchenettes, en suite bathrooms, a TV room and lounge, laundry room, lockers, luggage storage, and Internet access. No smoking, no drinking, and reservations are mandatory.

YWCA
80 Woodlawn East, 923-8454

HOSTELS — UNIVERSITY

When school's out during the summer months, many of Toronto's university and college residences turn into seasonal lodgings. Don't just show up on their doorsteps — most require reservations made well in advance.

GLENDON COLLEGE
487-6798

KNOX COLLEGE AT UNIVERSITY OF TORONTO
978-4503

NEILL-WYCIK COLLEGE
96 Gerrard East, 977-2320

During the year, this 28-storey high-rise is a co-operative dormitory for students from the nearby Ryerson Polytechnical and the University of Toronto. From May through August, the College rents single and double rooms by the night, week, or month. All rooms have telephones and the facility features laundry and kitchen access, daily housekeeping, and 24-hour front-door security.

NEW COLLEGE AT UNIVERSITY OF TORONTO
978-2464

ST. MICHAEL'S COLLEGE AT UNIVERSITY OF TORONTO
926-1300

TRINITY COLLEGE AT UNIVERSITY OF TORONTO
978-2522

UNIVERSITY COLLEGE AT UNIVERSITY OF TORONTO
978-2532

VICTORIA COLLEGE AT UNIVERSITY OF TORONTO
585-4524

WYCLIFFE COLLEGE AT UNIVERSITY OF TORONTO
946-3535

YORK UNIVERSITY
736-5020

HOTELS

Toronto has many first-class hotels — the Four Seasons, the Royal York, and the King Edward, among others. Here's a list of some alternative choices in or near the downtown core.

AMBASSADOR INN
280 Jarvis, 260-2608

BOND PLACE HOTEL
65 Dundas East, 362-6061

COMFORT HOTEL
15 Charles East, 924-1222

CROMWELL
55 Isabella, 962-5670

DAYS INN
1684 Queen East, 694-1177
30 Carlton, 977-6655

DELTA CHELSEA INN
33 Gerrard West, 595-1975

ESSEX PARK HOTEL
300 Jarvis, 977-4823

HOLIDAY INN
370 King West, 599-4000

HOTEL SELBY
592 Sherbourne, 921-3142

STRATHCONA HOTEL
60 York, 363-3321

WHITEHOUSE HOTEL
76 Church, 362-7491

INTERNET ACCESS

Free Internet access is available at several community centres and service groups. Generally, time must be booked in advance, and if you show up later than five minutes after the reserved start time, the booking is cancelled. For other locations with free Internet access, see Employment Centres and Libraries.

CENTRE FOR INDEPENDENT LIVING
205 Richmond West, 599-2458

Free. Two terminals.
Barrier-free.

CULTURE LINK
474 Bathurst, 923-4678
Free. Ten terminals. Two steps.

FRED VICTOR MISSION HUMAN RESOURCE CENTRE
145 Queen East, 364-8228
Free. 16 terminals.
Barrier-free.

INFOSTORE — INFORMATION ONLINE
900 Dufferin, 532-6443
$1/hour. Nine terminals.
Barrier-free.

NEIGHBOURHOOD INFORMATION POST
269 Gerrard East, 924-2543
Free. Three terminals.
Barrier-free.

RALPH THORNTON COMMUNITY CENTRE
765 Queen East, 392-6810
Free. Ten terminals. Barrier free.

ST. ALBAN'S BOYS AND GIRLS CLUB
843 Palmerston, 534-8461
Free. Two terminals.
Barrier-free.

TAMIL EELAM SOCIETY OF CANADA
861 Broadview, 463-7647
Free. Three terminals.
Barrier-free.

LEGAL ASSISTANCE

DOWNTOWN LEGAL SERVICES
44 St. George, 978-6447

HIV & AIDS LEGAL CLINIC
399 Church, 340-7790

NEIGHBOURHOOD LEGAL SERVICES
333 Queen East, 955-9915

UNIVERSITY OF TORONTO STUDENT LEGAL SERVICES
91 St. George, 978-6497

LEGALITIES

CIGARETTE SMOKING
Cigarette smoking is prohibited in all public buildings, including all stores, offices, and on public transit. Although most bars do not provide *non*-smoking areas, many restaurants allow smoking in designated areas only. Smoke-free establishments usually advertise themselves as such.

DRINKING LAWS
Alcohol can only be served in government-licensed restaurants and bars between the hours of 11 a.m. and "last call" at 2 a.m. There are even restrictions in some establishments that prevent customers from walking from one room to another with a drink in your hand — so don't even think of walking down Queen West as you chug a Moosehead. Beer, liquor, and wine are available for sale from government Beer Stores or LCBO (Liquor Control Board Of Ontario) outlets; the Amsterdam, Toronto's only microbrewery with its own retail outlet, is the exception (see listing page 44).

DRUG LAWS
While caffeine, nicotine, and alcohol are legal in Ontario, soft drugs such as marijuana and hashish as well as narcotics like heroin, cocaine, and crack are not. With the government's crackdown on soft drugs, grass and hash is now as expensive in Toronto as smack and blow. Go figure. And for some reason, codeine — a morphine derivative found in painkillers and cough medicine — is perfectly legal.

TRAFFIC LAWS
See Traffic Laws, page 246.

LIBRARIES

Libraries are a great resource — as well as books, they also carry current and back issues of popular magazines and a small selection of video tapes. Most branches also offer free Internet access. The hours listed below are when the Internet is accessible.

ANNETTE LIBRARY
145 Annette, 393-7692
Two terminals.
Monday to Thursday noon to 8:30 p.m.
Friday noon to 6 p.m.
Saturday 9 a.m. to 5 p.m.
Closed Sunday.
Barrier-free.

THE BEACH LIBRARY
2161 Queen East, 393-7703
One terminal.
Monday to Friday 10 a.m. to 8:30 p.m.
Saturday 9 a.m. to 5 p.m.
Closed Sunday.
Barrier-free.

SURVIVAL

BLOOR-GLADSTONE LIBRARY
1101 Bloor West, 393-7674

One terminal.
Monday to Friday 10 a.m. to 8:30 p.m.
Saturday 9 a.m. to 5 p.m.
Sunday 1:30 p.m. to 5 p.m.
Barrier-free.

CANADIAN LESBIAN AND GAY ARCHIVES
56 Temperance, Ste. 201, 777-2755

Closed Friday to Tuesday.

CITY HALL LIBRARY
100 Queen West, 393-7650

Two terminals.
Monday to Friday 11 a.m. to 4 p.m.
Closed Saturday and Sunday.
Barrier-free.

COLLEGE-SHAW LIBRARY
766 College, 393-7668

One terminal.
Monday to Thursday noon to 8:30 p.m.
Friday noon to 6 p.m.
Saturday 9 a.m. to 5 p.m.
Closed Sunday.
Barrier-free.

DANFORTH-COXWELL LIBRARY
1675 Danforth, 393-7783

One terminal.
Monday to Friday 10 a.m. to 8:30 p.m.
Saturday 9 a.m. to 5 p.m.
Closed Sunday.
Barrier-free.

DEER PARK LIBRARY
40 St. Clair East, 393-7657

One terminal.
Monday to Friday 10 a.m. to 8:30 p.m.
Saturday 9 a.m. to 5 p.m.
Closed Sunday.
Barrier-free.

DUFFERIN-ST. CLAIR LIBRARY
1625 Dufferin, 393-7712

One terminal.
Monday to Friday noon to 8:30 p.m.
Saturday 9 a.m. to 5 p.m.
Sunday 1:30 p.m. to 5 p.m.
Barrier-free.

FOREST HILL LIBRARY
700 Eglinton West, 393-7706

One terminal.
Monday to Thursday 10 a.m. to 8:30 p.m.
Friday and Saturday 9 a.m. to 5 p.m.
Closed Sunday.
Barrier-free.

GERRARD-ASHDALE LIBRARY
1432 Gerrard East, 393-7717

Two terminals.
Monday to Friday noon to 8:30 p.m.
Saturday 9 a.m. to 5 p.m.
Closed Sunday.
Barrier-free.

HIGH PARK LIBRARY
228 Roncesvalles, 393-7671

Two terminals.
Monday to Thursday 10 a.m. to 8:30 p.m.
Friday 10 a.m. to 6 p.m.
Saturday 9 a.m. to 5 p.m.
Closed Sunday.
Barrier-free.

LILLIAN H. SMITH LIBRARY
239 College, 393-7746

Includes Toronto author Judith Merrill's science-fiction, speculation, and fantasy archives as well as the Osbourne Collection of Early Children's Books.
17 terminals.
Monday to Thursday 10 a.m. to 8:30 p.m.
Friday 10 a.m. to 6 p.m.
Saturday 9 a.m. to 5 p.m.
Closed Sunday.
Barrier-free.

MAIN STREET LIBRARY
137 Main, 393-7700

One terminal.
Monday to Friday 10 a.m. to 8:30 p.m.
Saturday 9 a.m. to 5 p.m.
Closed Sunday.
Barrier-free.

MT. PLEASANT LIBRARY
599 Mt. Pleasant, 393-7737

One terminal.
Tuesday noon to 8 p.m.
Wednesday and Thursday noon to 6 p.m.
Friday 11 a.m. to 6 p.m.
Saturday 9 a.m. to 5 p.m.
Closed Sunday and Monday.
Barrier-free.

NORTHERN DISTRICT LIBRARY
40 Orchard View, 393-7610

Two terminals.
Monday to Friday 10 a.m. to 8:30 p.m.
Saturday 9 a.m. to 5 p.m.
Sunday 1:30 to 5 p.m.

Barrier-free.

PALMERSTON LIBRARY
560 Palmerston, 393-7680

One terminal.
Monday and Thursday 10 a.m. to 8:30 p.m.
Tuesday, Wednesday, and Friday 10 a.m. to 6 p.m.
Saturday 9 a.m. to 5 p.m.
Closed Sunday.

Barrier-free.

PAPE-DANFORTH LIBRARY
701 Pape, 393-7727

Three terminals.
Monday to Friday 10 a.m. to 8:30 p.m.
Saturday 9 a.m. to 5 p.m.
Sunday 1:30 to 5 p.m.

Barrier-free.

PARKDALE LIBRARY
1303 Queen West, 393-7686

13 terminals.
Monday to Friday 10 a.m. to 8:30 p.m.
Saturday 9 a.m. to 5 p.m.
Closed Sunday.

Barrier-free.

PARLIAMENT LIBRARY
269 Gerrard East, 393-7663

One terminal.
Monday to Friday 10 a.m. to 8:30 p.m.
Saturday 9 a.m. to 5 p.m.
Closed Sunday.

Barrier-free.

PERTH-DUPONT LIBRARY
1589 Dupont, 393-7677

Two terminals.
Tuesday to Thusday noon to 8:30 p.m.
Friday noon to 6 p.m.
Saturday 9 a.m. to 5 p.m.
Closed Sunday and Monday.

Barrier-free.

QUEEN-SAULTER LIBRARY
765 Queen East, 393-7723

One terminal.
Tuesday noon to 8:30 p.m.

Wednesday noon to 6 p.m.
Thursday noon to 8:30 p.m.
Friday noon to 6 p.m.
Saturday 9 a.m. to 5 p.m.
Closed Sunday and Monday.

Barrier-free.

RIVERDALE LIBRARY
370 Broadview, 393-7720

14 terminals.
Monday to Friday noon to 8:30 p.m.
Saturday 9 a.m. to 5 p.m.
Closed Sunday.

Barrier-free.

RUNNYMEDE LIBRARY
2178 Bloor West, 393-7697

Two terminals.
Monday to Friday 10 a.m. to 8:30 p.m.
Saturday 9 a.m. to 5 p.m.
Closed Sunday.

Barrier-free.

SANDERSON LIBRARY
327 Bathurst, 393-7635

One terminal.
Monday to Thursday 10 a.m. to 8:30 p.m.
Friday 10 a.m. to 6 p.m.
Saturday 9 a.m. to 5 p.m.
Sunday 1:30 p.m. to 5 p.m.

Barrier-free.

SPADINA ROAD LIBRARY
10 Spadina Road, 393-7666

One terminal.
Tuesday to Friday 10 a.m. to 8:30 p.m.
Saturday 9 a.m. to 5 p.m.
Closed Sunday and Monday.

Barrier-free.

ST. CLAIR–SILVERTHORN LIBRARY
1748 St. Clair West, 393-7709

Two terminals.
Monday 11 a.m. to 6 p.m.
Tuesday 11 a.m. to 7 p.m.
Thursday 11 a.m to 7 p.m.
Friday 11 a.m. to 6 p.m.
Saturday 9 a.m. to 5 p.m.
Closed Sunday and Wednesday.

Barrier-free.

ST. LAWRENCE LIBRARY
171 Front East, 393-7655

One terminal.

Tuesday to Friday noon to 8:30 p.m.
Saturday 9 a.m. to 5 p.m.
Closed Sunday and Monday.
Barrier-free.

TORONTO METRO REFERENCE LIBRARY
789 Yonge, 393-7000

70 terminals.
Monday to Thursday 10 a.m. to 8 p.m.
Friday and Saturday 10 a.m. to 5 p.m.
Saturday 1:30 to 5 p.m.
Closed Sunday.
Barrier-free.

URBAN AFFAIRS LIBRARY
55 John, 393-7131

Five terminals.
Monday to Wednesday 10 a.m. to 6 p.m.
Thursday and Friday 10 a.m. to 8 p.m.
Closed Saturday and Sunday.
Barrier-free.

WYCHWOOD LIBRARY
1431 Bathurst, 393-7683

One terminal.
Monday to Thursday 10 a.m. to 8:30 p.m.
Friday 10 a.m. to 6 p.m.
Saturday 9 a.m. to 5 p.m.
Closed Sunday.
Barrier-free.

YORKVILLE LIBRARY
22 Yorkville, 393-7660

One terminal.
Monday 10 a.m. to 6 p.m.
Tuesday 10 a.m. to 8:30 p.m.
Wednesday 10 a.m. to 6 p.m.
Thursday 10 a.m. to 8:30 p.m.
Friday 10 a.m. to 6 p.m.
Saturday 9 a.m. to 5 p.m.
Closed Sunday.
Barrier-free.

MEDICAL CLINICS

ACCESS ALLIANCE MULTICULTURAL HEALTH CENTRE
509 College, 324-8677

ALBANY MEDICAL CLINIC
200 Danforth, 461-9471

ANISHNAWBE HEALTH TORONTO
225 Queen East, 360-0486

Health services for indigenous people.

ANNEX MEDICAL CLINIC
515 Bloor West, 537-3513

BATHURST-RICHMOND MEDICAL CENTRE
626 Richmond West, 703-2303

CABBAGETOWN WOMEN'S CLINIC
302 Gerrard East, 323-0642

CHOICE IN HEALTH CLINIC
597 Parliament, 975-9300

CLARKE INSTITUTE OF PSYCHIATRY
250 College, 979-2221

HASSLE-FREE CLINIC (MEN)
556 Church, 922-0603

HASSLE-FREE CLINIC (WOMEN)
556 Church, 922-0566

THE HOUSE COMMUNITY HEALTH CENTRE
36B Prince Arthur, 927-7171

QUEEN STREET MENTAL HEALTH CENTRE
1001 Queen West, 535-8501

QUEEN-SPADINA MEDICAL CENTRE
455 Queen West, 869-3627

SHOUT CLINIC
467 Jarvis, 927-8553

WALK-IN DOCS CLINIC
809 Bloor West, 533-0081

THE WORKS
277 Victoria, 392-0520

Needle exchange.

MOTELS

BEACH MOTEL
2183 Lakeshore West, 259-3296

CASA MENDOZA INN
2161 Lakeshore West, 259-7671

THE EXECUTIVE MOTOR HOTEL
621 King West, 504-7441

HILLCREST MOTEL
2143 Lakeshore West, 255-7711

SEAHORSE INN
2095 Lakeshore West, 255-4433

PUBLIC TRANSIT

TORONTO TRANSIT COMMISSION
393-4636

Toronto's public transit system, the TTC, operates the city's network of subways, streetcars, buses, and LRTs (Light Rapid Transit). Subways run about every 10 minutes from 6 in the morning till 1:30 a.m., Monday to Saturday. Sunday subway service starts at 9 a.m. and continues till 1:30 a.m. Most bus routes and streetcar lines run from 5 a.m. to 1:30 a.m.

The Blue Night Network comprises interlinked buses and streetcar routes that run all night long. In the downtown area, these include the Queen, Dundas, College, and St. Clair streetcars as well as buses on Yonge, Bathurst, Bloor-Danforth, and Dufferin streets. Adult fare is two dollars cash or a ticket or token. Five tokens will cost you $8 and you can buy them at all subway stations and most convenience stores. Exact fares are required on all buses or streetcars — the operators are not required to make change (this is not a problem at subway stations). Day passes are available for $6.50, and monthly Metropasses are available for $83.

Until you know the system, always get a transfer when you pay your fare — unless you're changing the mode of transit at a subway station, you'll need a transfer when you're changing from the bus to the streetcar or from the LRT back onto the bus.

TTC CONNECTIONS TO AIRPORT
363-4636

The cheapest — and slowest — way to get to the airport is to take the 58A Malton bus from the Lawrence West station on the University subway line. It operates daily from approximately 6 a.m. to 1:30 a.m. with buses running as often as every 10 minutes during rush hour and at least once every 30 minutes at other times (from 9 a.m. on Sundays and holidays and running as often as every 20 minutes during peak hours and at least once an hour during off-hours). It arrives at Terminal Two of Pearson International Airport, turns around, and returns to Lawrence West station. Cost: $2.

TTC LOST AND FOUND
Bay Subway Station, 393-4100

RAVE HOTLINES

When raves first surfaced in the Toronto underground 10 years ago, they were illegal after-hours parties held in clandestine warehouse locations. Even now that the scene has gone commercial, the secrecy of where the rave will happen is still much of its attraction. And al-

though most events are perfectly legal, they're still advertised only by phone and on flyers found in record stores and clothing shops along Queen West, College, and Yonge streets. Here's a list of the latest hotlines — and since many of the promoters are fly-by-night operations, some of these numbers may already be obsolete.

ATOM MUSICA
760-3171

BEYOND — NEXT LEVEL
614-4067

BIG BUD
760-3270

DAYBREAKS HANG THE DJ
280-6499

DESTINY
631-8821

DOSE
760-3275

DUB SCIENCE
598-1665

E! NETWORK
208-3093

EFFECTIVE
760-3185

FIVE MONKEYS
760-3214

GOOD VIBES
760-3137

HULLABALOO
410-3813

JUMP
760-9300

LIFEFORCE
760-3322

LIQUID ADRENALINE
760-3166

LIQUID GROOVE
760-3234

LOVE (CONTINUUM)
760-3388

PUBLIC TRANSIT

TORONTO TRANSIT COMMISSION
393-4636

TTC CONNECTIONS TO AIRPORT
363-4636

TTC LOST AND FOUND
Bay Subway Station, 393-4100
See listings page 243

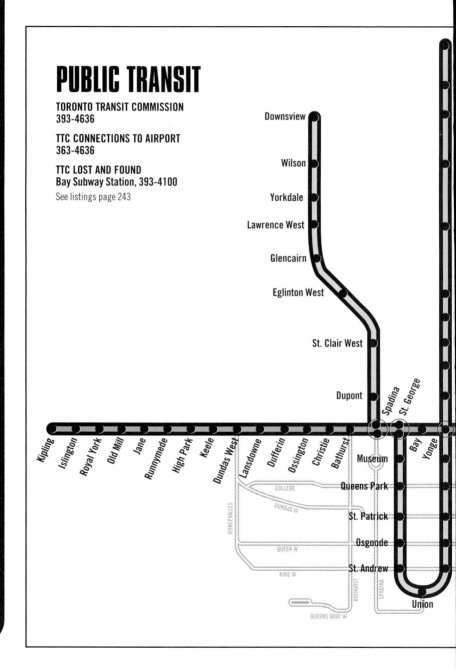

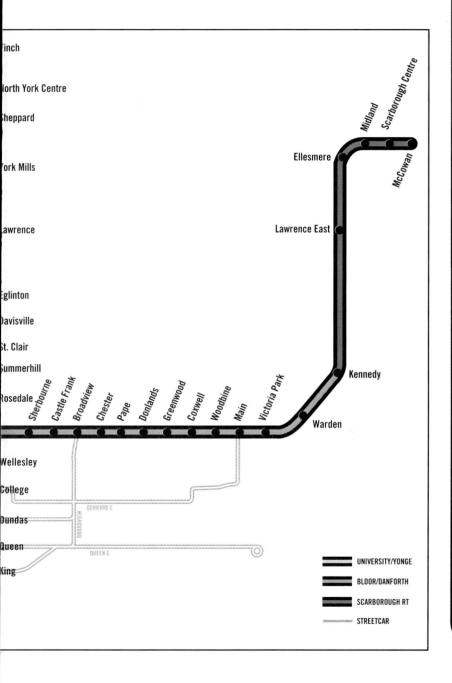

Finch

North York Centre

Sheppard

York Mills

Lawrence

Eglinton

Davisville

St. Clair

Summerhill

Rosedale

Sherbourne

Castle Frank

Broadview

Chester

Pape

Donlands

Greenwood

Coxwell

Woodbine

Main

Victoria Park

Warden

Kennedy

Lawrence East

Ellesmere

Midland

Scarborough Centre

McCowan

Wellesley

College

Dundas

Queen

King

GERRARD E

BROADVIEW

QUEEN E

UNIVERSITY/YONGE

BLOOR/DANFORTH

SCARBOROUGH RT

STREETCAR

MDMA
208-0307

MILK
202-8839

OM FESTIVAL
280-6218

PHRYL PRODUCTIONS
760-3161

RENEGADES
760-3305

SYNC
718-4820

SYROUS
760-3133

UTOPIA PRODUCTIONS
905/281-8947

X-STATIC
760-3730

TAXIS

BECK TAXI
751-5555

CO-OP CABS
504-2667

DIAMOND TAXI
366-6868

METRO CAB
504-8294

ROYAL TAXI
221-1187

YELLOW CAB
504-4141

TRAFFIC LAWS

FLASHING GREEN LIGHT
A flashing green light is an advance signal that means proceed.

PARKING
There are plenty of parking lots and meters throughout the city, and drivers who park in posted "No Parking" areas — whether on the street or on private property — are asking for trouble. Not only will you receive a $20-plus ticket, your car may be towed and im-

pounded. It costs about $200 — and a lot of aggravation — to get your vehicle back.

PEDESTRIAN CROSSWALKS
Pedestrian crosswalks are marked by large Xs painted on the roadway 200 feet in advance of the crossing. Pedestrians are required to signal their intent to use the crosswalk by activating the overhead flashing yellow lights and/or by pointing. Motorists are required by law to stop for them if they do so.

SCHOOL BUSES
When a school bus stops to let riders on or off, it sets off a flashing yellow light on its roof. Motorists travelling in both directions are required to stop until the light stops flashing.

SEAT BELTS
Seat belts must be worn at all times in automobiles and trucks. The police spot-check and fine unbelted motorists regularly.

STREETCARS
When a streetcar stops to pick up or let off riders, motorists are required by law to stop their vehicles behind the streetcar's rear doors.

TURNING RIGHT ON A RED LIGHT
In Ontario, it is legal to make a right-hand turn on a red light — unless otherwise posted.

TRAINS

GO TRANSIT
869-3200

UNION STATION
See listing page 113.

VIA RAIL
65 Front West, 366-8411

TRAVEL INFORMATION

AMERICAN EXPRESS
157 Yonge, 868-1044

TOURISM TORONTO
203-2500

TRAVELLER'S AID SOCIETY
Pearson International, 905/676-2868

TRAVELLER'S AID SOCIETY
Union Station, 366-7788

24–7 BOWLING ALLEYS

BOWLERAMA
Thorncliffe Market Place, 421-2211
115 Rexdale at Kipling, 743-8388
5429 Dundas East of Hwy. 427, 239-3536
Five-pin and ten-pin bowling. Computerized scoring.
Fully licensed.

24–7 CHEQUE CASHING

MONEY MART
688 Yonge, 924-1000

24–7 DRUG STORES

SHOPPERS DRUG MART
722 Yonge, 920-0098

24–7 FOOD STORES

BLOOR SUPER SAVE
384 Bloor West, 964-8318

DOMINION
425 Bloor West, 923-9099
83 Gould, 862-7171

FINE FOOD
637 Bay, 597-1300

RABBA
37 Charles West, 964-3409
40 Asquith, 967-5326
9 Isabella, 928-2300

SUPER FRESHMART
524 Church, 967-9484

24–7 GAS STATIONS

CAR CAFE
1001 Queen East, 461-1916

ESSO
153 Dundas West, 977-7790

24–7 GLASS REPAIR

METROPOLITAN GLASS
377 Dundas East, 362-1549

24–7 LAUNDROMATS

24 HOUR COIN LAUNDRY
566 Mt. Pleasant, 487-0233

24–7 LOCKSMITHS

SURE LOCKS
1045 Avenue, 486-5077

24–7 POOL HALLS

BILLIARDS ACADEMY
485 Danforth, 466-9696
See listing page 193.

CENTRAL BILLIARDS
468 Queen West, 504-9494
See listing page 21.

CLUB 24-7
553 Queen West, 361-6354
See listing page 21.

24–7 RESTAURANTS

COMMISSO BROTHERS AND RACCO
8 Kincourt, 651-7671
See listing page 222.

FRAN'S
20 College, 923-9867
See listing page 153.

FRAN'S
21 St. Clair West, 925-6337
See listing page 153.
One step at door, washrooms on same floor.

FRAN'S
45 Eglinton East, 481-1112
See listing page 153.
Barrier-free.

GOLDEN WHEAT BAKERY
652 College, 534-1107
See listing page 74.

MARS
432 College, 921-6332
See listing page 83.

MONTREAL'S DELICATESSEN
160 Adelaide West, 365-1212
See listing page 109.
440 Bloor West, 966-8881
See listing page 166.

PHO PASTEUR
525 Dundas West, 351-7188
See listing page 96.

7 WEST
7 Charles West, 928-9041
See listing page 153.

SUNSET GRILL
2006 Queen East, 690-9985
See listing page 203.

2 CHEZ
3 Charles East, 968-9078
See listing page 136.

VESTA LUNCH
474 Dupont, 537-4318
See listing page 166.

WEATHER

WEATHER INFORMATION
661-0123

WOMEN'S RESOURCES

ABORTION CARE CLINIC
256-4139

ABORTION RIGHTS ACTION LEAGUE — PRO CHOICE (CARAL)
961-1507

ADELAIDE RESOURCE CENTRE FOR WOMEN
392-9243

BARBRA SCHLIFER COMMEMORATIVE CLINIC
323-9149

BREAKTHROUGH YWCA
961-8100

CABBAGETOWN WOMEN'S CLINIC
302 Gerrard East, 323-0642

CHOICE IN HEALTH CLINIC
597 Parliament, 975-9300

COMMUNITY INFORMATION TORONTO
397-4636

DAVID KELLY LESBIAN AND GAY COUNSELLING PROGRAM
595-9618

EDUCATION WIFE ASSAULT
968-3422

INTERVAL HOUSE
924-1491

THE METROPOLITAN ACTION COMMITTEE ON VIOLENCE AGAINST WOMEN AND CHILDREN (METRAC)
158 Spadina Rd, 392-3135

MORGENTALER CLINIC
727 Hillsdale East, 932-0446

NATIVE WOMEN'S RESOURCE CENTRE
191 Gerrard East, 963-9963

NELLIE'S
275A Parliament, 461-1084

RIVERDALE IMMIGRANT WOMEN'S CENTRE
465-6021

S.O.S. FEMMES (FRENCH CRISIS LINE)
759-0138

SCOTT CLINIC
157 Gerrard East, 962-4108

SISTERING DROP-IN CENTRE
926-9762

SOUTH ASIAN WOMEN'S CENTRE
537-2276

TORONTO RAPE CRISIS CENTRE
597-8808

UNIVERSITY OF TORONTO WOMEN'S CENTRE
49 St. George, 978-8201

WOMEN'S COUNSELLING, REFERRAL AND EDUCATION CENTRE
525 Bloor West, 534-7501

WOMEN'S HEALTH IN WOMEN'S HANDS
2 Carlton, 593-7655

WOMEN'S OWN DETOX CENTRE (CRISIS LINE)
603-1462

YWCA WOMEN'S SHELTER
693-7342

YWCA WOODLAWN WOMEN'S EMERGENCY SHELTER
923-8454

INDEX

FOOD & DINING

ENTERTAINMENT

SHOPPING